LAWSUIT and ASSET PROTECTION

Complete Guide to Protecting and Insulating Your Hard-Earned Assets from Lawsuits, Judgment Liabilities and IRS

For Homeowners, Businessmen, Professionals, Consumers, Creditors or Debtors - and Their Attorneys, Accountants and Financial Planners

VIJAY FADIA

IMPORTANT

Although care has been taken to ensure the accuracy and utility of the information and forms contained in this manual, neither the publisher nor the author assumes any liability in connection with any use thereof. This publication is sold with the understanding that the publisher is not engaged in rendering legal, accounting or other professional service.

This manual contains sophisticated techniques, ideas and suggestions to help you develop your own financial and legal plan to suit your circumstances. Any such plan of necessity requires competent professional help before it is devised and implemented. This book should not be used as a substitute for professional assistance essential to planning your business, financial, tax and legal affairs.

Printed in the United States of America

Published by

HOMESTEAD PUBLISHING COMPANY, INC.
21707 Hawthorne Blvd., Suite 204
Torrance, CA 90503

Titles from Homestead Publishing Company

- **The Living Trust: A Cure for the Agony of Probate**
  - *also available in software version*
- **Lawsuit and Asset Protection Kit**
- **Estate Planning for the 1990s: A Practical Guide to Wills, Trusts, Probate and Death Taxes for Everyone**
- **How to Protect Your Assets, Perfectly Legally, from the Catastrophic Costs of Nursing-Home Care**
- **You and Your Will: A Do-It-Yourself Manual**
  - *also available in software version*
- **Money Manager** - *Windows Software for PC*
- **The Durable Power of Attorney**
- **The Legal Forms Kit** - *also available in software version*
- **How to Cut Your Mortgage in Half**
  - *also available in software version*
- **How to Deal with the IRS**
- **Facts About AIDS**
- **Stress Management**
- **Substance Abuse**
- **Child Abuse**
- **Teach Your Baby to Swim** - *Video*

What Our Customers Have to Say about the *Lawsuit and Asset Protection Kit*

"Dear Jay, As a landlord I believe my assets are particularly vulnerable to lawsuits for a variety of reasons. Before I had read Lawsuit and Asset Protection Kit, I had placed all my properties into revocable trusts (land trust). I then believed that these assets were completely "bullet proof" from creditors. After reading the Lawsuit and Asset Protection kit, I now realize these assets may not be as "bullet proof" as I originally thought.

"I was also just notified by one of my associates that an expert tax attorney who also gives tax seminars (from Newport Beach, CA), also highly recommends all the books/kits published by Mr. Fadia."

"So YES, I highly recommend the Lawsuit and Asset Protection Kit for anybody who has concerns over keeping their assets that they have worked for and earned over the years for themselves and their loved ones." P.H. Portland, CT

"Very good and well-written Kit. Gave me good ideas and procedures to use to protect assets. It's practical as it gives those of us who aren't sophisticated about law how to protect our assets." N.W.Y. Los Angeles, CA

"I've had several occasions to use the Lawsuit and Asset Protection Kit. It is a valuable reference in my library! I have more peace of mind thanks to your informative publication" P.F. Lihue, HI

"It is very effective...virtually a necessity for the working library of every independent businessman and professional." D.V.P. Flint, MI

"It was helpful in developing an overall estate plan. I've since reading it formed a family limited partnership and two corporations." W.K. Johnstown, PA

"Highly recommended." C.E.R. Washington, D.C.

"I've found it to be very informative and helpful. It has been placed with other important reference books in my library. Keep up the good work." J.K. Old Westbury, NY

"Excellent book. Your chapters on incorporation and trusts were very good." R.U. Buffalo, NY

"Many good idea's...in that it spells out in great detail how to set up corporations that are judgment proof." R.F.T. Northampton, PA

"Informative and easy to read. I am finding the legal loopholes and tax breaks without having to suffer through volumes of boring books in a legal library. Chapter 15 is worth the $39.95, especially the section on legally and simply precluding or terminating State Income Taxes! I'm starting my own electronic controls firm - with 100% profits and organizing as a proprietorship, I need to eliminate taxes and to be judgment proof." M.T. Huntington Beach, CA

"Excellent resource for reference material. I have used it to be able to have a greater understanding of laws that affect me. When I speak to my lawyer about items of concern I look it up in the Book, make notes, questions, ideas, and find our meetings much more fruitful. Lawyers have a greater respect for your questions. They seem surprised (and impressed) that a layman is so competent about legal issues." G.C. Glen Head, NY

"It contains a set of concise and explicit criteria clarifying the issues it presents in a readily understandable way, which I find useful (as a non-lawyer)." L.J.P. Tucson, AZ

Contents

Section VI

Section VII

Section VIII

Section IX

Section X

SECTION I

Protecting Jointly-Held Property from Creditors

1

Joint ownership is probably the most popular form of family ownership of property, while at the same time the least understood. It is estimated that more than three-fourths of all the real estate owned by married couples in the United States is held in joint tenancy. When you consider joint bank accounts, joint ownership of stocks and bonds, and joint safe deposit boxes it becomes apparent that joint ownership of property is by far the most prevalent form of ownership.

More important, such joint ownership of property is not limited to husbands and wives. It is quite common to see homes, bank accounts, even an automobile owned in joint tenancy by a mother and daughter, or by parents and a teenage son, or by two business partners.

When more than one person own the same property at the same time, they're said to be "co-tenants" of that property. Co-tenancy can be in several forms: joint tenancy, tenancy by the entirety, tenancy in common, and tenancy by partnership.

The problems often arise when a creditor of one owner tries to collect the debt owed by levying on the jointly-owned property. Can the creditor of one joint tenant reach the whole property? Can he at least reach his debtor's share of the property? Can he force a sale or a division of the property to satisfy the debt? In other words, do you have to worry about the creditors of your co-tenant or joint tenant? Can his creditors reach your money in the bank account or your share of the residence?

In this chapter we'll examine the rights of one co-tenant or joint tenant against the creditors of another, and the problems a creditor may encounter when he tries to levy the jointly-owned property of his debtor.

Joint Tenancy

A joint tenancy is a joint interest owned by two or more persons in equal shares with the express declaration that the title is held in joint tenancy. A joint tenancy may be created by the owner's conveying to two or more persons, as joint tenants, or by one of the owners conveying to himself and one or more persons as joint tenants.

Simultaneous Deaths

A joint tenancy in most jurisdictions must, however, be created by a written instrument and not by an oral agreement. In the event of simultaneous deaths, the joint tenancy is severed and the undivided interest of each tenant is divided as if he or she had survived the other. For instance, the joint property of husband and wife would be divided equally, so that one-half passes through the husband's estate and the other half through the wife's estate.

Illustration: A and B who own an asset as joint tenants die simultaneously. The right of survivorship is inoperative. One-half of the asset will be distributed in the estate of A as if A were the surviving joint tenant and the other half will be distributed similarly in the estate of B.

Joint tenancy conveys to each tenant equal and undivided interest in the property. However, if any one joint tenant conveys his interest, the joint tenancy is severed and the parties become tenants in common as to the conveyed interest.

Right of Survivorship

Joint tenancy has one feature that distinguishes it from all other forms of ownership: Upon the death of one of the joint tenants, the surviving tenant or tenants become the sole owners of the entire property by operation of law. The decedent's will has no effect on the disposition of a jointly-held property.

In some states, a joint tenancy between a husband and wife is presumed to be tenancy by the entirety. This form of ownership is similar to joint tenancy with a right of survivorship, except neither spouse may sever the tenancy without the other's consent.

Disadvantages

The principal disadvantage of joint tenancy lies in its general inflexibility and the inability of the tenants to dispose of the property by will, except upon the death of the survivor. In addition, since the entire interest in the property passes to the surviving tenant outright, all of it is subject to inclusion in the survivor's estate.

Joint tenancy form of ownership is not a will substitute and should not be used as such. It is almost invariably necessary for the joint tenants to have wills to dispose of other assets and the joint tenancy asset, if the testator is the survivor. A will is also necessary to appoint guardians for minor children.

Many individuals with small estates may own all of their assets in joint tenancy, and often married couples own their residences and checking accounts in joint tenancy. If the bulk of the family assets are held in joint ownership, they will pass to the survivor outright. The survivor, as absolute owner of the property, may dissipate it, reinvest it unwisely, or make injudicious gifts.

If the surviving spouse later remarries, some or all of the property may pass to his or her second spouse to the exclusion of the children of the first marriage. It's possible, for example, that the surviving spouse may put all the property received as the surviving co-owner into a new co-ownership with the spouse of the second marriage, or may leave all the property by will to such spouse.

Tenancy by the Entirety

A tenancy by the entirety is a special form of joint tenancy which may be used only by a husband and wife. Its origins can be traced to the English common law when property was transferred to husband and wife together. In early days, man and woman as a result of marriage, for legal purposes, were treated as a unification of the two people, so that their ownership of property (usually real estate) was not regarded as being owned by the two individuals, but by the "unity," or by the "entirety."

Under this concept the whole of the property is owned not by two people but rather by the unity created when the parties are married, and the two take title as a single person.

Because of this entirety concept, neither party, acting alone, could transfer his or her interest in the property held by the entirety, and on the death of either party, the survivor would own the whole property. In this respect, tenancy by the entirety works in the same fashion as a joint tenancy. The tenancy in the entirety operates until both parties agree to a transfer or until the marriage is dissolved by law or by the death of one of the parties.

Presently, twenty four jurisdictions recognize tenancy by the entirety in some form. The laws applicable to this form of ownership vary from state to state with certain basic similarity in concept and elements. Many states, however, have actually abolished tenancy by the entirety on the theory that it is out-moded and does not reflect the present-day attitude that husband and wife are individuals, notwithstanding their marriage relationship.

In many states that recognize tenancy by the entirety, there's often a presumption that when husband and wife take property as joint tenants, they're actually taking ownership as tenants by the entirety. To eliminate this presumption, if your intentions are to own the property in true joint tenancy, the title should read as "joint tenants and not as tenants by the entirety." It is important to consult your local state law to determine the full implications of various forms of property ownerships.

Comparing Tenancy by the Entirety with Joint Tenancy

The tenancy by the entirety has a common characteristic with joint tenancy in that there is a right of survivorship in both. That is, on the death of either owner, the survivor owns the whole property. However, there are important differences between the two.

First, a joint tenancy may be held by any number of persons, while a tenancy by the entirety may be held only by husband and wife.

Second, any one of the joint tenants by transferring his ownership to a third party can sever or terminate the joint tenancy, whereas a tenancy by the entirety may not be transferred unless both parties agree, and may not be severed except by dissolution of marriage, or by the death of one of the parties, or by agreement between husband and wife.

The right of a surviving spouse to own the whole property on the death of a spouse is one of the major advantages of holding property by the entirety. Such property passing to the surviving spouse becomes hers or his alone without going through probate, and without being subject to the claims of creditors of the deceased person (unless the property itself was pledged as collateral or security, such as a mortgage signed by both parties.) The surviving spouse may then dispose of the property as her or his own, regardless of any provision to the contrary in the will of the deceased spouse.

In the event of a simultaneous death of both spouses, the property would be distributed as if it was owned by them as tenants in common. In other words, one-half of the property would pass to the husband's estate and the other half to the wife's estate.

Different Types of Co-Tenancies and Their Characteristics - An Overview

Question	Joint Tenancy	Tenancy by the Entirety	Tenancy in Common
Survivorship rights?	Yes	Yes	No
Right to sell share?	Yes	No	Yes
Right to divide?	Yes	No	Yes
Can creditors reach share?	Yes	Maybe	Yes
Included in estate?	Yes (unless w/ spouse, then one-half)	Yes (one-half)	Only your share

Joint Tenancy vs. Trust

Question	Joint Tenancy	Trust
Avoids probate?	Probably	Yes
Can save estate taxes?	No	Yes
Protection from creditors' attack?	No	Yes
Provides for the unexpected?	No	Yes
Affected by disability of owner?	Yes	No
Affected by simultaneous death?	Yes	No
Affected by divorce?	Yes	No
Easy to contest?	Yes	No
Can provide for spouse, children and grandchildren?	No	Yes
Can protect from creditors of beneficiaries?	No	Yes
Can predict outcome?	No	Yes
Reduces overall costs and expenses?	No	Yes

Factors Affecting Creditors' Rights

Whether a creditor will be able to reach jointly-owned property depends primarily on three factors:

1. Whether the debtor (joint tenant or co-tenant) is alive or deceased at the time the creditor attempts to levy on the property.

2. Whether the property is held in a joint tenancy, a tenancy-in-common, or a tenancy by the entirety.

3. Applicable state law.

These factors will largely determine whether the creditor can reach the property in satisfaction of his debt.

While the Debtor Is Alive

Joint Tenancy

A creditor seeking to satisfy a debt owed to him may attach his debtor's interest in property held in a joint tenancy if the debtor/joint tenant is alive at the time of the attachment. (An attachment is a legal securing of property to satisfy a debt.)

The general rule followed by the courts is that during the life of a joint tenant, that joint tenant's undivided interest can be reached by his creditors. The theory behind this is that each joint tenant is able to sell or transfer his interest during his life, thus severing the joint tenancy between himself and his co-tenants and creating a tenancy in common between his buyer and the other co-tenants. Since each joint tenant can sell or otherwise freely transfer his interest, his creditor should be able to reach that same interest to satisfy a debt owed by the joint tenant to the creditor.

The creditor's attachment on the joint tenancy creates a result similar to when a joint tenant's interest is sold. The joint tenancy between the debtor and his co-tenants is destroyed and the creditor becomes a tenant in common with the other co-tenants. The other co-tenants remain joint tenants among themselves.

Case: The case of *Frederick v. Shorman* provides a good illustration of this result. In that case Hilda Bjornsen bought a piece of residential property in Cedar Rapids, Iowa, and had the deed state that she and her son, Robert, were joint tenants in the property with full rights of survivorship. Robert later married Yvonne and they had a daughter, Roberta. Robert and Yvonne were subsequently divorced and a judgment for child support was entered against Robert. When Robert failed to pay, Yvonne went to court and obtained an order that if Robert did not pay immediately, his property would be attached and sold to satisfy his obligations.

Hilda then brought an action in Lynn District Court in Iowa seeking to have the court declare that Yvonne could not attach the jointly-held property. She argued that when she added Robert as a joint tenant she had only intended to create a future right of survivorship in her son and not a present interest that could be attached by his creditors. "I was unmarried at the time I purchased the property," she told the court, "and he was my only child, my only heir, so naturally I put the house in his name, only if something happened to me, he would get the house."

Hilda also argued that she and Robert had agreed that Robert was to pay her one-half of the purchase price and maintenance on the property, but he never did. Since he never paid anything toward the property, he had no real interest in it and his creditors should not be able to touch it.

The district court agreed with Hilda's arguments and held that Yvonne was restrained from proceeding with her attachment and levy on the property. Yvonne appealed to the Supreme Court of Iowa.

The Iowa Supreme Court reversed the lower court's decision. It agreed with Yvonne that Robert and Hilda did indeed hold the property as joint tenants because the deed on the property clearly reflected this intent. It reached this conclusion despite the fact that Robert never paid for any of the property's cost. Since Yvonne brought her action while Robert was still alive, she had the right, as Robert's judgment creditor, to proceed with her sale of Robert's one-half undivided interest in the property.

Tenancy in Common

A creditor of a tenant in common may clearly attach the interest which his debtor owns in the tenancy in common. This is a well-settled principle in the law. It must be remembered, however, that the creditor stands in the shoes of his debtor, and therefore he can only take the interest which his debtor owned. In this event the creditor becomes a tenant in common with the other co-tenants.

Case: In a Colorado case, C.V. James and his family were tenants in common in a parcel of land in El Paso County, Colorado. Mr. James owned a three-fourths interest and his wife and children owned the other one-fourth interest in the property (tenants in common needn't have equal shares).

In 1931, William J. Fallon won a judgment against Mr. James in the district court of Boulder County. An order for collection on the judgment was subsequently issued, and the sheriff of El Paso County was ordered to collect the money owed. The sheriff levied upon the land and put the land up for sale so that the proceeds could be given to Fallon and the judgment could be satisfied. Mr. Fallon himself purchased the property at the sheriff's sale, and he received the sheriff's deed. The sheriff's deed, however, appeared to convey all the interest in the land. It made no mention of the three-fourths interest of Mr. James. Mr. Fallon went into possession of the land assuming he was owner of the whole property.

It was not until eighteen years later that Mr. James' wife and children claimed their one-fourth share of the property. Mr. Fallon resisted but the El Paso County District Court agreed with the wife and children. Fallon appealed.

The Supreme Court of Colorado also agreed with the wife and children and held that despite the fact that the sheriff's deed purported to convey all the interest in the land, the only interest the sheriff could levy upon was that of the debtor, C.V. James, and not upon the interest of the co-tenants. Only Mr. James' three-fourths interest could be reached by Fallon. Therefore, when Mr. Fallon bought the land, he stepped into the shoes of Mr. James, his debtor, and became a tenant in common in the land with Mr. James' wife and children. The wife and children were allowed to claim their interest in the land, even though so much time had elapsed.

Tenancy by the Entirety

Tenancy by the entirety is a special form of joint tenancy that can be used only by a husband and wife. Under this form of ownership, the whole of the property is owned not by two individual spouses but rather by the unity created by the marriage partners; the two married partners take title as a single person.

In the states that recognize tenancy by the entirety, neither spouse, acting alone, can sever such a tenancy. This creates unique problems for creditors who attempt to attach the husband's or wife's interest in the property (except in the case of a bankruptcy.)

As a general rule, if the husband wife are jointly liable on a debt, the property they hold as tenants by the entirety may be attached during their lifetime and sold for satisfaction of their debt. However, if only the husband or only the wife is individually liable on a debt, the creditor will usually not be allowed to seize that property.

Except for those states where tenancy by the entirety has been abolished or modified, creditors of the wife may not attach the property and have it sold. Since the wife herself is not allowed to sell her interest in a tenancy by the entirety, her creditors could gain no greater rights and therefore will likewise not be allowed to sell it. In effect, the wife's interest in the property is insulated from the claims of her individual creditors during her lifetime.

Except in those states (such as Massachusetts) where special protection is given by law to a principal residence or other property held under a tenancy by the entirety, a creditor of the husband may place a lien or attachment on the property since the husband has the sole right to possession during his life. However, as a general rule, the property will not be sold to satisfy the husband's debt so long as the wife is alive.

After the Death of the Debtor

Joint Tenancy

One of the essential characteristics of the joint tenancy with a right of survivorship is that the surviving tenant becomes owner of the whole property after the death of his joint tenant. In other words, by operation of law, the joint tenancy ceases to exist upon the death of the joint tenant.

One consequence of this characteristic of joint tenancy is that the creditors of a deceased joint tenant may not satisfy their debts from the jointly-held property. The theory behind this is that the property no longer belongs to the joint tenant's estate, but passes as the sole property of the surviving joint tenants. In other words, the creditors cannot reach the joint property because there's "nothing" to reach.

The creation of joint tenancy is deceptively simple. And as we've seen before, a very large portion of property owned by more than one person in the United States is held in joint tenancy with right of survivorship. But before you rush out to put all your property into joint tenancy, so as to put it out of reach of creditors after your death, you should carefully examine the tax and legal implications of joint tenancy, as well as exceptions to the rules. Consult a professional for proper guidance.

Exceptions

Although, as a general rule, a creditor cannot reach the jointly-owned property on the death of a debtor/joint tenant, there are two recognized exceptions to this rule:

First, if the joint tenancy was created to defraud the creditors it would be deemed a fraudulent conveyance and would be set aside.

Second, jointly-held funds are generally subject to the payment of federal or state taxes. In other words, you'll not be able to avoid the taxman by forming a joint tenancy.

A third exception would apply in those states that have specific laws regarding creditors' rights against joint property. South Dakota, for example, has a law that allows a creditor to sue a surviving joint tenant for the debts of a deceased joint tenant, and the creditor may reach the joint property to the extent of the deceased joint owner's contribution. And Washington seems to take the position that a joint tenancy shall not cause a creditor to lose his rights. But these states are definitely in the minority.

To the extent that the jointly-held property is subject to federal or state taxes, the surviving joint tenant (or tenant by the entirety) will still own the property but be subject to the payment of taxes. In fact, a lien (a legal attachment) automatically attaches to all property that is subject to tax in the deceased's estate. If there's not enough money to pay the tax out of other property, the jointly-held property may be sold to pay the tax.

Creditors and Joint Bank Accounts

Joint bank accounts between husband and wife or other members of the family or even between two unrelated parties engaged in a common business venture are quite common. It is important to realize the rights of creditors of one of the joint tenants in the event the creditor obtains a judgment against that joint tenant.

Can a creditor of one of the account holders attach the funds in the jointly-held account to satisfy the debt? Is he entitled to only one-half of the funds in the account or can he attach the entire account? Can he do so if the debtor is the non-contributing co-tenant (in other words, if the debtor is only an account holder in name without having contributed any money to the account)?

The answers to these questions depend upon the applicable state law and specific circumstances of the case.

In some states the law provides that each tenant of a joint bank account has a "vested" interest in the account. A vested interest is one which legally belongs to a person, giving him in effect an absolute ownership. Even in the absence of a specific state law, a court may rule that a creditor who has obtained a judgment against one of the joint tenants now stands in the shoes of the joint tenant and is able to withdraw the funds in the account just as the joint tenant himself is able to do. The following case illustrates the complications that arise with joint bank accounts.

Case: Benedict Track and his wife, Dorothy, opened a joint account at the Northwestern National Bank of Minneapolis. The account card they signed stated that all funds deposited would be the property of the depositors jointly with right of survivorship in each, and that each party had complete and absolute authority over the account and that either could withdraw any part, or all of the funds.

Benedict owed rent to an organization called Park Enterprises. Park sued Benedict and obtained a judgment against him, and went on to attach Benedict's bank account. Wife, of course, protested that the joint account was not attachable for her husband's debts. Further, she contended that some of the funds in the account were contributed by her and were her separate property, and therefore should not be reachable by Park. The lower court ruled that Benedict's creditor could reach what was Benedict's and allowed Park to reach one-half of the account. Benedict and Dorothy appealed.

The Supreme Court of Minnesota looked at things differently. The high court said that Park Enterprises not only could reach one-half of the account, but was entitled to recover all of the funds in the account up to the full amount necessary to satisfy the judgment against Benedict. The court reasoned that the contract covering the joint account allowed either of the account holders to withdraw the full balance without accounting to the other.

As this case shows, ownership of the funds in a joint bank account may or may not end up the way the parties intend, depending upon the actual circumstances and the applicable state law. Some states have laws establishing a presumption of a certain intent on the part of the joint tenants, while the laws of other states may establish conclusively that the parties intended a true joint tenancy. In short, ownership of funds in a joint bank account is somewhat unpredictable and the results may or may not be to your liking.

Protecting the Tenancy-by-the-Entirety Property from the Claims of Creditors

Does ownership of a property in tenancy by the entirety afford any protection against the claims of creditors of one of the spouses? Many people are under the impression that if they own a property in tenancy by the entirety, the property would be insulated against the claims of creditors.

The fact is this may or may not be true, depending upon the circumstances.

The determining factor is whether the creditors are creditors of husband or wife, or both, and more importantly, whether the applicable state law recognizes tenancy by the entirety and the extent to which it allows a creditor to reach such property.

Generally speaking, if a husband and wife are jointly liable on a debt, that is, if they both have signed the promissory note and/or both agreed to pay the debt, then any property they own, whether individually, jointly, or as tenants by the entirety may be subject to attachment by their creditors and sale for non-payment of the debt. On the other hand, if the debt is incurred by either husband or wife individually, then the property owned as tenants by the entirety is usually not subject to attachment and sale to satisfy the debt of one of the spouses.

Of course, if the property is pledged as security for the debt (such as on a mortgage), then that property may clearly be sold to satisfy non-payment of the debt.

Fraudulent Conveyance

Most states have adopted the Uniform Fraudulent Conveyance Act (or similar act), which states that a party may not gratuitously transfer property to another (including a transfer into a co-tenancy) if his intent in doing so is to defraud his creditors. The Uniform Act says that such an intent is presumed if the transfer thereby renders the party insolvent.

Some cases have held that if a party puts his property in a joint tenancy in order to defraud a creditor, then that creditor may reach the jointly-held property on his debtor's death. For example, the New York Court of Appeals in 1967 decided in a case that if mutual funds were placed in joint accounts to defraud a creditor, that creditor could reach the funds at the debtor's death.

Creditors' Rights in a Bankruptcy

The right of a creditor to reach a jointly-held property is generally more restrictive as long as the debtor has not filed for bankruptcy. Once in bankruptcy, the creditor may be able to go farther. The federal Bankruptcy Code has established some special rules for joint tenancy when one of the joint tenants is declared bankrupt by a federal court.

When a person is the subject of bankruptcy proceedings, all his property is under the jurisdiction of the court and becomes the property of the "trustee" in bankruptcy. This will include his interest as a joint tenant, tenant in common, or tenant by the entirety.

Under the Bankruptcy Code, the trustee in bankruptcy may sell the property of the bankrupt co-tenant under any of the various forms of co-tenancy and apply the proceeds of the share of the bankrupt co-tenant to satisfy the bankrupt co-tenant's debts. It is up to the non-bankrupt co-tenant to properly claim his share of the proceeds of the commonly-held property before they are applied to satisfy the debts.

If a non-bankrupt co-tenant is the true "owner" of jointly-held property in which the bankrupt is his co-tenant, he must prove to the court that none (or only a part) of the commonly-held property should be subject to the bankruptcy proceedings. This could prove quite difficult and, even if successful, could result in considerable expense.

Illustration: Father creates a joint bank account with his Son. Father contributes all the money and lists his Son as a joint tenant only as a matter of convenience. Later Son files for personal bankruptcy and, as the law requires, lists the joint bank account with his Father as an asset. Under the Bankruptcy Code Father must prove to the court that he contributed all the funds in the account before he can recover them.

If instead of a bank account he had opened a brokerage account, registered jointly with his bankrupt Son, he would be able to recover only one-half the value of the securities, since the other half would have been considered a completed gift to his Son. The Son or his creditors would be entitled to that one-half regardless of the fact that Son had made no contribution.

In some states, exception against a bankruptcy sale is provided for certain property. For example, principal residence held in tenancy by the entirety may be protected against a bankruptcy sale. Remember, however, that this is more of an exception than the rule. You should check the laws of your state to see if you're entitled to any special protection.

> **The manner in which you own a property may have the most significant impact on your asset protection and estate planning strategies. It will determine the disposition of the property upon your death, it may affect the claims of creditors, and it definitely will have federal estate, income and gift tax implications.**

Agreement to Convert Joint Tenancy to Tenancy in Common

Agreement made, effective _____ [date], by and between _____ _____, of _____ [address], County of _____, State of _____, and _____ _____, of _____ _____, [address], County of _____, State of _____.

RECITAL

The parties to this agreement desire that the property, both real and personal, now owned by them in joint tenancy and not as tenants in common be converted and held by them as tenants in common, and not as joint tenants with right of survivorship.

SECTION ONE

OWNERSHIP RIGHTS

It is agreed that from and after the effective date of this agreement all the real and personal property owned by the parties to this agreement, whether presently held in joint tenancy by the parties, or presently owned by either of the parties in that party's own name, shall be owned by each of the parties as follows:

An undivided _____ percent (_____%) interest therein shall be the separate property of _____, and _____ _____ assigns and transfers to _____ _____ all of such transferor's right, title, and interest in and to such undivided _____ percent (_____%) interest in the same.

An undivided _____ percent (_____%) interest therein shall be the separate property of _____, and _____ _____ assigns and transfers to _____ _____ all of such transferor's right, title, and interest in and to such undivided _____ percent (_____%) interest in the same.

SECTION TWO

CONVEYANCES

The parties further agree to execute and deliver any deed or other instrument, and to do any act, necessary to effectuate this agreement.

SECTION THREE

GOVERNING LAW

This agreement shall be governed by, construed, and enforced in accordance with the laws of the State of _____.

SECTION FOUR

ASSIGNMENT OF RIGHTS

The rights of each party under this agreement are personal to that party and may not be assigned or transferred to any other person, firm, corporation, or other entity without the prior express and written consent of the other party.

In witness whereof, each party to this agreement has caused it to be executed at _____ *[place of execution]* on the date indicated below.

_____

_____

Signatures and date(s) of signing

[Acknowledgments]

Creditors' Rights in Community Property States

2

The system of community property ownership prevailing in the United States today is essentially an inheritance from the Spanish and can be traced in written form to the Visi Gothic Code of 690 A.D. The community property system was originally adopted by eight states: Louisiana, Washington, Texas, New Mexico, Nevada, California, Idaho and Arizona. Wisconsin became the latest state to adopt community property system in 1985.

History

The community property system, as originally brought from Spain or Mexico, has undergone varying degree of development in these states and the laws in these states are far from uniform.

Husband Controlled All Property

Over the years, husband, as a rule, was the domineering partner in the community. Husband more or less exercised complete control of his separate property, of the community property, and of the wife's separate property. In many cases, wife had no capacity to contract debts. The community was generally subject to debts of the husband but rarely subject to debts of the wife.

Starting from the early to mid-19th century, state legislatures made periodic changes in the community property laws, a result of which was to increase the rights of married women. For example, in 1913 married women in Texas were given control of the separate property which they had brought into the marriage or acquired later by gift or inheritance. California, in 1917, provided that the wife had to join in any instrument by which the husband conveyed, encumbered, or leased for more than one year any community real property.

For the most part, however, the general rule of inequality between sexes prevailed. The right of a married woman to enter into contracts and to manage community property was substantially restricted across the board.

Equality between Spouses

Major reform toward bringing sexual equality into community property did not take place until the 1960's. The effect of these new reforms has been to equalize the rights and responsibilities of partners in marriage. Now, women have equal power to manage community property, just as they have the full power to contract and manage their separate property. Community property is now subject to debts of the wife under the same principles that made property subject to the husband's debts.

Creditors' Rights in General

Common Law States

In non-community property states, also known as common law states, the question of what property a creditor of the husband or wife may reach to satisfy the creditor's debt is relatively simple. If the debt is owed by the husband, his property may be reached. If the debt is owed by the wife, her property may be reached. Thus, if a husband was indebted to the creditor, creditor would obtain a judgment against the husband and then execute on the husband's property.

If both husband and wife are liable on the debt, and the liability is joint and several as it usually is, judgment can be obtained against either or both and the property of either or both, may be reached by execution. In other words, the fact that two individuals are married does not directly affect either their liability for obligations incurred or the property that may be reached by their creditors.

Community Property States

In contrast, in a community property state, the fact that two individuals are married is of paramount importance in determining, first, who is liable for the debt, and second, what property may be reached after a judgment has been obtained by a creditor.

When a married person in a community property state incurs a debt, it needs to be determined whether the debt is of that particular individual's separate obligation, a community obligation, an obligation of the other spouse because the contracting party was acting as the spouse's agent, or any combination of the above.

Thus, for example, if a wife enters into a contract to purchase an automobile, she may be purchasing it on her own and not purchasing it either on behalf of her husband or the community. On the other hand, it is also possible that she is purchasing the automobile for the community and thus obligating the community for the debt. In the event that she is purchasing the vehicle as an agent for her husband, she is obligating only him and his property.

While analyzing a creditor's claim against a specific property of a married couple, the following questions need to be answered:

1. Does the creditor have a claim sounding in contract or in tort?

2. Is the debt a separate debt of one of the spouses or a community debt?

3. Is the creditor attempting to reach community property or the separate property of one or both spouses?

4. Does the property the creditor is attempting to reach represent earnings of one of the spouses?

5. If the property is community property, is the creditor attempting to reach all of it or only the interest of one of the spouses in it?

6. Is the claim one that arose before or after the marriage?

7. What is the statutory and case law of the jurisdiction? There's little uniformity among the laws of various community property states.

Separate and Community Property

In general, property that one of the spouses brings to the marriage continues to be his or her separate property during marriage. Gifts and bequests of property to one spouse during the marriage are also the separate property of that spouse, as is property inherited under the intestacy laws.

All other property is community property, including that which is earned by either spouse during the marriage and profits from community property accumulated by the couple. Commingling of separate property generally transmutes it to community property, and there is a general presumption that property obtained by either spouse during the marriage is community property.

Two aspects of community property deserve mention in the context of creditors' rights. Earnings of a spouse during the marriage are generally community property, but are sometimes treated differently than other community property when creditors of the other spouse are attempting to reach them to satisfy a separate debt.

More complex is the question of whether a spouse's interest in the community property is liable for the spouse's separate debts. A spouse does not have the right to withdraw his or her interest in the community and to make it separate property, and, in absence of divorce or separation, there is no right to have the community property partitioned. However, this does not necessarily mean that a creditor should not be able to reach a spouse's interest in the community in order to satisfy that spouse's separate debt.

Separate and Community Debts

The distinction between separate and community property is fairly clear from the statutes and case law of all community property jurisdictions. The same cannot be said of community debts and separate debts. Except for New Mexico, no other jurisdiction has a statutory provision defining separate and community debts.

Obligations incurred prior to the marriage or after a separation or divorce are universally denominated as the separate obligation of the spouse incurring the debt. On the other hand, debts incurred during the marriage are generally community obligations.

If the resulting debt was from a contract made on behalf of the community or if the activity giving rise to a tort obligation was designed to benefit the community, the presumption again is that, if that was incurred during marriage by either spouse, it is a community obligation.

The law in New Mexico is more definite. By statute, it defines separate debts as those incurred prior to the marriage or after either a divorce or separation, and as those debts "contracted by a spouse during the marriage, which are identified by a spouse to the creditor in writing at the time of its creation as a separate debt of the contracting spouse," or which are obligations resulting from a "separate tort committed during marriage." In New Mexico, the statute also provides for a judicial decree that a debt is a separate debt. Community debts are defined simply as all debts incurred by either spouse during marriage that are not separate debts.

Liability of Marital Community

The concept of marital community discussed in this chapter, a concept common to Texas and California, must be distinguished from that found in other community property states, such as Arizona, New Mexico or Washington, for example.

Law in Arizona, New Mexico and Washington

In the latter states, the marital community might be viewed as an independent or quasi-independent entity capable of incurring obligations or debts, and for which husband and wife may at times act as agents. Under this system, the intent with which a spouse contracts is relevant in determining the extent of liability; if a spouse contracts for the benefit of the community, or contracts as an agent of the community, then the community property may be liable, but not otherwise.

	Community Debts	Separate Debts
Arizona	Must be satisfied first from community property, then from separate property of contracting spouse. Separate property of non-contracting spouse not liable.	If contracted before 9/1/73, may be satisfied only from separate property of contracting spouse. If contracted after 9/1/73, may be satisfied from separate property of contracting spouse and from community property to the extent of contracting spouse's contribution thereto.
New Mexico	May be satisfied from community property and from separate property of contracting spouse. Separate property of non-contracting spouse not liable.	May be satisfied from separate property of contracting spouse and from one-half of the community property.
Washington	May be satisfied first from community property and from separate property of contracting spouse. Separate property of non-contracting spouse not liable.	May be satisfied only from the separate property of the debtor spouse. Pre-nuptial credtors of a spouse may also reach that spouse's community property earnings.

Law in California, Texas and Idaho

This approach to community property law, commonly called the "community debt" doctrine, is rejected in California and Texas, which provide by statute that at least some of the community property will be liable for the debts of either spouse regardless of the purpose for which the spouse incurred them.

In California, Texas and possibly in Idaho, proper analysis requires that marital obligations not be analyzed in terms of "community" and "separate" debts. In those jurisdictions, obligations are attributed to the husband or the wife, or to both of them jointly.

The "marital community," a concept common to California and Texas, is not an entity separate and distinct from husband and wife. It neither acts nor contracts as principal or through agents.

In Texas and California, the community of marriage owes nothing and owns nothing. A spouse's efforts during marriage are community efforts but not the community's efforts; property earned by a spouse during marriage is community property but not the community's property. The "community" does not own property or incur obligations; husband and wife do, either individually or jointly.

The liability of marital property is not affected by the purpose for which a spouse contracts; whether a spouse contracts for the benefit of himself or herself individually, or for the benefit of both marital partners, is irrelevant in determining the liability of marital property for debts of either spouse.

Summary

1. Generally, a community debt is a debt incurred by either spouse for the purpose of benefiting the community, as distinguished from a debt incurred for the benefit of a contracting spouse's separate estate only. If a spouse and the third party with whom the spouse deals agree that any obligations are those of the contracting spouse alone, any resulting debt is separate.

2. California, Texas and Idaho do not recognize the community/separate debt distinction. In those states debts are attributed to spouses individually or jointly, as the case may be. "Community debt" and "separate debt" are inappropriate analytical categories in those jurisdictions.

3. Louisiana and Nevada are community property jurisdictions whose community property laws may differ significantly from those of the other states. Therefore, they are omitted from the chart above.

A basic concept of community property law is that of marital effort. Property acquired by the efforts of either spouse during marriage is community property. Property acquired before marriage or that acquired afterward by gift or inheritance is the separate property of that spouse.

The separate property of a spouse is generally liable for all contracts of that spouse.

How to Avoid Joint Liability on Your Spouse's Debts

Under the modern community property statutes, both spouses now have the power to obligate the community property for their contracts. On the other hand, with the exception of the "necessaries" of life, neither spouse may unilaterally obligate the separate property of a non-contracting spouse for debts of a contracting spouse.

Where a debt is a joint obligation of husband and wife, all of the community property together with the separate property of the respective spouses, will be liable for the debt.

Generally speaking, joint liability is readily established in the context of marriage. For example, where one spouse pays bills of the other spouse, that spouse would be held jointly liable for subsequent debts incurred by the other spouse. In one case, by making even a single payment, one spouse is said to have clothed the other contracting spouse with apparent authority to contract joint debts.

Steps to Take

Spouses seeking to avoid joint liability on marital debts should take precautionary measures. For example, a wife who wishes to avoid liability for her husband's purchases should make clear to the husband, and immediately to the seller if she is billed for the debt, that her husband acted without her authority or consent. If she desires to pay that debt in full or in part, she should inform the seller that payment by her does not constitute a regular practice and that her husband does not have authority to make future purchases for which she will make payment.

Alternatively, she might make a gift of funds to the husband, or execute a partition agreement with him, so that he may pay the debt with his separate property.

Spouses should avoid making loans to the other spouse to enable the other spouse to pay debts or to start a separate business in which the other spouse might contract debts; such a practice has rendered the lending spouse liable for subsequent debts of the borrowing spouse. Again, a partition or gift of property may accomplish the same results without risking joint liability.

Overview of Rules and Exceptions

The following general statements illustrate the complexity of rules surrounding separate or community property and rights of creditors to reach it to satisfy either the separate or joint debts of marital partners. Keep in mind that these statements are entirely general, and for every categorization, there is a host of exceptions, and rules and exceptions vary from state to state. The statements are provided here only as a very general overview of property laws in community states.

✓ **The general presumption in community property states is that all property acquired during marriage is community property.**

✓ **Separate property is property acquired before marriage and that property acquired afterward by gift, device, descent or bequest; community property is all other property acquired during marriage.**

✓ **Property traceable to separate property is separate property.**

✓ **The separate property of a spouse is ordinarily not subject to the liabilities of the other spouse.**

✓ **The separate property of a spouse is liable for the payment of debts contracted by either spouse for the necessaries of life.**

✓ **Specific items of separate property of a non-contracting spouse may be reached on a theory of fraud or constructive fraud.**

✓ **Generally, spouses are free to alter the status or ownership rights of marital property by contract, partition agreement or gift, but such transactions may not prejudice the rights of pre-existing creditors, and creditors of a contracting spouse may reach specific separate property in the hands of the non-contracting spouse, if that property can be traced to the contracting spouse's fraud.**

For example, if a debt-ridden spouse transfers half the cash receipts from the sale of a community property car to his wife by gift with an intent to defraud the creditors, the creditors of that spouse would be able to reach the cash in the hands of the other spouse even though the transaction was effective as a gift between the spouses.

✓ **The California rule is that community property is subject to the debts of either spouse contracted before or after marriage, except that neither spouse's earnings are liable for premarital debts of the other spouse.**

✓ The Texas rule is that community property which is subject to the joint control of the spouses is liable for the debts of either which were contracted before or during marriage, or that community property, subject to the sole control of a spouse, is not subject to any non-tortuous liabilities of the other spouse.

✓ The form in which record title to real property is held is conclusive in favor of good faith purchasers for value, without notice of contrary claims.

✓ If for some reason record title to real property is in the name of the spouse not having actual authority to convey any interest therein, third party purchasers and creditors may nevertheless rely upon the form of title. For instance, in Texas the unilateral conveyance is conclusively valid in favor of third parties acting in good faith without notice.

✓ Judgments for or against one spouse in actions involving community property are not necessarily binding upon the other spouse.

✓ Agreements between spouses determining or altering the status of property are generally valid.

✓ Antenuptial contracts are generally valid in California and Texas.

✓ Marital partners may alter the status of property by postnuptial partition or contract.

✓ Marital partners may alter the status of property by conduct creating an inference that a gift has been made.

Community Property Laws in Individual States

Here we'll briefly examine the statutes that delineate the liability of separate or community property for the satisfaction of separate or community debts in various community property states.

Arizona

A. The separate property of a spouse shall not be liable for the separate debts or obligations of the other spouse, absent agreement of the property owner to the contrary.

B. The community property is liable for the premarital separate debts or other liabilities of a spouse, incurred after September 1, 1973 but only to the extent of the value of that spouse's contribution to the community property which would have been such spouse's separate property if single.

D. Except [when joinder of both spouses is required] in § 25-214, either spouse may contract debts and otherwise act for the benefit of the community. In an action on such a debt or obligation the spouses shall be sued jointly and the debt or obligation shall be satisfied: first, from the community property, and second, from the separate property of the spouse contracting the debt or obligation.

California

A. Except as otherwise expressly provided by statute, the community property is liable for a debt incurred by either spouse before or after marriage, regardless which spouse has the management and control of the property and regardless whether one or both spouses are parties to the debt or to a judgment for the debt.

B. The earnings of a married person during marriage are not liable for a debt incurred by the person's spouse before marriage...they remain not liable so long as they are held in a deposit account in which the person's spouse has no right of withdrawal and are uncommingled with other community property, except property insignificant in amount...

Calif. Civ. Code § 5122 provides in part:

A. A married person is not liable for any injury or damage caused by the other spouse except in cases where he or she would be liable therefor if the marriage did not exist.

B. The liability of a married person for death or injury to person or property shall be satisfied as follows:

1. If the liability of the married person is based upon an act or omission which occurred while the married person was performing an activity for the benefit of the community, the liability shall first be satisfied from the community property and second from the separate property of the married person.

2. If the liability of the married person is not based upon an act or omission which occurred while the married person was performing an activity for the benefit of the community, the liability shall first be satisfied from the separate property of the married person and second from the community property.

Idaho

The major statutory provision is Idaho Code § 32-912, set forth in Chapter 7, which provides that either husband or wife may bind the community property by contract with an exception for the sale, conveyance or encumbrance of realty, joint action is then required.

Idaho exempts some separate property from liability for certain community obligations. Idaho Code § 32-912 provides, in part: "any community obligation incurred by either the husband or the wife without the consent in writing of the other shall not obligate the separate property of the spouse who did not consent."

Louisiana

La. Stat. Ann. -Civ. Code art. 2360 as follows:

An obligation incurred by a spouse during the existence of a communityproperty regime for the common interest of the spouses or for the interest of the other spouse is a community obligation.

A separate obligation of a spouse is one incurred by that spouse prior to the establishment or after termination of a community property regime, or one incurred during the existence of a community property regime though not for the common interest of the spouses or for the interest of the other spouse. An obligation resulting from an intentional wrong not perpetrated for the benefit of the community, or an obligation incurred for the separate property benefit of a spouse to the extent that it does not benefit the community, the family, or the other spouse, is likewise a separate obligation.

Reimbursement may only be made to the extent of community assets, unless the community obligation was incurred for the ordinary and customary expenses of the marriage, or for the support, maintenance, and education of children of either spouse in keeping with the economic condition of the community. In the last case, the spouse is entitled to reimbursement from the other spouse even if there are no community assets.

Nevada

Nev. Rev. Stat. 123.050:

Neither the separate property of a spouse nor his share of the community property is liable for the debts of the other spouse contracted before the marriage.

New Mexico

N. Mex. Stat. 1978 § 40-3-9:

A. "Separate debt" means:

(1) a debt contracted or incurred by a spouse before marriage or after entry of a decree of dissolution of marriage; [or legal separation]. . . .

(3) a debt designated as a separate debt of a spouse by a judgment or decree of any court having jurisdiction;

(4) a debt contracted by a spouse during marriage which is identified by a spouse to the creditor in writing at the time of its creation as the separate debt of the contracting spouse; or

(5) a debt which arises from a tort committed by a spouse before marriage or after entry of a decree of dissolution of marriage or a separate tort committed during marriage.

B. "Community debt" means a debt contracted or incurred by either both spouses during marriage which is not a separate debt.

§40-3-10: A. The separate debt of a spouse shall be satisfied first from the debtor spouse's separate property, excluding that spouse's interest in property in which each of the spouses owns an undivided equal interest as a joint tenant or tenant in common. Should such property be insufficient, then the debt shall be satisfied from the debtor spouse's one-half interest in the community property or in property in which each spouse owns an undivided equal interest as a joint tenant or tenant in common, excluding the residence of the spouses. Should such property be insufficient, then the debt shall be satisfied from the debtor spouse's interest in the residence of the spouses . . . . Neither spouse's interest in community property or separate property shall be liable for the separate debt of the other spouse.

B. The priorities or exemptions established in this section for the satisfaction of a separate debt must be claimed by either spouse under the procedure set forth in Section 42-10-13 NMSA 1978, or the right to claim such priorities or exemptions is waived as between a spouse and the creditor.

C. This section shall apply only while both spouses are living, and shall not apply to the satisfaction of debts after the death of one or both spouses.

§ 40-3-11: A. Community debts shall be satisfied first from all community property and all property in which each spouse owns an undivided equal interest as a joint tenant or tenant in common, excluding the residence of the spouses. Should such property be insufficient, community debts shall then be satisfied from the residence of the spouses, except as provided in Section 42-10-9 NMSA 1978. Should such property be insufficient, only the separate property of the spouse who contracted or incurred the debt shall be liable for its satisfaction. If both spouses contracted or incurred the debt, the separate property of both spouses is jointly and severally liable for its satisfaction.

B. The priorities or exemptions established in this section for the satisfaction of community debts must be claimed by either spouse under the procedure set forth in Section 42-10-13 NMSA 1978 or the right to claim such priorities or exemptions is waived as between a spouse and the creditor.

C. This section shall apply only while both spouses are living, and shall not apply to the satisfaction of debts after the death of one or both spouses.

Texas

The text of **Vernon's Ann. Tex. Stat. Family Code § 5.61** is as follows:

(a) A spouse's separate property is not subject to liabilities of the other spouse unless both spouses are liable by other rules of law.

(b) Unless both spouses are liable by other rules of law, the community property subject to a spouse's sole management, control, and disposition is not subject to:

(1) any liabilities that the other spouse incurred before marriage; or

(2) any nontortious liabilities that the other spouse incurs during marriage.

(c) The community property subject to a spouse's sole or joint management, control, and disposition is subject to the liabilities incurred by him or her before or during marriage.

(d) All the community property is subject to tortious liability of either spouse incurred during marriage.

The Texas approach to marshaling is also unique; it is left to the discretion of the judge by **Vernon's Ann. Tex. Stat. Family Code § 5.62:**

(a) A judge may determine, as he deems just and equitable, the order in which particular separate or community property will be subject to execution and sale to satisfy a judgment, if the property subject to liability for a judgment includes any combination of:

(1) a spouse's separate property;

(2) community property subject to a spouse's sole management, control, and disposition;

(3) community property subject to the other spouse's sole management, control, and disposition; and

(4) community property subject to the spouses' joint management, control, and disposition.

(b) In determining the order in which particular property will be subject to execution and sale, the judge shall consider the facts surrounding the transaction or occurrence upon which the suit is based.

Washington

Washington has been unusual in making community property responsible for the payment of only community liabilities and certain premarital debts. Because most separate debts could not be collected from community property and most community debts could not be collected from separate property, the distinction between community and separate liabilities was more important (and more frequently litigated) than in other community property states.

The separate property of a spouse is not liable for the separate debt of the other spouse.

Wisconsin

Wis. Stat. 1985-86 § 766.55 provides in part:

(1) An obligation incurred by a spouse during marriage, including one attributable to an act or omission during marriage, is presumed to be incurred in the interest of the marriage or the family. A statement separately signed by the obligated or incurring spouse at or before the time the obligation is incurred stating that the obligation is or will be incurred in the interest of the marriage or the family is conclusive

evidence that the obligation to which the statement refers is an obligation in the interest of the marriage or family, except that the existence of that statement does not affect any interspousal right or remedy.

(2) After the determination date all of the following apply:

(a) A spouse's obligation to satisfy a duty of support owed to the other spouse or to a child of the marriage may be satisfied only from all marital property and all other property of the obligated spouse.

(b) An obligation incurred by a spouse in the interest of the marriage or the family may be satisfied only from all marital property and all other property of the incurring spouse.

(c) 1. An obligation incurred by a spouse before or during marriage that is attributable to an obligation arising before marriage or to an act or omission occurring before marriage may be satisfied only from property of that spouse that is not marital property and from that part of marital property which would have been the property of that spouse but for the marriage.

2. An obligation incurred by a spouse before, on or after January 1, 1986, that is attributable to an obligation arising before January 1, 1986, or to an act or omission occurring before January 1, 1986, may be satisfied only from property of that spouse that is not marital property and from that part of marital property which would have been the property of that spouse but for the enactment of this chapter.

(cm) An obligation incurred by a spouse during marriage, resulting from a tort committed by the spouse during marriage, may be satisfied from the property of that spouse that is not marital property and from that spouse's interest in marital property.

(d) Any other obligation incurred by a spouse during marriage, including one attributable to an act or omission during marriage, may be satisfied only from property of that spouse that is not marital property and from that spouse's interest in marital property, in that order.

(2m) Unless the dissolution decree or any amendment to the decree so provides, no income of a nonincurring spouse is available for satisfaction of an obligation under sub. (2)(b) after entry of the decree. Marital property assigned to each spouse under that decree is available for satisfaction of such an obligation to the extent of the value of the marital property at the date of the decree. If a dissolution decree provides that the nonincurring spouse is responsible for satisfaction of the obligation, the obligation may be satisfied as if both spouses had incurred the obligation.

SECTION II

Your Legal Rights as a Consumer

3

The Fair Debt Collection Practices Act of 1978 (FDCPA) offers to consumers some of the most comprehensive benefits and protections provided by any federal or state law regulating the activities of debt collectors. Although the Act applies to a relatively small portion of the debt collection industry, its influence is wide-spread and significant. Several states have adopted regulations and statutes fashioned on the broad standards and detailed proscriptions of the Act, and have brought all collectors of debt under their coverage.

Introduction

The FDCPA became law on March 30, 1978. It establishes general standards of proscribed conduct for debt collectors in detail, restricts abusive collection practices, and provides specific rights and remedies for consumers. In particular, consumer is protected from invasion of privacy, harassment, abuse, false or deceptive representations and unfair or unconscionable collection methods. Specific debt collection acts prohibited include late night or repetitive phone calls and false threats of legal action.

The Act gives consumer the right to require a collector to stop all collection contacts. It requires a collector to deal with consumer's attorney when consumer has one. It gives consumer the right to require a collector to verify the existence, legality or amount of the debt it's attempting to collect.

Who Is a "Debt Collector?"

In order to fully understand the protections afforded by the Fair Debt Collection Practices Act, it is necessary to determine if the person or agency is in fact a "debt collector" as defined by the Act. If the person is not a debt collector, then the protections of the Act would not apply. So let's look at the definition of the term "debt collector" and exclusions from that term.

1. Any Person Whose Principal Business Is Collecting Debts Is a "Debt Collector"

Under this definition most debt collection agencies are covered by the FDCPA, whether or not they own the debts they collect. The definition covers flat-rate debt collectors which are "companies hired by a creditor for a flat fee simply to mail debtors letters requesting payment directly to the creditor," and credit counselors who, for a profit, arrange for payment of a consumer's debts.

Creditors are expressly excluded from the definition of "debt collector." There are, however, many creditors whose primary business is collecting debts, both delinquent and non-delinquent. Sales finance companies, such as General Motors Acceptance Corporation and General Electric Credit Corporation, whose principal business is purchasing and collecting consumer transactions, generated by a retailer clearly come within the scope of the Act, although they may appear to be excluded at first glance.

An attorney, if acting as an agent of a collection agency and not a creditor, would be covered under the Act. Conversely, a collection agency's employees may be excluded from coverage as the creditor's agents where they collect on a creditor's premises, in the creditor's name, and with the creditor's supervision.

2. Any Person Who Regularly Collects Debts Owed to Another Is a "Debt Collector"

The phrase covers the collection of delinquent debts by one creditor for another. Many creditors enter into "reciprocal collection agreements" to collect each other's debts in areas where one is located and the other is not.

For example, if a bank's debtor moves to a distant state, the bank may enlist the aid of a bank in the distant state to collect the debt, while agreeing to perform similar services for the distant bank.

3. Creditors Using False Names Are "Debt Collectors"

Under this phrase, a creditor not otherwise covered would be subject to the Act if it uses a name other than its own which suggests the involvement of a third-party collector, or poses as a collection agency, or uses a third party's name in its collection efforts. This would include, for instance, a creditor who mails letters written by a debt collection agency using the agency's letterhead. A creditor mailing collection letters on an attorney's letterhead is also covered under this definition.

This section was designed to cover principally companies in the business of "flat-rating," and also persons who incidentally design or supply deceptive collection forms. "Flat-rating" is the practice of designing or selling to creditors form letters with the flat-rater's name on the letterhead, thereby falsely suggesting the flat-rater's active participation in the collection process.

4. Repossession Companies Are Treated as "Debt Collectors" Under Certain Circumstances

The Act is aimed at companies that principally repossess automobiles.

5. Lawyers Regularly Collecting Consumer Debts Are Now Covered by All FDCPA Provisions

Effective July 9, 1986 the limited attorney exemption in the Fair Debt Collection Practices Act was eliminated. An attorney who regularly collects consumer debts is now subject to all provisions of the FDCPA.

Who Is Not a "Debt Collector?"

As we've seen above, the requirements of the Fair Debt Collection Practices Act apply only to "debt collectors" as defined by the Act. It is necessary to know who is not a debt collector. The law specifically provides for ten exceptions.

1. Creditor's Employees Collecting in the Name of the Creditor Are Specifically Excluded

This section excludes from most FDCPA requirements creditor's in-house collectors who use a creditor's true business name. By implication, creditor corporations collecting their own debts in their own name are also excluded because they can only act through their employees and officers.

2. A Commonly-Owned or Affiliated Corporate Collector Collecting Only for Its Affiliates Is Specifically Excluded If It Is Not Principally a Debt Collector

This exception applies to debts transferred from one corporate affiliate or commonly-owned organization to another, so long as the transferee is not principally a debt collector and collects transferred debts only for corporate affiliates. For example, one finance company branch may transfer a debt to a corporate affiliate in another city or state because the consumer owing the debt has moved.

3. State and Federal Officials Performing Their Duties Are Specifically Excluded

This exception applies to marshals and sheriffs who are attempting to collect particular debts in their official capacities. The exception does not apply to a private collection agency hired to collect debts for a state or federal agency.

4. Process Servers Are Specifically Excluded

This exclusion applies, for example, to a sheriff serving a subpoena upon a witness to appear in an action for debt.

5. Bona Fide Non-Profit Consumer Credit Counselors Are Specifically Excluded

Most cities have non-profit counseling services or adjustment bureaus established and maintained by major credit extenders. Their principal function is to accept referrals of financially distressed consumers and help them arrange out-of-court plans to pay their creditors in an orderly fashion. To qualify for the exclusion, the counseling agency must be non-profit, must engage in such service in good faith, and must receive and distribute payments, as well as provide financial counseling.

6. Attorneys Acting as Attorneys for Clients in the Clients' Names Were Specifically Excluded Before 1986

This exclusion was repealed in 1986.

7. Persons Collecting Debts as Part of Bona Fide Fiduciary or Escrow Arrangements Are Specifically Excluded

As a fiduciary, a bank trust department may hold notes, accounts receivable and judgments owed trusts, estates and guardian accounts. In its capacity as trustee, executor or guardian, the trust department has legal ownership of such obligations as well as the legal duty to collect them. The specific exemption applies to activities carried out by bank trust departments, escrow companies, and other bona fide fiduciaries.

8. An Extender of Credit Collecting on Behalf of Another a Debt It Originally Extended Is Specifically Excluded

This section excludes from the general coverage of the Act a credit extender's collection in its own name of a debt that it originally extended and then sold or assigned to another creditor while remaining responsible for some or all aspects of collection.

For example, a retailer may assign its retail credit contracts to a bank but retain responsibility for collecting delinquent assigned accounts. He would be exempted from the provisions of the FDCPA. Similarly, a mortgage servicing company that remains responsible for collecting a mortgage it originated but no longer owns would be exempted too.

9. Persons Collecting Debts Not in Default When Obtained Are Specifically Excluded

This exclusion applies to mortgage service companies and others who service outstanding debts for others, so long as the debts were not in default when taken for servicing.

10. Enforcer of a Security Interest in an Account Used as Collateral for a Commercial Loan Is Specifically Excluded

Retailers and lenders sometimes use consumer accounts receivable as collateral for their own commercial loans. Upon default by the retailer or lender, the secured party collects the payments due on the retailer's or lender's consumer accounts receivable. In such situations, the secured party may not be considered a debt collector under this section.

What Transactions Are Covered?

Under the FDCPA Only Consumer Debts Are Covered

This definition limits the application of the Act to activities involved in the collection of consumer debts, incurred primarily for personal, family or household purposes, whether or not such obligations have been reduced to judgment. Commercial debts are not within the scope of the Act.

Debts such as rent, medical expenses, utility, insurance, claims under student loans, parking tickets and credit cards are covered under the provisions of the FDCPA. It also includes dishonored checks if such checks were used for consumer purposes.

FDCPA Covers Only Debts Allegedly Owed by a Natural Person

The term "consumer" means any natural person obligated to pay any debt. Artificial entities, such as corporations, cannot be consumers.

The private remedies provided by the Act are available to "any person." This would include employers, creditors, relatives, friends and neighbors affected by violations connected with consumer transactions.

For example, if a collector calls a consumer's friend asking him or her to talk to the consumer about a debt, both the consumer and friend have a standing to sue under the provisions of the Act prohibiting third-party contacts.

Restrictions on Abusive Debt Collection Practices

The FDCPA restricts the times and places a debt collector may contact a consumer, limits third-party contacts and prohibits contacting a consumer represented by an attorney. These restrictions, along with others, protect the consumer's right to privacy and the security of the consumer's relationships with third parties, including attorneys, co-workers and employers. This was considered an "extremely important protection" when Congress passed the Act.

1. FDCPA Prohibits Contacts at Unusual or Inconvenient Times or Places

Without the prior consent of the consumer given directly to the debt collector, or order from court, a debt collector may not communicate with a consumer in connection with the collection of any debt at any unusual time or place or a time or place known or which should be known as inconvenient to the consumer.

In the absence of any knowledge to the contrary, a debt collector is obliged to assume that the convenient time for communicating with a consumer is after 8 a.m. and before 9 p.m. local time at the consumer's location. Under this section, a collector may not contact a consumer during daytime hours if he has knowledge that the consumer works at night.

Collection contacts could be inconvenient for the consumer for many other reasons: the consumer might be entertaining friends, eating a meal, or attending to an illness in the family. According to the FDCPA, Sunday is an inconvenient or unusual time.

Inconvenient or unusual places to contact a consumer about a debt would include a neighbor's home, hospital or funeral parlor. Work places seem inherently inconvenient places to contact many types of workers, such as assembly line workers, restaurant workers or nurses.

As a general rule, the following types of telephone calls may be illegal:

- calls at odd hours of the day and night;
- repeated calls;
- calls to friends, neighbors, relatives, children, employers, and places of employment;
- threatening calls; and
- calls asserting falsely that legal process is about to be served.

2. A Collector May Not Contact a Consumer It Knows to Be Represented by an Attorney

This prohibits consumer contacts by a collector who knows the consumer is represented by an attorney with respect to the debt. Once the collector learns that the consumer is represented by an attorney, the collector must deal exclusively with the attorney and should not contact the consumer even to confirm the attorney's retention.

If the attorney fails to respond to the collector's communications within a reasonable amount of time, the consumer forfeits the protection against collector contacts.

3. Collectors Are Restricted in Contacting Consumers Who Are at Work

This section protects consumers from interference on their jobs. Collectors are held responsible for general knowledge that workers in certain occupations do not receive mail, phone calls or visits at work except in emergencies; such occupations include factory, construction, school, hospital and retail jobs.

Additional Restrictions on the Activities of a Debt Collector

In addition to the restrictions placed on the times and places a debt collector may contact a consumer, the FDCPA places additional restrictions on the activities of a debt collector.

1. Informing Most Third Parties Including Consumer's Employer, Friends, and Relatives of Consumer's Indebtedness Is Prohibited

This is one of the most important protections of the FDCPA accorded to the consumer. Other than to obtain location information of a consumer, a debt collector may not phone, write, or visit a consumer's employer, relatives (except spouse), friends, or neighbors about a debt, except with the consumer's direct prior consent, with court permission, or to enforce a post-judgment judicial remedy.

A debt collector is permitted to contact third parties in order to learn the consumer's residential address and phone number or his or her work address. Even when obtaining this limited information, however, the debt collector is not permitted to reveal the indebtedness of the consumer and cannot reveal the collection agency name unless it is requested.

While communicating with a consumer by mail, a collector may not use a name or other information on the envelope indicating that its contents pertain to debt collection, since other people may see the envelope addressed to the consumer.

2. Obtaining Location Information About a Consumer from Third Parties Is Strictly Regulated

The Act strives to protect the consumer's right to privacy, by prohibiting a debt collector from communicating the consumer's personal affairs to third parties. It nonetheless recognizes the debt collector's legitimate need to seek the whereabouts of missing debtors. Accordingly, this section permits a debt collector to contact third persons for the purpose of obtaining the consumer's location under certain guidelines.

• While contacting a consumer, the debt collector's employees must use their own individual names or consistently-used and recorded aliases. The employee may not reveal the collector's trade name except upon request and then must reveal the true legal name.

• When contacting a third party, the collector may state only that "he is confirming or correcting location information concerning the consumer;" the collector may not state that the consumer owes a debt.

• The collector may contact a third party for location information only once unless the collector reasonably believes that the third party's information was erroneous or incomplete and that the third party now has correct or complete information. According to the FDCPA, the collector may only once leave word with the consumer's friend or relative to have the consumer contact the collector.

• The collector may not use postcards to obtain location information. He may not use any name, language, or symbol in any communication or on any envelope indicating that it is in the collection business, or indicating the communication relates to debt collection.

• Once the collector knows that the consumer is represented by an attorney, and can determine the attorney's name and address, it may contact only the attorney for location information, unless the attorney fails to respond to the collector's contact within a reasonable time.

If a debt collector uses harassment, trickery or other deceptive means to obtain location information, it would be violating other provisions of the Fair Debt Collection Practices Act.

3. Consumer May Waive by Direct Prior Consent Protections from Collection Contacts

By direct prior consent, a consumer may waive the protections of the Act and allow a collector to communicate with him or her at inconvenient or unusual times or places, when represented by an attorney, or at his or her place of employment. The consumer may also give prior consent to the collector to make third-party contacts.

4. FDCPA Prohibits Conduct Serving to Harass, Oppress or Abuse

The Act generally prohibits harassing, oppressive and abusive conduct by debt collectors. The following case points out what constitutes such proscribed conduct.

In *Rutyna v. Collection Accounts Terminal, Inc.,* the collector sent the consumer a letter stating:

You have shown that you are unwilling to work out a friendly settlement with us to clear the above debt.

Our field investigator has been instructed to make an investigation in your neighborhood and to personally call on your employer.

The immediate payment of the full amount or a personal visit to this office will spare you this embarrassment.

In ruling against the collector, the court held:

Without doubt defendant's letter has the natural (and intended) consequence of harassing, oppressing, and abusing the recipient. The tone of the letter is one of intimidation, and was intended as such in order to effect collection. The threat of an investigation and resulting embarrassment to the alleged debtor is clear....Defendant's violation of (Section) is clear.

(a) Debt Collectors May Not Use or Threaten Violence or Criminal Conduct

The Act prohibits violent and criminal collection activities, directed not only against the consumer, but also against the consumer's children, friends and other third parties.

(b) Collectors May Not Use Obscene, Profane or Abusive Language

The prohibition against abusive, profane and obscene language would include name-calling, racial or ethnic slurs and other derogatory remarks.

(c) The Act Generally Prohibits Publishing a List of Allegedly Defaulting Debtors

This section prohibits, among other acts, posting of "deadbeat lists" or "shame lists" in the window of a collection agency or publishing such lists in local newspapers.

(d) FDCPA Prohibits Advertising a Debt for Sale in Order to Coerce Payment

This provision prohibits advertising a list of accounts for sale; this prevents shaming the debtor by listing his or her name publicly in the advertisement.

(e) FDCPA Prohibits Repeated or Continuous Telephone Calls Intended to Annoy, Abuse or Harass

This provision limits the frequency and duration of telephone calls a debt collector may place. It applies not only to actual telephone conversations, but also to causing a telephone to ring; for example, redialing after a consumer has hung up the telephone. The protection is available not only to the consumer but also to other persons such as the consumer's babysitter.

How many phone calls would constitute too many calls? A debt collector is almost certainly within his rights to call the debtor more than once. For example, he may call on the day before and on the day after a promised payment. But six phone calls in an hour or a day probably would violate this section.

Incidentally, Massachusetts restricts debt collection calls to two per week at home and one per month at work.

(f) An Employee of a Collector Must Provide Meaningful Disclosure of His or Her Identity When Telephoning

This provision prohibits anonymous phone calls by requiring collection employees to disclose their personal identities and the employer for whom they work.

FDCPA Prohibits False, Deceptive or Misleading Representations and Collection Methods

Under this section the Act prohibits a variety of conducts which would be branded as false, deceptive or misleading. The following is a summary of such conducts.

1. Collectors May Not Use False, Deceptive or Misleading Representations or Collection Means

An example of a deceptive collection practice may be a threat of a lawsuit, because either the suit is not intended by the collector when the threat was made, or was not as imminent as represented, or was beyond the collector's present contractual or legal authority.

Threats of actions other than a lawsuit may also be deceptive. Such deceptive threats include threat of referral to the creditor for legal action, referral to an attorney, referral to a credit reporting agency, or other harm to the consumer's credit rating. Contacting third parties, adding charges to the collector's claim, pursuing post-judgment remedies before suit is filed, etc. may also be deceptive.

2. Collectors May Not Falsely Imply That They Are Vouched for, Bonded by, or Affiliated with the Government

This provision is intended to prohibit a collector from impersonating a government official, such as a law enforcement officer. It also prohibits using a business name that implies governmental affiliation.

3. Collectors May Not Falsely Represent the Character, Amount or Legal Status of Any Debt

This section prohibits a false representation that a debt exists. Such misrepresentations may occur, for example, when:

- Debts are alleged to arise out of unordered mail merchandise (which is treated as a gift under federal law);
- Debts are claimed for which the statute of limitations has expired;
- Debts are claimed against individuals not legally obligated for them, such as a consumer's unobligated relative;
- Debts are claimed which have been discharged in bankruptcy.

A collector misrepresents the "amount" of a debt when it fails to give a consumer credit for payments received or adds illegal, unauthorized or unapproved charges to the balance of the debt.

A collector misrepresents the "legal status" of a debt by attempting to collect money on a non-existent judgment, by threatening immediate garnishment of a consumer's wages when judgment has not been taken, or by claiming that a debt is due after expiration of the statute of limitations.

4. Collectors May Not Falsely Represent Any Services Rendered or Compensation to Which They Are Entitled to for the Collection of a Debt

When a "flat-rate" collector falsely represents that he'll engage in collection activities beyond mailing a series of dunning letters, he has indulged in a prohibited practice.

5. FDCPA Prohibits Falsely Implying That a Person Is an Attorney or That a Communication Comes from an Attorney

This provision prohibits a collector from actually or implicitly impersonating an attorney by mailing form letters carrying an attorney's letterhead and signature.

6. FDCPA Prohibits Implying That Non-payment of Any Debt Will Result in the Arrest or Imprisonment of Any Person or the Seizure, Garnishment, Attachment or Sale of Any Property or Wages of Any Person Unless Such Action Is Lawful and the Debt Collector or Creditor Intends to Take Such Action

7. FDCPA Prohibits Threatening Illegal or Unintended Action

This important provision prohibits the use of threats by a collector that he does not intend to carry out or that are illegal. For example, a creditor is unlikely to follow through with a lawsuit or repossession if:

- The debt is relatively small;
- There is a dispute involving the debt;
- The creditor in the past has exhibited a policy or tendency not to pursue such action;
- The appropriate court is too far away from the collector or creditor so as to make it cost ineffective or impractical for legal action; or
- The collector does not have the authority to sue either under state law or under the collector's agreement with the creditor.

Under these circumstances a threat by the collector would be prohibited since the threatened action would be either unlawful or unintended.

8. FDCPA Prohibits Falsely Implying That Transfer of a Debt Will Preclude a Consumer's Claim or Defense or Will Subject the Consumer to a Practice Prohibited by the Act

This provision was designed to prohibit a covered creditor or a collector from making direct or implied false threats to transfer a consumer's account to another, harsher collector or to an attorney or to a repossession agency.

9. FDCPA Prohibits Misrepresenting That the Consumer Committed a Crime or Engaged in Other Misconduct in Order to Disgrace the Consumer

An example of such a prohibited action would be a statement by a collector to the consumer that it is a crime merely to write a dishonored check, because bad check laws usually have other prerequisites, such as a specific intent by the consumer to write such a check.

10. FDCPA Prohibits Communicating or Threatening to Communicate False Credit Information Regarding a Consumer

This provision prohibits, for example, threats to tell third parties without explanation that a consumer refuses to pay a debt when either the consumer is unobligated or the debt is in dispute.

11. FDCPA Prohibits Using or Distributing Written Material That Gives a False Impression of a Source, Authorization or Approval

This provision prohibits such common debt collection practices as simulating legal process, and using false legal documents that may imply governmental affiliation. In general, the types of form letters prohibited are:

- letters creating false impression that they were approved by the collector's state licenser;
- letters sent by a collector using an attorney's letterhead stationery;
- letters representing the collector to be a credit reporting agency;
- letters sent by a creditor on a collection agency's stationery.

12. FDCPA Prohibits Using False Representations or Deceptive Means to Collect or Attempt to Collect a Debt or to Obtain Information About a Consumer

Under this section even unsuccessful attempts to collect debts by deceptive means are prohibited. Some examples of the violations are:

- misrepresentation by a collector that he only has authority to accept payment in full;
- use of a letter that resembles telegram to create a false sense of urgency and expense;
- false implication that the collector is providing legal advice to the creditor;
- failure to reveal the collector's close association with the creditor.

13. Except When Acquiring Location Information from a Third Party, the Collector Must Clearly Disclose in All Communications That the Debt Collector Is Attempting to Collect a Debt and That Any Information Obtained Will Be Used for That Purpose

A collector may not disclose the debt collection purpose of a phone call to most third parties when leaving messages for the consumer. The collector must, however, disclose the collection purpose to the consumer when the consumer returns the phone call.

14. FDCPA Prohibits Falsely Implying That Accounts Have Been Transferred to Innocent Purchasers for Value

This provision prohibits a debt collector from misrepresenting, among other things, that it purchased an account when in fact it was paid a flat rate for its collection activities or a contingent fee for its accounts. Such misrepresentations may suggest to the consumer that the collector has already paid the consumer's debt and now the collector is innocently collecting an account for the overreaching creditor.

15. Falsely Implying That Documents Are Legal Process Is Prohibited

A collection letter closely resembling the format, words, and type size and style of a court summons or complaint simulates legal process and is proscribed.

16. FDCPA Prohibits Using Any Business Name Other Than the True Name of the Debt Collector's Business

This provision does not require that an affirmative disclosure be made of the collector's name; it only requires that a business use its true name if one is used at all.

17. Falsely Implying That Documents Are Not Legal Process Is Prohibited

This provision prohibits a collector from representing that a consumer need only send in payments upon being sued, when in fact legal inaction by the consumer will result in a default judgment.

18. FDCPA Prohibits Falsely Implying That the Collector Operates or Is Employed by a Credit Reporting Agency

---

FDCPA Prohibits the Use of Unfair or Unconscionable Means in Debt Collecting

---

There is a general prohibition against unfair or unconscionable collection practices not covered under other sections. A practice may be unfair without being harassing, abusive or sharp. Under this section vulnerable consumers, such as the illiterate and infirm, are given particular protection.

The following practices are specifically prohibited.

1. Collecting Any Amount Not Permitted by Law Is Prohibited

This provision prohibits collection of any amount (including interest, dishonored check charges, service charges, litigation costs, late or other expenses incidental to the principal obligation) unless such amount is expressly authorized by the agreement creating the debt or permitted by law.

2. Soliciting, Accepting and Depositing Post-Dated Checks Are Restricted

The purpose of this section is to prevent a common abusive debt collection practice of forcing a consumer to write a postdated check and then pressuring him to make it good under the threat of criminal prosecution.

3. Causing Expenses to a Person by Concealing the Collection Purpose of a Communication Is Prohibited

This section prohibits a collector from placing a collect telephone call or telegram to a consumer without having first notified the consumer to expect it and without having announced its collection purpose.

4. Repossession or Threats of Repossession Are Prohibited When There Is No Right or Intent to Repossess or When the Property Is Exempt from Repossession

5. Using a Postcard to Communicate with a Consumer Regarding a Debt Is Prohibited

6. FDCPA Prohibits Using Any Language or Symbol, Other Than the Debt Collector's Address on Any Envelope When Communicating with a Consumer by Use of the Mails or by Telegram, Except That a Debt Collector May Use His Business Name If Such Name Does Not Indicate That He Is in the Debt Collection Business

Asserting Your Rights against a Bill Collector

4

The Fair Debt Collection Practices Act (FDCPA) encourages consumers to exercise their rights against possibly abusive debt collection practices. In most cases they can exercise their rights without the assistance of a lawyer. There are basically three rights:

Right to Stop Collection Contacts

This provision requires a debt collector to halt its routine collection efforts upon receiving either a written request from a consumer to seize collection efforts or a written refusal to pay the debt. After receiving the notice, the collector may contact the consumer only to advise that its collection efforts are being terminated and that it or the creditor intends to invoke specified remedies.

Under the Act, the collector or creditor can specify only those remedies that are ordinarily invoked by such debt collector or creditor. Remedies not ordinarily pursued by the collector may be specified, but only if they are intended to be pursued in the particular case. When a collector falsely threatens a consumer with an extraordinary action, a violation of this section may have occurred.

Verification of a Debt

The FDCPA gives consumers the right to obtain verification of a debt from the collector. This is intended to minimize instances of mistaken identity of a debtor, or mistake over the amount or existence of a debt.

Within 5 days after the initial communication with a consumer in connection with the collection of a debt, a debt collector is required to send to the consumer a written notice containing the amount of the debt; the name of the creditor to whom the debt is owed; a statement that unless the consumer, within 30 days after receipt of the notice, disputes the validity of the debt, the debt will be assumed to be valid by the debt collector; a statement that upon written demand within 30 days by the consumer, the debt collector will obtain verification of the debt or a copy of the judgment against the consumer and that such verification will be mailed to the consumer by the debt collector; and finally, a statement that upon the consumer's written request within the 30-day period the debt collector will provide the consumer with the name and address of the original creditor, if different from the current creditor.

Additionally, if the consumer notifies the debt collector in writing within the above 30-day period disputing the debt, or requesting the name and address of the original creditor, then the debt collector must cease collection of the debt until the consumer is supplied with the verification of the debt, or a copy of the judgment, or the name and address of the original creditor.

Consumer May Direct Application of Payments When a Collector Holds Multiple Accounts

If a consumer owes multiple debts and makes a single payment to any debt collector holding multiple accounts, such debt collector must apply the payment in accordance with the consumer's directions, and may not apply such payment to any debt which is disputed by the consumer.

This provision gives consumer the right to decide how to allocate payments among multiple debts being collected by the same collector. For instance, he may wish to give preference to a secured debt over an unsecured debt.

In addition to the above rights, the FDCPA also places certain restrictions on the activities of a debt collector.

Restrictions against Bringing Suits in Inconvenient Forums

A debt collector who brings a legal action on a debt against a consumer must bring such action only in the judicial district in which such consumer signed the contract sued upon or in which the consumer resides. In a case involving real property, such action can be brought only in a judicial district in which such real property is located.

How to Protect Yourself against Abusive Medical Bill Collection Practices

5

More than any other kind of debt, debts incurred for medical services are probably the most debilitating to a consumer's financial well-being. It is a matter of national disgrace that a large segment of our population is neither covered by private medical insurance, nor is eligible for public assistance programs, such as Medicare or Medicaid. An unexpected mishap or a minor emergency requiring a short stay in a hospital would wipe out most families' savings.

What are the common defenses available to a consumer against abusive medical bill collectors?

Fortunately, consumers have a variety of health and consumer law defenses to debt collection efforts by doctors, hospitals, and their collection agencies. Federal and state laws place significant restrictions on abusive debt collection practices.

Federal Law

The Fair Debt Collection Practices Act (FDCPA) prohibits abusive, deceptive and unfair debt collection practices. For example, it provides consumers with the right to:

- obtain verification of the debt;
- terminate collection efforts; and
- be sued in a convenient forum.

In addition to generally prohibiting abusive, deceptive, and unfair debt collection practices, the FDCPA also specifies that certain conduct is a *per se* violation of the FDCPA. For example, sending of post cards to debtors, late night phone calls, false threats of suit, and most third-party contacts to collect a debt are violations of the Act.

Although the FDCPA applies primarily to collection agencies and usually not to creditors, from a practical standpoint, most health care providers, such as hospitals and doctors, typically employ collection agencies in their debt collection efforts. In all likelihood, a consumer would be dealing with an outside collection agency employed by the health care provider.

Moreover, while hospitals and doctors are generally "creditors" not subject to the FDCPA, there are a number of instances in which these creditors and affiliated collection entities may be subject to the Act. For example, if a hospital's internal bill collector misrepresents that he or she is calling from a collection agency, both the employee and hospital would be subject to the provisions of the FDCPA.

Federal Trade Commission, mindful of the potential for misrepresentation and deceptive practices in the health care field, has adopted several rules to safeguard the consumer. For instance, a hospital staff attorney's plan to send collection letters on his letterhead, which indicates he is a private practitioner and does not disclose his hospital employment, is a violation of the FDCPA, and subjects both the hospital and attorney to FDCPA sanctions.

In another case, where a non-profit hospital created a separate collection organization to collect debts for itself and other health care providers, the use of an attorney letterhead by the collector's staff attorney, without indicating the attorney's employment by the collector violated the FDCPA, subjecting the collector and attorney to a liability. If a hospital hires a debt collection agency and holds a common ownership interest, the agency should indicate its affiliation with the hospital when collecting the hospital's debts, unless the agency is actually independent of the hospital.

A creditor violating the FDCPA is liable for actual damages (which include damages for emotional distress), statutory damages, attorney's fees and court costs. Most courts have also granted class junctive relief.

State Remedies for Medical Debt Harassment

In the consumer's arsenal, there is even a more effective weapon than the FDCPA. State laws as opposed to federal statutes or FTC actions provide a broader line of defense for a besieged consumer.

State debt collection statutes were passed in the 1960's and 1970's to protect consumers against abusive debt collection practices. State remedies for health debt collection harassment often utilize state debt collection statutes, state unfair and deceptive acts and practices (UDAP) statutes, the tort of intentional infliction of emotional distress and other remedies.

The advantage of state action over federal enforcement is that state laws generally allow a consumer to proceed directly against the health care provider as well as against the collection agency for abusive collection tactics. The consumer in a private action can recover attorney's fees, actual damages and sometimes statutory damages.

In some states, unfair and deceptive action practices statutes provide for recovery of double or treble actual damages as well as attorney's fees. Thus, a harassed consumer with substantial actual damages might be well advised to proceed under the UDAP statute than the FDCPA.

If a debt collector is dealing with a person known to be handicapped or convalescing, the court is likely to impose a greater duty of care. An aggrieved consumer in these circumstances would be able to assert the claim of tort of infliction of emotional distress - a cause of action very commonly used in abusive debt collection practices. The advantage of this tort is the likelihood of recovery of punitive damages in an egregious case where the collector's malice is readily apparent.

Duress as a Defense to a Hospital Collection Action

A debtor facing a hospital collection action can assert an important contractual defense, that the hospital's contract was extracted from the consumer under duress. For example, a hospital's requirement that the patient (or a relative or friend of a patient) agree to pay the patient's medical bills in order for the patient to be admitted or discharged may give rise to the complete contractual defense of duress.

There are three basic elements of duress:

Creditor's Exercise of Coercion

There can be no duress unless there is a threat to do some act which the party threatening has no legal right to do. For example, hospitals are generally not required to admit emergency patients. In order to assert the defense of duress, there must be county or state or other governmental regulations that call for compulsory emergency admittance.

Similarly, the act or threat of a hospital detaining a person by refusing to discharge the patient until a bill is paid is improper since it amounts to false imprisonment. Such an act would clearly fall under coercion.

Debtor's Loss of Volition as a Result of the Coercion

This is the second element of duress. For example, a patient initially refuses to sign a note, but then relents under a threat of detention and signs the note. The threat has resulted in the debtor's loss of volition.

A Promissory Note or Contract Must Be Executed as a Result of the Wrongful Coercion

This element rounds out the claim of duress. The patient must have been forced to execute a contract or promissory note that he or she would otherwise not have done.

A few years ago, Washington Post had reported an instance where a hospital had brought a $56,000 suit against a patient's widow who had signed an agreement believing it was necessary to gain admittance for her husband, who was in great pain and vomiting while waiting for emergency treatment. He later died in the hospital of cancer. The jury voided the bill.

Your Guide to Protection from Harassment by Bill Collectors

6

> The following summary of the protections afforded by the Fair Debt Collection Practices Act is excerpted from a publication put out by the Bureau of Consumer Protection in the Federal Trade Commission.

If you use credit cards, owe money on a loan, or are paying off a home mortgage, you are a "debtor." Most Americans are.

You may never come in contact with a debt collector. But if you do, you should know that there is a law to make sure you are treated fairly. The Fair Debt Collection Practices Act was passed by Congress in 1977 to prohibit certain methods of debt collection. Of course, the law does not erase any legitimate debt you owe.

The following questions and answers may help you understand your rights under the Debt Collection Act.

What debts are covered?

Personal, family, and household debts are covered under the Act. This includes money owed for the purchase of a car, for medical care, or for charge accounts.

Who is a debt collector?

A debt collector is any person, other than the creditor, who regularly collects debts owed to others. Under a 1986 amendment to the Fair Debt Collection Practices Act, this includes attorneys who collect debts on a regular basis. The Act does not apply to attorneys who only handle debt collection matters a few times a year.

How may a debt collector contact you?

A debt collector may contact you in person, by mail, telephone, or telegram. However, a debt collector may not contact you at inconvenient or unusual times or places, such as before

8 a.m. or after 9 p.m., unless you agree. A debt collector may not contact you at work if the debt collector has reason to know that your employer disapproves.

Can you stop a debt collector from contacting you?

You may stop a debt collector from contacting you by writing a letter to the collection agency telling them to stop. Once the agency receives your letter, they may not contact you again except to say there will be no further contact or to notify you that some specific action will be taken, if the debt collector or the creditor intends to take such action.

May a debt collector contact any other person concerning your debt?

If you have an attorney, the collector may not contact anyone but the attorney. If you do not have an attorney, a debt collector may contact other people, but only to find out where you live or work. In most cases, the collector is not allowed to tell anyone other than you or your attorney that you owe money. Collectors are usually prohibited from contacting any person more than once.

What is the debt collector required to tell you about the debt?

Within five days after you are first contacted, the debt collector must send you a written notice telling you the amount of money you owe; the name of the creditor to whom you owe the money; and what to do if you believe you do not owe the money.

If you believe you do not owe the money, may a debt collector continue to contact you?

The debt collector may not contact you if, within 30 days after you are first contacted, you send the collector a letter saying you do not owe the money. However, a debt collector can begin collection activities again if you are sent proof of the debt, such as a copy of the bill.

What types of debt collection practices are prohibited?

Harassment. Debt collectors may not harass, oppress, or abuse any person. For example, debt collectors may not:

- use threats of violence of harm to the person, property, or reputation;

- publish a list of consumers who refuse to pay their debts (except to a credit bureau);

- use obscene or profane language;

- repeatedly use the telephone to annoy someone;

- telephone people without identifying themselves;

- advertise your debt.

False Statements. Debt collectors may not use any false statements when collecting a debt. For example, debt collectors may not:

- falsely imply that they are an attorney or government representative;

- falsely imply that you have committed a crime;

- falsely represent that they operate or work for a credit bureau;

- misrepresent the amount of the debt;

- indicate that papers being sent are legal forms when they are not.

Also, debt collectors may not say that:

- you will be arrested if you do not pay your debt;

- they will seize, garnish, attach, or sell your property or wages, unless the collection agency or the creditor intends to do so, and it is legal;

- actions will be taken against you which legally may not be taken.

Debt collectors may not:

- give false credit information about you to anyone;

- send you anything that resembles an official document from a court or government agency;

- use a false name.

Unfair Practices. Debt collectors may not engage in unfair practices in attempting to collect a debt. For example, debt collectors may not:

- collect any amount greater than your debt, unless allowed by law;

- deposit a post-dated check before the date on the check;

- make you accept collect calls or pay for telegrams;

- take or threaten to take your property unless this can be done legally;

- contact you by postcard.

What control do you have over payment of debts?

If you owe several debts, any payment you make must be applied to the debt you choose. A debt collector may not apply a payment to any debt you believe you do not owe.

What can you do if you believe a debt collector broke the law?

You have the right to sue a debt collector in a state or federal court within one year from the date you believe the law was violated. If you win, you may recover money for the damage you suffered. Court costs and attorney's fees also can be recovered. A group of people may sue a debt collector and recover money for damages up to $500,000, or one percent of the collector's net worth, whichever is less.

Where can you report a debt collector for an alleged violation of the law?

Report any problems with a debt collector to your state Attorney General's office. Many states also have their own debt collection laws and your Attorney General's office can help you to determine your rights.

If you have a question about your rights under the Fair Debt Collection Practices Act, the Federal Trade Commission may be able to assist you. While the FTC cannot intervene in individual disputes, information from consumers about their experiences is vital to the enforcement of the Act. Contact any of the FTC offices listed below.

6th & Pennsylvania Avenue, N.W.
Washington, D.C. 20580
(202) 326-2222

1718 Peachtree Street, N.W.
Atlanta, Georgia 30367
(404) 347-4836

10 Causeway Street
Boston, Massachusetts 02222
(617) 565-7240

55 East Monroe Street
Chicago, Illinois 60603
(312) 353-4423

118 St. Clair Avenue
Cleveland, Ohio 44114
(216) 522-4210

8303 Elmbrook Drive
Dallas, Texas 75247
(214) 767-7053

1405 Curtis Street
Denver, Colorado 80202
(303) 844-2271

11000 Wilshire Boulevard
Los Angeles, California 90024
(213) 209-7890

26 Federal Plaza
New York, New York 10278
(212) 264-1207

901 Market Street
San Francisco, California 94103
(415) 995-5220

915 Second Avenue
Seattle, Washington 98174
(206) 442-4655

How to Stop Debt Collection Harassment without Litigation or Bankruptcy 7

Debt collection harassment can take an enormous toll on the financially-strapped consumer in more ways than one. Abusive collection efforts and outrageous conduct by the collector can result in severe emotional distress for the consumer and his family. The consumer, without exception, is already in dire financial straits when he's subjected to the abuse and humiliation by the debt collector.

The emotional stress and anxiety created as a result of abusive debt collection can manifest itself in the form of many physical ailments: loss of appetite, nausea, loss of weight, ulcers, headaches, impotence, frigidity, hysteria, irritability, heart attack, angina, etc. The embarrassment, humiliation and intimidation can also affect the consumer's family life and job performance.

What can you, as a consumer, do to avoid being the victim of abusive debt collection practices?

Strategies to Stop Debt Collection Harassment

Litigation is a definite possibility in certain egregious debt collection cases. A successful lawsuit may not only result in a recovery of actual and statutory damages but also in punitive damages which will have a general deterrence on the future conduct of the collector.

However, litigation is not a practical solution in many instances. For example, the conduct may not be sufficiently outrageous, the requirement of legal proof may be lacking, the consumer may not have maintained proper documentation to support the allegations of misconduct and, finally, legal counsel may be hard and expensive to obtain. In other words, litigation at best is a costly and uncertain weapon and beyond the reach of most consumers.

Bankruptcy, by definition, is a weapon of last resort. It will stop all collection efforts immediately, but the cost of bankruptcy in terms of future credit and emotional trauma is high and is not an acceptable solution for many consumers.

However, there are strategies that can help alleviate a consumer's distress from debt collection abuses without resorting to a lawsuit or bankruptcy. All of these strategies are predicated on the number of important rights afforded to consumers under the Fair Debt Collection Practices Act (FDCPA). These rights include:

- **The right to terminate future collection contacts;**
- **The right to stop contacts at work if the employer prohibits them;**
- **The right to stop contacts at work if they are inconvenient;**
- **The right to obtain verification of a debt;**
- **The right to direct application of payments to a specific debt being collected by the debt collector.**

Strategy 1: Ask Collector to Terminate Contacts

The federal Fair Debt Collection Practices Act requires collection agencies to terminate collection contacts once the consumer notifies the debt collector in writing that the consumer refuses to pay a debt or that the consumer wishes the debt collector to cease further communications with the consumer. The Act generally does not cover creditors collecting their own debts, and thus they do not have to honor such requests. Nevertheless, in practice most creditors do comply with such requests.

The actual implementation of this strategy would require the consumer to write the collector detailing his present financial inability to pay the debt, a reasonable assessment of his future outlook and realistic repayment schedule, the abusive tactics of the collector's employees and the distress such tactics have caused the consumer and his family. The letter should then request the collector to terminate all future collection contacts.

A copy of the letter should also be sent to the creditor making him aware of its collection agency's abusive practices. In an egregious case, a copy should also be sent to the local Better Business Bureau which would precipitate an investigation if there was a history of repeated misconduct.

Sample Letter to Debt Collector Requesting Termination of Collection Contacts

John Smith
123 Main Street
Los Angeles, CA 90015

March 10, 1989

ABC Collection Agency
500 S. Broadway
Los Angeles, CA 90007

Re: Your demand to pay $710.00
       Sears Roebuck, Acct. No. _____

Gentlemen:

    Under the federal Fair Debt Collection Practices Act, 15 U.S.C.A. § 1692 c(c), I'm asking you to terminate your debt collection communications to me.

    About two months ago, I was hospitalized for an emergency heart by-pass surgery. Since then I've been unable to return to work. Doctors expect that I should be sufficiently recovered to perform my job duties in another 45 days. My wife has found a part-time job in the meantime, but her earnings are not sufficient to make any payment on the above debt.

    Please note that your collection letter indicated the amount of the debt as $710. My records show the amount to be no more than $605.

    I would also like to point out that your employees have engaged in illegal collection practice by calling me at 6:30 in the morning on March 2, 1989, and then making repeated phone calls during the day. Such calls have caused a great deal of distress to me and my family.

    When I'm able to go back to work, I hope to make small payments toward paying off the debt. In the meantime, I'll appreciate your understanding in the matter.

Very truly,

John Smith

cc: Sears Roebuck
       1200 Alameda
       Los Angeles, CA 90017

       Better Business Bureau
       450 Oak Street
       Los Angeles, CA 90005

Strategy 2: Complaint to Consumer Protection Agencies

Another strategy to stop collection harassment is for the consumer to write letters to state and federal agencies charged with enforcing the laws against debt collection abuses.

Most government agencies as a practical matter do not take action against an isolated instance of debt collection abuse but, if there has been a documented history of complaints against a particular collection agency, your letter may just produce an inquiry from the enforcement agency. Also, a copy of your letter sent to the collection agency and creditor may result in voluntary cessation of further harassment.

The complaint letter should be addressed to the Federal Trade Commission, Bureau of Consumer Protection, Washington, D.C., 20580, for most non-banking transactions. Copies of the letter should be sent to the state attorney general's office, consumer protection division in the local district attorney's office and also to any other regulatory agencies connected. If the collector's abusive behavior appears routine (e.g., the deception or harassment appears in a form letter), this should be pointed out to the enforcement agency.

Sample Letter Complaining of Debt Collection Abuses
to Federal Trade Commission

John Smith
123 Main Street
Los Angeles, CA 90015

March 10, 1989

Federal Trade Commission
Bureau of Consumer Protection
Division of Credit Practices
Washington, D.C. 20580

Gentlemen:

I am writing to complain of abusive debt collection practices by ABC Collection Agency, 500 S. Broadway, Los Angeles, CA 90007 and request that you investigate this matter.

1. The collection agency is demanding a payment of $710 for a debt that according to my records is no more than $605. Neither the collection agency nor the creditor has taken any steps to investigate this dispute.

2. The collection agency has contacted my parents and my neighbor regarding this particular debt. I believe such contacts are illegal.

3. An employee of the collection agency has called me at 6:30 in the morning and then has made repeated calls during the day. The person has used abusive, insulting, and derogatory language during these calls.

4. The collection agency has made repeated threats to take legal action against me unless I made a full payment against the said debt. However, to this date they have done nothing more than send dunning letters and make repeated phone calls, which goes to prove their threat of legal action was deceptive and illegal.

5. I've asked the collection agency to terminate all collection contacts with me. However, this request has gone unheeded.

Due to a medical emergency I've been unable to work at my job for the past two months. I'm doing my best to get back on my feet. In the meantime, I would appreciate any assistance from your agency in this matter.

Very truly yours,

John Smith

cc: Attorney General's Office
       Bureau of Consumer Protection
       Sacramento, CA 97345

       ABC Collection Agency
       500 S. Broadway
       Los Angeles, CA 90007

       Sears Roebuck
       1200 Alameda
       Los Angeles, CA 90017

Strategy 3: Complaint to the Collector about the Amount of Debt

If you dispute the amount of debt for any reason (erroneous billing, services not rendered, payments not applied) you should immediately write to the collection agency asking it to investigate. The federal Fair Debt Collection Practices Act requires debt collection agencies and lawyers (but generally not creditors) to stop collection efforts until they investigate the disputed debt, as long as the consumer's written request was received within 30 days of the first communication from the collector regarding the debt.

If the dispute involves a revolving charge account, a credit card account, or an electronic transfer of money, federal regulations specify that if a consumer, within 60 days of receiving an erroneous bill, sends a letter to the creditor disputing the billing, the creditor must re-examine the bill. In most such cases, collectors will generally stop their collection efforts and investigate the matter.

Strategy 4: Have a Lawyer Send a Letter Requesting the Collector to Stop Contacts

The Fair Debt Collection Practices Act requires collection agencies to stop contacting a consumer known to be represented by a lawyer, as long as the lawyer responds to the collection agency's inquiries within a reasonable time. Creditors, although not covered by the FDCPA, will, too, generally honor such requests from a debtor's lawyer.

In most cases, a letter from the consumer asking a collector to stop collection contacts would produce results. Many consumers experiencing temporary financial difficulties go to a lawyer with the intention of filing a bankruptcy when all they actually need is relief from a few abusive bill collectors collecting unsecured debts. A letter from a lawyer as shown below will produce immediate results, i.e., termination of collection contacts.

Sample Letter from a Lawyer Requesting Termination of Collection Contacts

Law Offices of
Smith, Jones, & Little
2001 Avenue of the Stars
Century City, CA 90055

March 25, 1989

ABC Collection Agency
500 South Broadway
Los Angeles, CA 90007

Re: John Smith
     Sears Roebuck, Acct No. _____
     Demand to pay $710.00

Gentlemen:

This is to advise you that Mr. John Smith is represented by the law offices of Smith, Jones & Little. In the matter of the above-mentioned indebtedness you are advised to direct any future contacts regarding this or other accounts of my client to me. You're asked to cease all contacts with my client forthwith.

I've been advised by Mr. Smith that your employees have engaged in certain prohibited debt collection practices.

In particular, your agency has made contacts to my client at 6:30 in the morning and has made repeated phone calls during the day. Such practices have caused my client and his family severe emotional distress. Any continued harassment by your employees will aggravate that distress.

You should also be advised that my client disputes the amount of the debt as explained in his letter of March 10, 1989 to you. To this day, he has received no response from you.

My client is presently undergoing certain physical problems and has been laid off from work temporarily. He intends to pay the correct amount of the debt as soon as he is able to. In the meantime, I would appreciate your cooperation in this matter.

Very truly yours,

Bob Jones

cc: Federal Trade Commission
     Bureau of Consumer Protection
     Division of Credit Practices
     Washington, D.C. 20580

Strategy 5: Propose a Workout Agreement with the Creditor

Many consumers, after being sufficiently harassed by a collection agency, will succumb to the pressure and agree to pay the debt, in installments.

You should approach this strategy only after doing a realistic evaluation of your future financial prospects that will take into account the urgency of other debts and the extent of legal recourse available to the creditor. You may discover that a creditor, even after taking a judgment against you, would be unable to satisfy it under your current financial circumstances. In other words, take a long and hard look at all your debts and then assign priority to them in terms of adverse impact on your cash flow.

As a rule, most creditors and collection agencies take the initial position that they must receive the entire outstanding balance in one payment. They'll urge the consumer to borrow from a finance company or relatives, or obtain a bill consolidation loan at much higher interest rates to pay off the debt. But, if the debt is not secured with a collateral and has a low interest rate or no interest (e.g., medical bills), it is to the consumer's advantage to stretch out the payments on this debt so that secured debts and debts with higher interest and late charges may be paid first. Through skillful negotiations a consumer can get a collector to agree to a realistic installment payment plan.

A note of caution: You should never fall in the trap of giving the collector a post-dated check as part of a workout arrangement. Writing a check without sufficient funds to cover it is a crime under certain circumstances. Many collectors demand post-dated checks, knowing that the consumer will not be able to make the check good when the time comes and they'll be able to use it as a leverage to extract cash payment from the consumer under the threat of criminal prosecution.

Legal Remedies against Abusive Debt Collectors 8

There are basically two areas of redress available to a consumer who has been subjected to abusive debt collection practices.

Statutory Relief

The consumer can seek relief under the Fair Debt Collection Practices Act or various state consumer protection statutes. The purpose of the FDCPA is to protect consumers from abusive debt collection practices and at the same time provide effective remedial measures.

A debt collector who violates the FDCPA while collecting a consumer debt is usually subject to suit by "any person" affected by the violations. As a remedy, the successful consumer may recover actual damages, statutory damages, attorney's fees, costs and perhaps punitive damages and injunctive relief.

Note, however, that the FDCPA provides a one-year statute of limitations for private actions. In other words, a consumer claiming to have been injured due to any FDCPA violations must bring an action within one year from the date on which such a violation occurs.

Tort Relief

The principal remedy against abusive debt collection practices is still an action in tort. There are distinct advantages and disadvantages to a tort approach to abusive debt collection conduct.

One major advantage of a tort claim is that it allows you to proceed against creditors and their agents who generally may not be subject to the Fair Debt Collection Practices or other state consumer protection statutes. These statutes are usually limited to debt collection agencies. Another major advantage of tort claims in many states is the availability of punitive or exemplary damages for various conduct which is malicious or reckless.

The major disadvantage of a tort claim is that many states impose a much higher standard of proof on the consumer claiming to have been injured by the outrageous conduct of the debt collector than is generally required under consumer protection statutes.

Action under Tort

Various tort theories may be available to a harassed debtor. These include:

- **Intentional infliction of emotional distress (or mental anguish)**
- **Invasion of right of privacy**
- **Intentional interference with employment relationships**
- **Defamation**
- **Malicious prosecution**
- **Abuse of process**

In this chapter, we'll briefly look at these legal remedies available to a consumer against abusive debt collectors.

Intentional Infliction of Emotional Distress

The theory of tort of intentional infliction of emotional distress was principally developed as protection against abusive debt collection practices. To be successful under this theory, the creditor's conduct must be:

- intentional, reckless, or negligent;
- outrageous or unreasonable;
- undertaken without a legal privilege; and
- the proximate cause of mental distress, severe mental distress or physical injury to the debtor.

In most jurisdictions a consumer has only to prove emotional distress even though there was no physical injury to recover damages. The legal proof required to show the degree of outrageousness and the severity of distress vary from court to court. The conduct must be "so outrageous in character, and so extreme in degree, as to go beyond all bounds of decency, and to be regarded as atrocious, and intolerable in a civilized community."

Generally, a collector is entitled to take any reasonable steps necessary to collect a debt. The collector can legally notify the debtor of the status of the debt, remind the debtor to pay and warn him of the legal consequences of default. A debt collector will also be within his rights to threaten the consumer with a poor credit rating if he did not pay the debt. Similarly, threats of wage assignment or garnishment are permissible too. Contacting the debtor's employer for employment verification is also accepted by courts.

To illustrate the tort of intentional infliction of emotional distress, we should look at some actual cases:

•   In a case where a debt collector made a series of calls to a debtor, became abusive, warned the debtor to "stay out of Minnesota if you know what's good for you and your family," and attempted to collect interest not owed, there was sufficient evidence of extreme and outrageous conduct to justify jury award of $6,000, damages for emotional distress and damages of $3,900 for attorney's fees for defending the prior suit.

•   In another case where threatening, harassing, and obscene statements by a debt collector caused the debtor heart attack and severe mental distress, an action in tort was sustained.

•   In another case where a veterinarian had threatened to do away with little children's dog unless mother paid charges for treating the dog, such a threat could be found to be extreme, outrageous and intolerable in present day society.

•   A lawsuit was sustained where a consumer alleged that a collector threatened him with loss of job and credit blacklisting, harassed him by phone at home and at work, placed phone calls (some long distance, collect) to the consumer's friends, relatives and employers, sent him late night telegrams and subjected him to a barrage of letters and insults.

•   A buyer's allegation that a seller placed a threatening phone call at 11:00 p.m. concerning a disputed debt to the house of the buyer's neighbor, resulting in the buyer's being called to that house and humiliated before others and causing an extended illness was sufficient to sustain a cause of action for intentional infliction of emotional distress.

Invasion of Privacy

The right to privacy is recognized in some form in most jurisdictions. Again, it is not necessary to prove that physical harm was done to the consumer.

Courts generally recognize that creditors have a right to use reasonable means to collect their debts, but they also recognize that this right must be balanced against the consumer's right to privacy. In other words, the debt collector's conduct must be beyond "reasonable bounds" or be "highly offensive" before being held actionable.

Here are some actual cases involving invasion of privacy:

• A creditor who phoned a consumer's home 8 or 10 times a day for two weeks, phoned the consumer three times in 15 minutes at work (at school), called her employer and her landlord, and phoned at late hours, concerning a partially disputed debt, leading the consumer to suffer nervousness, anguish, humiliation, loss of sleep, loss of a roommate and fears for her employment was found guilty by invasion of privacy.

• In another case a female debt collector called the debtor's wife and sister-in-law and, without identifying herself except as "Doris," insinuated that she had an extramarital relationship with the debtor. A suit for invasion of privacy was justified in this instance.

• A plaintiff was awarded $2,700 for his impaired credit, mental anguish, humiliation and embarrassment caused when a store accidentally issued a credit card to the plaintiff's brother in the plaintiff's name, and then served plaintiff with suit at his job after being informed of the error.

• In this context, public disclosure of private facts even though true would invite a suit for invasion of privacy. For example, a 5 foot by 8 foot sign listing debtors in a store window would constitute invasion of privacy. In another instance, listing a plaintiff's name under a list headed "NO CHECKS" in plain view of customers at a retail store checkout counter would be sufficient to sustain an invasion of privacy lawsuit.

• A consumer who alleged that her creditor yelled at her in his store and also in front of neighbors about an unjustly inflated bill was awarded $4,000 damages for invasion of privacy, emotional distress and impaired health.

Intentional Interference with Employment Relationships

If a collector threatens to cause a loss of job or takes steps which puts the consumer's job in jeopardy, and as a result of the collector's actions the consumer loses his job, he would be able to pursue remedy under this theory of tort.

The following cases illustrate the tort of employment interference:

• A consumer who refused to settle a claim with an insurer who in turn threatened his current employer with cancellation of the entire insurance policy which resulted in loss of his employment, pursued an action in tort against the insurer. A court award of damages was upheld on appeal.

• An employee was fired two days after a creditor had threatened to cause the termination of the job if the employee did not immediately pay one delinquent installment. The creditor's conduct was actionable for actual damages to the fired employee.

• A plaintiff was awarded $7,600 after a creditor, who was on the board of the hospital where plaintiff worked, obtained a resolution from the board that the plaintiff be fired if a disputed debt of $325.35 was not paid.

Defamation

In debt collection cases, tort under defamation theory arises either from a letter to the consumer's employer or from publication of a list of debts allegedly due (a "deadbeat list"). Ordinarily, a credit report given to other creditors is privileged.

Malicious Prosecution and Abusive Process

Both of these torts apply to wrongful use of judicial processes. For example, a creditor who initiates a bad check prosecution solely to cause payment of a disputed debt may be liable for malicious prosecution.

• $25,000 in general damages and $5,000 in punitive damages were awarded in a malicious prosecution case where payee brought bad check charges against the plaintiff as a result of giving a NSF check for a pre-existing, disputed debt.

Fighting Back against Abusive Collection Practices

Here is how two consumers fought back against abusive debt collection practices.

A CitiBank Visa cardholder brought suit against Citicorp Credit Services, Inc., (CCSI) for its allegedly abusive debt collection practices. The cardholder sought damages under the Federal Fair Debt Collection Practices Act and brought a state law claim for intentional infliction of emotional distress. Although the court dismissed the cardholder's suit under the FDCPA, it allowed the cardholder's suit for intentional infliction of emotional distress to go forward.

First, a brief background.

In 1986, the cardholder fell behind in his Visa payments; the unpaid balance exceeded $5,000. CitiBank and CCSI made numerous attempts to collect the debt, both by mail and by phone. The cardholder wrote to CCSI, explaining that medical emergencies and related expenses prevented him from making the required payments, and informed CCSI that he would make partial payments. CCSI, however, continued to make harassing phone calls. The phone calls were made both to his home and to his office.

As a result, the cardholder brought suit against CCSI in federal court. At trial, the cardholder testified that CCSI would not listen to his explanation for the delinquency. He stated that CCSI's repeated phone calls caused both physical and emotional damages and that his wife had been "reduced to tears." CCSI and Citicorp argued that their behavior was within the bounds of the law and entirely proper.

The court, however, was sympathetic to the cardholder's claim for intentional infliction of emotional distress. The essential element of a claim for intentional infliction of emotional distress is that the defendant engage in conduct that is "so insulting as naturally to humiliate" the target of the conduct. In fact, the claim of intentional infliction of emotional distress was largely developed in response to abusive debt collection practices.

In this case, the cardholder alleged that CCSI's conduct was intended to distress him and his wife and that such distress was forseeable. Moreover, he argued that he and his wife suffered emotional and physical complaints due to CCSI's actions. The court found that his claims merited a hearing before a jury and allowed him to continue with his lawsuit. Should he prove his allegations, he would be entitled to damages (*Meads v. Citicorp Credit Services, Inc.,* Civ. Act. No. 287.182 (S.D. Ga. May 10, 1988).)

There is yet another potent weapon in the armour of a consumer. The Federal Racketeering Influence and Corrupt Organizations (RICO) Act is a broad statute prohibiting specific types of illegal conduct by an enterprise, including outrageous debt collection conduct.

In a suit against a debt collection agency, it was alleged that the collector violated RICO by seeking illegal "collection charges" of $20 or more from consumers on their dishonored checks and threatening arrest and criminal prosecution if the charge was not paid. These acts allegedly constituted extortion and mail fraud, crimes specifically within the scope of RICO prohibitions. The case was settled by a stipulated judgment against the collection agency and its owner, providing injunctive relief, termination of business and corporate dissolution of the agency, and treble damages to the plaintiffs. *(Downey v. The Goodwin Agency, Inc.,* 8 Clearing House Rev. 553 (Clearing House No. 13,878) (M.D. Ga. 1974) (consent judgment)).

RICO is a powerful weapon in the hands of an aggrieved judgment debtor. He can collect reasonable attorney's fees if he proves his case in the court. In addition, the law provides for treble damages which is a strong deterrent against abusive debt collection practices.

RICO can also be used when credit is extended or debt collected at interest rates greatly in excess of the maximum legal rate. RICO has been generally used in criminal prosecutions. But as the above case demonstrates, it can also be used effectively to counter abusive practices of debt collection agencies.

SECTION III

Locating the Missing Debtor

9

Assuming the debt is a valid debt, locating the debtor is the first step in any collection effort. Let's face it, without the debtor you cannot get to the second base. All your efforts, whether judicial or extrajudicial, are of little value if you cannot find the debtor.

While statutes in every state gives the judgment creditor many tools and remedies in locating and seizing a debtor's assets, they do not offer him much help in finding the judgment debtor. In many states, the judgment creditor can subpoena relatives, business associates, employers and all those in contact with, or who have knowledge of, the judgment debtor and question them. However, in all probability, those served with the subpoena will try to evade the process, be untruthful and frustrate every effort of the judgment creditor to locate the debtor. From a practical standpoint, the judgment creditor will face general reluctance from court to hold the witnesses in contempt of court and punish them for not complying with court process.

Consequently, when it comes to locating the judgment debtor, a creditor is pretty much left on his own and he has to use his imagination and resourcefulness to achieve the desired result.

A Word of Caution

In trying to locate the missing debtor, you must keep in mind the provisions of the Fair Debt Collection Practices Act. The creditor can only obtain information from a third party concerning the location of the debtor and not reveal that a debt is due. The creditor should be careful not to divulge any information which may reflect on the debtor's character. By carefully following a few simple steps, you'll be able to steer clear of any claim by the debtor that you have breached his right to privacy or defamed his character.

Skip-Tracing

Not all debtors intentionally hide their whereabouts from their creditors. Failure to notify a creditor of the change in address may be inadvertent. The debtor who has left the area or moved to another address without informing the creditor, either intentionally or due to an oversight, is called a skip. The attempt to locate this debtor is known as "skip-tracing."

How can you tell if a debtor has become a skip?

This generally is not hard to figure out. The two most common indicators are that the phone lines are disconnected and the mail is being returned. A quick check with the phone company to see if there is a new phone number or with the post office to see if there is a forwarding address will confirm that the debtor has become a skip.

There are other obvious indicators that may confirm your suspicions. You may receive inquiries from other creditors and encounter evasiveness of friends and neighbors concerning the debtor's location. The debtor's checks may be returned due to non-sufficient funds; loss of employment or problems related to the debtor's personal life, such as separation or divorce will also tip you off that the debtor is about to or has become a skip.

Debtor's File

Before initiating the location effort, you as a creditor should first carefully review the documentation of the transaction that led to the creation of the debt. This may include the rental or loan application, references and the debtor's payment records. In all cases, the debtor's file should be the first step in your search for the missing debtor.

If you have maintained good documentation, the debtor's file would provide a wealth of information that will help you locate the debtor. The file would reveal the debtor's former addresses and employers' names and addresses. As the debtor makes payments during the course of the transaction, you should note the number and location of the bank account and any change of address information. This information is very valuable in locating the debtor who has defaulted.

The file also may reveal information regarding other credit transactions entered into by the debtor, such as auto loans, credit cards, student loans, etc. You can obtain additional information by contacting other creditors to determine whether they are having problems with their accounts. Creditors are generally very helpful in providing information concerning a debtor as they, too, might be facing a similar situation in the future.

Other creditors can provide or confirm names of employers, relatives, friends and other people that might be helpful in locating the debtor. They can advise whether their accounts are current and how much is being paid presently on those accounts. Other creditors can also furnish information concerning pending lawsuits against the debtor.

If the debtor's file reveals the names of any ex-spouses or in-laws, then the creditor must make a special effort to contact these references. These people sometimes provide more information concerning the debtor than a friend or close relative.

A check of public records including motor vehicle registrations, public utilities, schools, and real estate recordings might also reveal the debtor's new whereabouts.

Using Telephone to Locate the Debtor

The telephone is clearly the least expensive and least time-consuming tool you can use in locating the debtor. Contacting third parties through the telephone has the added advantage that the contact may appear more informal and the sources are likely to be more expansive regarding the debtor's location and his current activities.

If the debtor is no longer working or has changed jobs, ask to speak to the payroll department to determine where the last check was mailed or whether a forwarding address has been left. It is also permissible to ask the employer to have one of the debtor's close friends contact you at that person's convenience. Naturally, you should not reveal your business name or the purpose of the call, but a phone number and the name of a specific person to contact should be given.

You'll be surprised at the wealth of information that you can obtain from telephone books and by making telephone calls to the debtor himself, his friends, neighbors and relatives. Get hold of a reverse street address telephone book and contact some of the neighbors of the debtor. If the debtor lives in an apartment house, contact his neighbors in the apartment house by calling them directly.

Do not feel bashful or intrusive; ask neighbors anything you wish to know concerning the debtor. People in general like to talk and you're only trying to collect what's owed to you. If you know anything about the debtor's business, job, children, or hobbies, use this information to convey an impression that you are a close acquaintance of the debtor. This in turn will allow your contacts to expand on what they know about the debtor. You may find out where the debtor does his banking, what kind of a car he owns, where he parks his car, where he works, and other valuable information that will be sufficient not only to locate the debtor but also his hidden assets that may satisfy the debt.

Getting Information from Credit Bureaus

Many financial institutions, landlords and businesses subscribe to credit bureau services, and they're a valuable source of information. A credit bureau report will reveal the inquiries made by other creditors concerning the debtor. It will give you the debtor's social security number, date of birth, previous addresses, and a list of other creditors. It will also reveal any lawsuits or judgments in existence. Information on lawsuits, drunk driving or other convictions, divorce proceedings, evictions, etc. should be used to canvass public records for potential leads.

Using School Records to Locate the Debtor

If the debtor's file reveals that the debtor has children, then by contacting the neighborhood schools you can determine whether those children are still enrolled, or whether they have been transferred to another school. School enrollment records often provide valuable leads. If a child is enrolled in college or is at least 18 years of age, then it is within the bounds of skip-tracing techniques to ask that child the new address of the parent.

Using Mail to Locate the Debtor

If the efforts to locate the debtor through telephone contacts fail, then using the mail is often the next recourse.

One technique that professional collection agencies, skip-tracers and creditors frequently use to locate debtors involves using registered mail addressed to a fictitious name in care of the debtor, and marked "deliver to addressee only." Such a letter will be forwarded to the new address with the new address marked on the envelope. Of course, when it reaches the new address it will not be delivered because of the notation "deliver to addressee only." When the envelope is returned to the sender, it will have the forwarding address of the debtor.

Similarly, registered letters sent in care of debtor's name to unions and professional organizations of which the debtor is a member and marked "deliver to addressee only" will provide fruitful results.

Freedom of Information Act - How to Use It to Locate the Debtor

The Freedom of Information Act is a federal law passed in 1966 requiring various governmental agencies to make available to the public certain information. A creditor can use this law to locate the missing debtor.

For instance, a debtor has moved from his present address without notifying the creditor. If he has left a forwarding address with the post office, you can use the Act to learn his new address. Send a letter to the postmaster at his last known address along with $1 in service fee as follows:

Dear Postmaster,

Pursuant to the Freedom of Information Act, please provide the forwarding address of the following person. Enclosed is $1 fee and a stamped return envelope for your convenience.

_____

Name

_____

Last address

_____

_____

Thank you,

Signed _____

You'll promptly receive the new address if it was left with the postmaster.

Sometimes, you may have the address of the debtor which is nothing more than a post office box. In such a case, the Freedom of Information Act has been useful in obtaining the street address. Postal regulations require that a street address be given on the application for a post office box. This information is kept on file at the post office. Again, write a letter to the postmaster asking for the debtor's street address.

Using Legal Process to Locate the Debtor

If all else fails in locating the debtor, you may have to resort to the use of legal process. State statutes often give creditors the right to subpoena witnesses and custodians of records in order to locate a judgment debtor. This means of locating the debtor should be used only as a course of last resort, since it is the most expensive and time-consuming means.

Before resorting to the legal process, you should send a letter to the previous employer of debtor asking for relevant information about him.

Employer Name
Address
City, State, Zip

Re: Judgment creditor vs. Judgment debtor
     Judgment amount: $_____
     Case No. _____

Gentlemen:

The above-named judgment creditor has obtained a judgment against the named judgment debtor on the said date.

I would like to request any information in your possession that may aid in execution of judgment. Specifically, would you please furnish the following information on the above-named judgment debtor:

Date of employment: _____

Nature of duties: _____

If terminated, date of termination: _____

Name and address of new employer: _____

_____

References, if any: _____

Your cooperation in this matter will be greatly appreciated and would obviate any need for further legal process necessitating your personal appearance in court.

A self-addressed envelope is enclosed for your reply. Thanking you in advance,

                              Very truly yours,

                              Signed _____

Essential Steps to Locating the Missing Debtor

1. Check the debtor's file for any clues. Loan or rental application, checks or other payment records, references, letters, etc.

2. Check the telephone information operator for the new telephone number and address.

3. Send $1 to the postmaster of the district or town where he previously lived and ask for any forwarding address that may have been left.

4. Call phone numbers found in the debtor's file that may unearth potential new leads.

5. Call the debtor's former employers or speak to his co-workers or friends and ask them to have the debtor contact you.

6. Speak to any references given on a credit or rental application, especially relatives, friends, ex-spouses or in-laws.

7. Contact the local credit bureau and obtain a credit report.

8. Contact the neighbors using the reverse street address telephone directory.

9. Obtain information from the motor vehicle bureau, veterans agencies, courthouse records, county recorder, or other public agencies.

10. Finally, check the neighborhood schools, churches or synagogues.

How to Protect Yourself as Judgment Creditor

✓ Whenever possible, try to make husband and wife "jointly and severally" liable on any debt. Obtain both signatures on any contract, note or lease agreement. It's obviously easier to collect a judgment against both husband and wife than against just one spouse.

✓ If a debtor's financial position and credit history appear weak, do not hesitate to demand a co-signer or guarantor of payment. Much to your surprise, parents, relatives, friends and even employers will often guarantee repayment of a debt.

✓ Maintain a complete and accurate file on the debtor. Loan or rental application, employment history, trade and banking references, personal references, marital history, credit report, delinquencies, judgments, bankruptcies and other legal proceedings, real or personal property recordings - all these provide a wealth of information in locating a missing debtor and eventually in collecting the debt.

✓ During the course of a transaction, update your file periodically: debtor's new address, divorce or remarriage, bank location and debtor's account number, new job, etc. Keep in mind, a well-documented file means fewer collection problems.

✓ Once the debtor becomes delinquent, proceed promptly and firmly. If you've allowed the delinquency to reach an unmanageable level, the debtor will have little incentive to cure it. Also, the longer you wait in following up, the more difficult the collection of a judgment will be.

✓ If you procrastinate in your collection efforts, the debtor is likely to move to a new location without informing you; he may close his bank accounts or transfer funds to put them beyond your reach; he may transfer ownership of his home or vehicles to his parents or friends; or, he may get his friendly boss to reduce his salary to half of what it is.

✓ Where a debtor is liable to a creditor for two or more debts, the creditor generally has the right to direct to which debt a payment shall be applied. Use this to your advantage wherever possible. For instance, apply the payment to an older debt or to a debt that may be legally more difficult to prove and enforce, or one that's unsecured.

Judgment Debtor Interrogatories

10

Once a judgment has been obtained, a creditor can make any reasonable inquiry into the debtor's financial affairs. This inquiry can take the form of interrogatories propounded on the judgment debtor in aid of execution. Written interrogatories are often referred to as a poorman's discovery technique; they are cost effective and, as a preliminary step, are of immense help in discovering a defendant's assets and his ability to pay on the debt.

Generally, the debtor inquiry can be as broad as necessary to determine the true status of the defendant's financial condition. If the judgment debtor resists such inquiry, a motion can be filed for contempt or to impose sanctions. If the court finds that the defendant willfully failed to answer questions or evaded interrogatories propounded by the creditor, costs and fees may be awarded to the creditor.

On the following pages is a set of questions designed to elicit sufficient information to the judgment creditor about the defendant's financial condition.

Sample Interrogatories for Judgment Debtor

---

1. Give your name, including any nicknames or other names used.

2. Give your present residence address.

3. Give your residence telephone number.

4. Give your social security number.

5. Give your age and the date of your birth.

6. State where you were born.

7. State your marital status and, if married, state your spouse's full name, social security number, and date of birth.

8. State whether your spouse is presently employed, and if so, give your spouse's employer and state how long your spouse has been so employed.

9. State your spouse's present residence address.

10. Do you have any children? If so, state each child's full name, residence address, and date of birth.

11. List all the places where you have lived in the past year by stating the street address, any post office address, city, state, zip code, and for each place, give the dates during which you lived there.

12. Give your occupation.

13. Who is your employer?

14. What is the address where you work?

15. What is the telephone number where you work?

16. Do you work part-time anywhere?

17. Give the dates during which you have been employed by your present employer.

18. State all business ventures you have engaged in during the past year and for each give:

(a) The name of the business.
(b) Its address.
(c) The beginning and ending dates of your association with said business.
(d) Identify other persons associated with the business.
(e) Describe the purpose of the business.
(f) State whether you still own any interest in the business.

19. State all partnerships in which you have been engaged in during the past year and for each give:

(a) The name of the partnership.
(b) The partnership address.
(c) Beginning and ending dates of the partnership business.
(d) Identify the partners.
(e) The purpose of the partnership business.
(f) State whether you still own any interest in the partnership.

20. Give the amount of income you received from your trade or profession for the past year.

21. Give the amount of the income your spouse received for the previous year.

22. List income from other sources, including but not limited to investments, interest, dividends, pension funds, profit sharing plans, and trust funds by identifying each source and the amount of money received for the past year.

23. Give the date and place of filing of your last state income tax returns and federal income tax return.

24. List all accounts you have with any banks, credit unions, savings and loan associations, or other financial institutions you have maintained either in your name or together with any person for the past year, and for each account, state:

(a) The name of the financial institution.
(b) Its address.
(c) The name on the account.
(d) The account number.
(e) The average balance in the account for the previous year.
(f) The current balance of the account.

    (g) Whether any IRA accounts exist.

    (h) The location of the IRA account.

    (i) The amount in the account.

25. Give all safe deposit boxes you have kept since one year prior to the entry of the judgment and give:

    (a) The bank or other institution where it is located.

    (b) The address of that institution.

    (c) The name or names on the box.

    (d) Describe in detail the contents of the box.

26. Identify each person who has possession or custody of any financial records reflecting your financial condition during the past year.

27. List anything you have in your possession which belongs to someone else.

28. Have you ever filed bankruptcy, and if so, state the date of filing, the name of the bankruptcy court, the location of the bankruptcy court, the nature of the proceedings, and the name of the attorney who represented you.

29. List all outstanding obligations, the name of the creditor, address of the creditor, amount due, and the amount of payments.

30. Have you ever been a defendant or a plaintiff in a lawsuit in the past five years? If so, for each action, state:

    (a) The name of the court.

    (b) The location of the court.

    (c) The case number.

    (d) The type of proceeding.

    (e) The result or outcome.

    (f) Identify the attorney who represented you.

31. List all of your properties that have been taken by a court order, attached, executed, or foreclosed since the entry of the judgment against you, and for each item of property, state:

    (a) Its description.

    (b) The name and location of the court that ordered seizure of the property.

    (c) The type of the case and case number.

    (d) The date the property was seized.

32.   Have you paid off any accounts within the past year and if so, what was the collateral or security?

33.   If you have co-signed with any person to repay a debt, list the following for each debt:

(a)   The identity of the person to whom the debt is owed.
(b)   The place the debt was incurred.
(c)   The nature of the debt.
(d)   The identity of the person with whom you co-signed.
(e)   The amount due.

34.   List any loan you have made to any of your relatives since the entry of the judgment against you and for each such loan:

(a)   Identify the relative's name and address.
(b)   State the relative's relationship to you.
(c)   State the amount of the loan.
(d)   State when the relative received the proceeds of the loan.
(e)   State the amount repaid and the date of repayment, if repaid.
(f)   State the present balance.
(g)   State the consideration for any loan.

35.   List any loans that you have received from any relatives in the past year and for each such loan, state:

(a)   The name and address of the relative.
(b)   The relative's relationship to you.
(c)   The amount of the loan.
(d)   The date you received the proceeds of the loan.
(e)   The amount you have repaid and the date of repayment, if repaid.
(f)   The present balance.
(g)   Whether any relative holds a perfected security interest in any of your property.

36.   List all losses you have suffered from fire, theft, or gambling within the last year and for each such loss:

(a)   Describe the property.
(b)   State how it was lost.
(c)   Give the date of loss.
(d)   State the value of the property.

    (e) State whether an insurance claim for the loss has been filed and if so, identify the insurance company.

    (f) State whether an insurance claim has been paid and if so, identify the insurance company making the payment and the amount of the payment.

    (g) Has the property been recovered.

37.   List all of your real estate and personal property you have sold, traded, pawned or given away since the entry of the judgment against you and for each item of property, state:

    (a) Description of the property

    (b) The date of the transfer.

    (c) The identity of the person whom it was transferred.

    (d) The relationship to you of the person to whom it was transferred.

    (e) The consideration you received in return for the property.

38.   List any of your property that has been returned to or repossessed by a creditor or secured party during the past year and for each item of property, state:

    (a) The name of the creditor or secured party.

    (b) A description of the property.

    (c) The value of the property.

    (d) The date it was returned or repossessed.

39.   List any other creditors, including wages, commissions, or funds that you may owe any employee or other person and for each such employee or other person, state:

    (a) The name of the employee or other person.

    (b) The amount due.

    (c) When contracted.

    (d) The nature of the work or reason for the debt.

40.   Name any person or business that owes you money or is indebted to you in some manner.

41.   Do you owe any federal, state or local taxes and if so, state:

    (a) The identity of the government branch to which it is owed.

    (b) The amount due.

    (c) The type of tax.

    (d) The place incurred.

    (e) The place assessed.

42. Do you make any alimony or child support payments in connection with a divorce, dissolution of marriage, or separation agreement, and if so, state:

    (a) The name of the person to whom it is paid.
    (b) The amount of payment.
    (c) The name of the court.
    (d) The date of the decree.
    (e) The type and the case number.

43. List any inheritances that you have received within the past year and for each such instance, state:

    (a) The source of the inheritance.
    (b) The monetary amount received and description of any property and its value.
    (c) The date you received the proceeds.

44. If you owe any debts for which you have pledged any of your property as a guarantee for payment, list the following for each debt:

    (a) The name of the person or business to whom the debt is owed.
    (b) A full and complete description of the pledged property.
    (c) The value of the property.
    (d) The date the debt was incurred.
    (e) Identify the document you signed in pledging the property.
    (f) The amount due on the debt.
    (g) Where any lien is recorded or filed.

45. Have you made any written statements or completed any applications or financial affidavits concerning your financial situation within the past year? If so, state:

    (a) The name of the person or business receiving the statement, application, or financial affidavit.
    (b) The date made.

46. With respect to any parcel of real property which you may own or in which you may have an interest, including a leasehold interest, state:

    (a) Its address.
    (b) Its legal description.
    (c) The original purchase price.
    (d) The balance on each mortgage on the property.

(e) The identity of the mortgage holder.

(f) The date of each mortgage.

(g) The market value of the property.

(h) Identify the person in possession of the property.

(i) Identify any leases on the property.

(j) Book and page number and where recorded.

47. Identify any stocks, bonds, annuities, negotiable instruments and securities that you own either individually or with someone else, and if jointly owned, identify each other owner and state that owner's interest in the property.

48. List the jewelry, watches, rings, artworks, stamp collections, coin collections, artifacts and antiques that you own and the estimated value of each.

49. List all the household appliances that you own and for each item, state:

(a) The year, make, and model including the serial number.

(b) The value.

(c) Identify all co-owners.

(d) Whether any liens exist.

50. List all the household furniture that you own and for each item, state:

(a) A full and complete description.

(b) The value.

(c) Identify all co-owners.

(d) Whether any liens exist.

51. List any livestock that you may own and state for each:

(a) The description.

(b) The address where it is located.

(c) The market value.

(d) Identify all documents pertaining to its registration, certification, or lineage.

(e) Identify any joint owner.

52. List all the automobiles or other motor vehicles including mobile homes and trailers that you own or are presently buying and for each item, state:

(a) The year, make, model, identification number, and certificate of title number.

(b) Its location.

(c) Identify any co-owners.
(d) The market value.
(e) Whether any liens exist.

53. List any farming equipment that you own and for each item, state:

(a) The description, including the year, make, model, and identification number.
(b) The address of its location.
(c) Identify any co-owners.
(d) The market value.
(e) Whether any liens exist.

54. List all machinery, equipment, and tools of business or other tools that you own or have an interest in and for each, state:

(a) The description.
(b) The address of its location.
(c) The identity of all co-owners.
(d) The market value.
(e) Whether any liens exist.

55. List all office equipment, furnishings, and supplies which you own and for each item, state:

(a) The description.
(b) The address of its location.
(c) The identity of all co-owners.
(d) The market value.
(e) Whether any liens exist.

56. Do you own a personal computer or other computer hardware or software and if so, state:

(a) The description.
(b) The address of its location.
(c) The identity of all co-owners.
(d) The market value.
(e) Whether any liens exist.

57. List all other personal property owned by you not previously listed including but not limited to: ships, boats, motorcycles, airplanes, cameras, guns, campers, golf clubs, sporting equipment, stereo systems, video cassette recorders, and musical instruments and for each item, state:

(a) The description, including year, make, model, identification or serial number, certificate of title number.

(b) The address of its location.

(c) The value.

(d) The identity of any co-owners.

(e) Whether any liens exist.

58. Identify each patent, copyright or trademark in which you have an interest and state its value.

59. List any interest you have in property now being held by someone else, including but not limited to interest in land, money, stocks, bonds, bequests, or other personal property and for each item, state:

(a) The identity of the person holding the interest.

(b) The description of the property.

(c) The address of the location of the property.

(d) The nature of your interest in the property.

(e) The value of your interest in the property.

60. List any insurance policies you own and for each such policy, state:

(a) The identity of the insurance company.

(b) The cash value of the policy.

(c) The type of insurance.

(d) The face value.

(e) The item or person insured.

(f) The annual premium.

61. Do you have money in any pension or retirement fund where you now work or have worked previously and if so, state:

(a) The name and address of employer.

(b) The name of the fund.

(c) The amount due you.

(d) The terms and provisions upon which it will be paid to you or your beneficiaries.

62. Do you have any money or security now posted as a bond? If so, state:

(a) The amount of the bond.

(b) The reason for the bond.

63. Identify all books, papers, and deeds relating to your estate, business, trade or property which you have not previously disclosed in your answers to these interrogatories and for each identify the person who has possession of it, if not in your possession.

64. Are you the beneficiary of any trust? If so, state the circumstances of the trust.

65. Do you have deposits with any utility or telephone companies? If so, state:

   (a) The name and address of the entity.
   (b) Amount of deposit.
   (c) When such deposit is due to be returned to you.

Examination in Supplementary Proceedings

IN THE _____ COURT

COUNTY OF _____

STATE OF _____

CASE NO. _____

_____ vs. _____
Plaintiff/Judgment Creditor   *Defendant/Judgment Debtor*

Name _____ Spouse _____

SS# _____ Dr. Lic. _____ SS# _____ Dr. Lic. _____

Address _____ How long _____ Phone _____

No. of dependents and relationship _____

Employed by _____ Occupation _____ How long _____

Address _____

Salary $ _____ How paid _____ When _____

Employer of spouse _____ Occupation _____ How long _____

Salary $ _____ How paid _____ When _____

Interest in any business _____

Other income _____

Own home ___ Value $_____ Mtgs. $_____ Equity $_____ Date of homestead _____

Name of mortgagee _____ Payments $ _____ When _____

Rent _____ Amount $ _____ Per Month _____ Due _____

Landlord's name and address _____

Interest in other real estate _____ Encumbered _____ Description _____

Bank _____ In whose name _____

Checking or savings _____ Last bank account _____ Closed _____

Safe deposit box _____ Where _____

Cash on person $ _____ Cash elsewhere _____

Stocks, bonds, securities _____

Life insurance _____ Amount $ _____ Yearly premium $_____

Jewelry _____ Interest in estate _____

Auto or interest therein _____

Registered owner _____ Legal owner & address _____

Value $_____ Payments $_____ per _____ Unpaid balance $ _____

Other vehicles _____

Ever filed for bankruptcy _____ When _____ Where _____

Property pledged or pawned_____

Debts owed to debtor _____

Debts owed by debtor_____

Names of parents _____ Address _____ Phone _____

Names of relatives or friends_____ Address_____ Phone _____

Promise to pay _____

Remarks _____

_____

Dated : _____ (Signed) _____

Judgment Debtor

SECTION IV

Using Exemption Laws to Protect Property

11

A judgment debtor has a very potent weapon in his arsenal against a creditor who's attempting to seize his assets to satisfy a debt: Exemption laws.

The federal government and all states, by constitutional or statutory provision, insulate certain property of the debtor from seizure by his creditor. The protected property is referred to as exempt property; if property is exempt and the debtor has taken all the necessary procedural steps to claim the exemption, creditors cannot attach the exempt property to the extent of the exemption without the consent of the debtor.

In effect, the debtor retains all rights of ownership of exempt property. He retains the right to possess, sell, encumber and use the property.

All exemption laws have three basic purposes:

- Protection of the debtor;

- Protection of the debtor's family;

- Protection of the society.

The amounts and types of exemptions provided under various statutes are far from uniform among the states. Nonetheless, many items of exempt property are common to most states.

Homestead Exemption

All but six jurisdictions provide a homestead exemption designed to safeguard the home for the debtor and his family. This exemption represents one of the most significant rights of debtors. First homestead exemption law was enacted in Texas in 1839 and now every state has enacted homestead protection statute, in one form or another.

Who and What Is Protected

The homestead exemption applies to real estate owned and occupied by the debtor. Generally, homestead exemption is available on single-family homes. However, in many states it is now extended to condominiums or apartments, and in some cases to mobile homes.

In most states, the debtor has to be the head of a family in order to claim homestead exemption, and the homestead must be used as the family's primary residence. Once a homestead has been established, the exemption is generally not lost if the debtor ceases temporarily to occupy his residence. In many states the homestead exemption survives death and possibly divorce. Some states now make the homestead available to single persons.

Amount of Protection

The value, size, and type of property that is eligible for homestead protection varies greatly from jurisdiction to jurisdiction. Most homestead statutes limit the exemption by size, value or both.

Texas, for instance, has perhaps the most liberal homestead statute in the nation. Texas has a homestead exemption of 200 acres in rural areas without regard to value, and of $10,000 in value at time of acquisition of urban property without regard to subsequent improvements. Under these liberal provisions, a $10,000 vacant lot bought in an urban area with improvements of $100,000 would be completely exempt. Similarly, a $100,000 house built on rural property would be completely exempt. In other states, the amount of the exemption is not related to the amount of acreage, but only to the dollar value.

Debts against Which the Homestead Is Protected

Exemption laws differ with respect to when a debtor must establish his homestead in relation to when the debt asserted against it arose. Most states extend homestead protection regardless of when the homestead was acquired or declared. In these jurisdictions the debtor generally may protect his exemption merely by asserting it after the sheriff levies on the land or before the property is sold. However, a number of states provide that the homestead is not exempt from debts incurred before it was acquired.

Claiming Homestead Exemption

The judgment debtor or claimant is often required to assert the right to the homestead exemption. In many states, the debtor must record a homestead declaration in the real estate records. However, some states now provide for an automatic homestead exemption upon occupancy by the homeowner as a principal residence.

The relationship between judgment lien law and the homestead exemption often creates perplexing issues. Most states provide that a judgment lien does not attach to homestead property. Thus, a purchaser of the homestead property takes it free of the judgment creditors' claims, even though the purchaser claims no homestead exemption in the purchased property. On the other hand, in some states the judgment lien usually does attach to the property, to the extent that the property exceeds the size or value of the allowed homestead exemption.

Life Insurance Exemption

The first life insurance exemption statute was enacted in 1840. Currently, every state grants significant exemptions for life insurance from collection by the owner's creditors. In many states, the exemption is extended against creditors of the beneficiary.

In addition to exemptions for individual life insurance policies, many states provide for exemption of term insurance as well as group life insurance.

Amount Protected

Many states place no limitation on the amount of life insurance which is exempt. Some jurisdictions limit the exemption by placing a dollar ceiling on the face amount of the policies held by the insured. In these states, if the face amount exceeds the ceiling, creditors of the insured can reach payable proceeds which exceed the limitation.

All of these statutes exempt insurance proceeds payable to a qualified beneficiary upon insured's death. In addition, the exemption usually extends to the cash surrender value of the policy. Many states exempt the proceeds which are paid upon the death of the insured from the reach of the beneficiary's creditors as well.

Exemption of life insurance proceeds is justified on the basis that it affords protection to dependents of the insured. However, many states grant the exemption even if persons other than dependents are beneficiaries.

Other Exemptions

Welfare Payments

Slightly more than half the states place the most significant type of public assistance, aid to families with dependent children, beyond the reach of creditors. Some states grant exemptions for other types of public assistance such as aid to the blind, the elderly and the disabled. The statutes not only prohibit a creditor from garnishing the state for payments to be made to the debtor but also exempt the assistance money after it has been paid to the debtor.

Retirement Income

The federal and state governments exempt funds paid through public retirement programs. In addition, many statutes protect the income from a variety of private retirement programs.

All social security payments are exempt from all types of legal process. By a variety of statutes, states exempt different forms of private retirement plans.

Alimony and Child Support

Although alimony and child support payments represent an important type of support income, these payments are seldom exempted from the claims of either the payor's or the payee's creditors.

Other Exempt Income

Most states exempt unemployment and workmen's compensation payments. Similarly, most states grant either a limited or complete exemption for disability and health insurance payments.

Appendix to Section IV: Income Exemptions of Each State

Both federal and state legislation exempt specified income of a judgment debtor from the reach of creditors by the use of garnishment or other judicial process.

Federal legislation provides a basic wage exemption pursuant to Title III of the Consumer Credit Protection Act (CCPA) and provides some specific exemptions principally related to federal payments and the Employee Retirement Income Security Act (ERISA). Under ERISA, pensions generally cannot be garnished.

Congress has legislated a major exception to these specific federal income exemptions. Pursuant to the Child Support Enforcement Act of 1975, the income exemptions are not applicable as to enforcement of alimony or child support decrees.

Under the federal wage exemption scheme established by CCPA, the maximum part of the aggregate disposable earnings of an individual for any work week that is subject to garnishment may not exceed the lesser of (1) 25% of his disposable earnings for that week or (2) the amount by which his disposable earnings for the week exceeds 30 times the federal minimum hourly wage.

CCPA does permit a greater garnishment to enforce court support orders. "Disposable" earnings are defined as that part of an individual's gross compensation for personal services that remains after deduction of amounts required by law to be withheld.

Although CCPA preempts state garnishment laws that permit greater garnishment than that provided by CCPA, more protective state exemption law still can apply instead of CCPA.

Under state exemption laws, creditors' access to the debtor's income may be further curtailed. Indeed, a few states, such as Florida and Texas, flatly prohibit garnishment of wages. The state wage exemption statutes affect various forms of income, including wages, pensions, and public assistance payments.

Specific income exemptions enacted by each state are enumerated below:

Arizona	50% of earnings for thirty days prior to levy for use of family.
Alabama	30% of weekly disposable income or amount by which disposable earnings per week are in excess of 50 times federal minimum hourly wage.
Alaska	Earnings of judgment debtor not to exceed $350 for head of family, $200 for single man for personal services rendered within 30 days preceding levy of execution where necessary to support debtor's family.
Arkansas	Wages for sixty days exempt provided statement is filed that wages are less than $200 if single, and $500 for a family. First $25 a week net wages exempt.
California	Greater than 50% or portion exempt by federal statute of the earnings of the defendant or judgment debtor received for his personal services rendered at any time within thirty days next preceding the levy of attachment or execution.
Colorado	Earnings 70%, 35% if single.
Connecticut	Greater amount 75% of disposable earnings per week up to greater of 65% or amount equal to 40 times federal minimum hourly wage.
Delaware	Earnings: 90% in New Castle County, 60% in Kent and Sussex, not exempt if self-employed. Liability for balance applies only to necessities of life.
District of Columbia	Greater of 75% of disposable earnings per week or amount of disposable earnings per week equal to 30 times federal minimum hourly wage. Withhold by garnishee-employer 90% of first $200 of gross wages, payable in a month in excess of $200 or under $500.
Florida	All earnings exempt except for alimony and support payments at discretion of court.
Georgia	Greater of 75% of disposable earnings per week or amount by which disposable earnings exceed 30 times the federal minimum hourly wage.

Hawaii	95% of first $100, 90% of next $100, and 80% of gross wages in excess of $200 per month or equivalent per week.
Idaho	Earnings 75% for his personal service rendered within thirty days preceding levy if necessary for use of family supported by his labor; provided that if garnishment be founded upon debt for necessaries, exemption shall not exceed 50% of wages or salary due at time of service of execution or attachment. In no case shall exemption exceed $100 at any one time.
Illinois	Earnings: 85% with minimum of $50 per week if single, or $65 if head of household, and maximum of $200 per week.
Indiana	75% of disposable earnings per week in excess of 30 times federal minimum hourly wage.
Iowa	75% of disposable earnings for week or amount by which disposable earnings exceed 30 times federal minimum hourly wage, whichever is greater. Maximum amount that can be garnished in any year is $250 for each creditor.
Kansas	75% of disposable earnings for week or amount by which disposable earnings exceed 30 times federal minimum hourly wage, whichever is greater. Exemption inapplicable to support orders.
Kentucky	Greater of 75% of disposable income per week or amount by which disposable earnings exceed 30 times federal minimum hourly wage. Exemption inapplicable to support orders.
Louisiana	75% of disposable earnings for any week, but not less than $70 on loans in excess of 10%. Lenders forbidden to use garnishment.
Maine	Greater of 75% of disposable earnings for week or amount by which disposable earnings exceed 10 times federal minimum hourly wage.

Maryland	Wages $150 exempt multiplied by the number of weeks in which said wages were earned or 75% of such wages, whichever is greater; except that in Caroline, Worcester, Kent and Queen Anne counties, exemption for any work week shall be greater of 75% of wages due or 30 times federal minimum wage.
Massachusetts	Wages for personal labor or services exempted from attachment to amount of $125 per week. Exemption of $75 of personal income which is not otherwise exempt by law.
Michigan	Householder with family, 60% exemption with following limitations: On first garnishment, maximum $50 per week for labor of one week. For more than one week's labor, maximum $90 and minimum $60. As to subsequent garnishments for one week's labor, maximum per week is $60 and minimum $24. For a period of more than 16 days, maximum is $60 and minimum $30. Employee, not householder with family, first garnishment 40% exemption with $50 maximum, $20 maximum and $10 minimum.
Minnesota	75% of net wages due at time of attachment, garnishment, or levy or 8 times the number of business days and paid holidays, not greater than 5 per week in the pay period, times the federal minimum hourly wage, whichever is greater. Where debtor has been on relief, exemption for a period of six months from date of return to private employment.
Mississippi	75% of wages or salaries of resident laborer or employee.
Missouri	Greater of (1) 75% of weekly earnings, (2) weekly amount equal to 30 times federal minimum hourly wage or (3) 90% of work week earnings.
Montana	All earnings for forty-five days preceding garnishment, limited to 50% exemption.
Nebraska	Greatest of 75% of disposable earnings or amount equal to 30 times federal minimum hourly wage or 85% of disposable earnings if wage earner is head of family.

Nevada	The greater of 75% of disposable earnings or the amount by which disposable earnings exceed 30 times the minimum federal hourly wage.
New Hampshire	Wages for labor performed after service of writ: wages for labor performed before service exempt unless action founded on debt on judgment issued by state court. In such cases wages equal to 50 times federal minimum hourly wage are exempt. Special exemption for small loan law debt.
New Jersey	Earnings 90% if debtor earns $7,500 a year or less. If more than $7,500, garnishee fixed by court.
New Mexico	Greater of 75% of debtor's disposable earnings or of excess of 40 times federal minimum hourly wage rate. Disposable earnings is that part of the debtor's salary remaining after deduction of amounts required to be withheld by law.
New York	Earnings 90%, unless less than $85 per week is earned. Balance is payable as installments.
North Carolina	Earnings sixty days preceding garnishee, if necessary for support of family.
North Dakota	Greater of 75% of debtor's disposable earnings or of excess of 40 times federal minimum hourly wage.
Ohio	Greater of 82 1/2% of the debtor's disposable income or 175 times federal minimum hourly wage. Statutory scheme preempted by Federal Consumer Protection Act.
Oklahoma	Earnings: 75% ninety days; 100% shown to be necessaries for support of family; single man, 75% of wages.
Oregon	Greater of 75% of disposable earnings for week or amounts by which disposable earnings exceed 30 times the federal minimum hourly wage.
Pennsylvania	100% of all wages. Does not apply to support orders of court.

Rhode Island	Earnings: $50 plus salary and wages of dependents; 100% for debtor on relief; and all earnings one year after off-relief.
South Dakota	100% of all earnings within sixty days, if necessary for support of family. However, 15% may be attached for judgment for food, fuel, or medicines.
Tennessee	Wages to 50%, minimum $20, maximum $50 per week; if single, 40%, $17.50 and $40 per week respectively; $2.50 per week addition for each dependent.
Texas	All wages for personal services.
Utah	Married man or head of family: one half of earnings for 30 days prior to levy if his earnings are necessary for family support. Minimum exemption of $50 per month on judgments arising from debts on consumer credit sales greater of 75% disposable earnings per week or 30 times federal minimum hourly wage.
Vermont	75% of disposable earnings for that week or excess of 30 times federal minimum hourly wage, whichever is greater.
Virginia	75% of disposable earnings for that week or excess of 30 times federal minimum hourly wage, whichever is greater. Exemption is inapplicable to court order for support.
Washington	The greater part of 40 times of the state hourly minimum wage or of 75% of disposable earnings of defendant is exempt from garnishment. Disposable earnings means that part of the earnings remaining after deductions of the amount required by law to be withheld.
West Virginia	$20 per week minimum of 80% of wages due or to become due within one year after issuance of execution.
Wisconsin	Greater of 75% of debtor's disposable earnings or excess of 30 times federal minimum hourly wage. Disposable earnings means that part of earnings after deduction of required by law to be withheld. Employees with depend-

ents: basic exemptions, $120 plus $20 per dependent for each 30-day period prior to service of process. Maximum exemption, 75% of income. Employees without dependents, basic exemption of 60% of income for each 30-day period prior to service of process. Minimum $75. Maximum $100.

Wyoming

Judgments on consumer credit sales, home or loan, greater of 75% of disposable earnings or excess over 30 times federal minimum hourly wage. Otherwise 50% of earnings for personal service 60 days before levy if necessary for use of resident family.

Appendix to Section IV: Exemptions under Section 522(d) of the Bankruptcy Code

(d) The following property may be exempted under sub-section (b) (1) of this section:

(1) The debtor's aggregate interest, not to exceed $7,500 in value, in real property or personal property that the debtor or a dependent of the debtor uses as a residence, in a cooperative that owns property that the debtor or a dependent of the debtor uses as a residence, or in a burial plot for the debtor or a dependent of the debtor.

(2) The debtor's interest, not to exceed $1,200 in value, in one motor vehicle.

(3) The debtor's interest, not to exceed $200 in value in any particular item, in household furnishings, household goods, wearing apparel, appliances, books, animals, crops, or musical instruments, that are held primarily for the personal, family, or household use of the debtor or a dependent of the debtor.

(4) The debtor's aggregate interest, not to exceed $500 in value, in jewelry held primarily for the personal, family, or household use of the debtor or a dependent of the debtor.

(5) The debtor's aggregate interest, not to exceed in value $400 plus any unused amount of the exemption provided under paragraph (1) of this subsection, in any property.

(6) The debtor's aggregate interest, not to exceed $750 in value, in any implements, professional books, or tools, of the trade of the debtor or the trade of a dependent of the debtor.

(7) Any unmatured life insurance contract owned by the debtor, other than a credit life insurance contract.

(8) The debtor's aggregate interest, not to exceed in value $4,000 less any amount of property of the estate transferred in the manner specified in section 542 (d) of this title, in any accrued dividend or interest under, or loan value of, any unmatured life insurance contract.

SECTION V

Law of Fraudulent Transfers

12

Few areas of law are more elusive and less understood than the law of fraudulent transfers. For judgment debtors and creditors alike, fraudulent transfers is an area full of booby-traps. Without a proper understanding of the law both are very likely to run into a host of problems.

As a first step in any kind of financial planning undertaken to protect the assets from potential judgment creditors, it is necessary that you become thoroughly familiar with the applicable state laws on fraudulent conveyances and the Federal Bankruptcy Code. Ignorance of these laws may cause you to engage in transfer of assets which could be set aside as fraudulent to creditors.

Introduction

If a creditor is seeking collection of delinquent debts or enforcing a judgment, it is very likely that the debtor may be delinquent with other creditors too. The debtor may attempt to protect his assets from the reach of creditors by secreting them or by transferring them to third parties. Typically, such transfers are for less than fair consideration, and almost always with a "string" attached to allow the debtor to reclaim the property after the financial woes have disappeared.

If the debtor were legally capable of doing this, creditor's collection efforts would be thoroughly frustrated. However, beginning in the Sixteenth century with the Statute of Elizabeth, creditors have been able to set aside such transfers as "fraudulent conveyances".

In the United States, basically two types of fraudulent conveyance statutes have been adopted by the various states. One is the direct descendant of the Statute of Elizabeth; the other, adopted by about half the states, is the Uniform Fraudulent Conveyance Act.

The Uniform Act is essentially a restatement of the Statute of Elizabeth. It did not so much change the law of fraudulent conveyances as it clarified its principles, streamlined its procedures, and relieved lawyers and judges of the need to produce tortuous legal reasoning in order to justify many cases under the old Statute of Elizabeth.

History

The law of fraudulent conveyances is generally considered to have begun with the English Statute 13 Elizabeth, c.5(1570), which provided:

I. For the avoiding and abolishing of feigned, convenor and fraudulent feoffments, gifts, grants, alienations (and) conveyances...which...are devised and contrived of malice, fraud, covin, collusion or guile to the end purpose and intent, to delay, hinder or defraud creditors...

II. Be it therefore...enacted...that all and every...conveyance...to or for any intent or purpose before declared and expressed shall be...deemed and taken (only as against that person...whose actions...are, shall or might be in any wise disturbed, hindered, delayed, or defrauded) to be clearly and utterly void, frustrate and of none effect...

IV. Provided that this Act...shall not extend to any interest...conveyed...upon good consideration and bona fide law fully conveyed or assured to any person...not having at the time of such conveyance or assurance to them made, any manner of notice or knowledge of such covin, fraud or collusion...

The statute was read to mean that conveyances made with the intent to hinder, delay or fraud creditors are not actually void, but rather are voidable as to creditors who were hindered, delayed or defrauded, the conveyance remaining valid as between grantor and grantee. However, from an early point, the courts concluded that the creditor did not actually have the transfer voided, but rather could proceed directly in the transferred property.

Twyne's Case

The earliest notable case on fraudulent conveyances, and one whose implications live to this day was the very famous *Twyne's Case,* 3 Coke 80b, 76 Eng. Rep.809 (Star chamber 1601). Actually, *Twyne's Case* was a good study of basic human nature.

It recognized that debtors who subjectively intend to cheat their creditors objectively tend to act in certain ways. Thus, when these observable manifestations are found, they can serve as evidence of the debtor's subjective fraudulent intent. As other courts have put it, these objective, observable facts are badges, evidences, or marks of fraudulent intent.

In the *Twyne's Case* a debtor was obligated to two creditors and, upon suit by one of the creditors, secretly transferred to the other creditor substantially all of his property. The debtor retained possession of the property conveyed and continued to manage it as his own. When the suing creditor obtained judgment and sought to levy upon the property, he was prevented from doing so on the ground that the property belonged to the other creditor.

The court held that the debtor's conveyance was fraudulent, and in recognition of the difficulty creditors faced in proving actual fraudulent intent to hinder or delay creditors' collection efforts, developed so-called "badges of fraud" to assist creditors in carrying their weighty burden of proof. The badges of fraud simply refer to circumstances indicative of the intent to defraud.

Specifically, in *Twyne's Case,* the court held that the conveyance was secretly made, that it was made pending litigation, that the transfer was general, without exception of the debtor's apparel or any other necessaries of life, and that the debtor retained possession of the property conveyed and used it as his own.

Modern-Day Adaptation

The notion of "badges of fraud" emanating from the Statute of Elizabeth ultimately found its way into jurisdictions of the United States and remains intact in roughly one-half of the states today. The fraudulent conveyance statutes in the states are basically modernized versions of the Statute of Elizabeth, providing creditors with the ability to avoid transfers made by debtors with the intent to hinder, delay or defraud creditors' collection efforts. The courts have variously held that the presence of one or more "badges" constituted either evidence, prima facie evidence, or conclusive evidence of fraudulent intent.

Twyne's Case also raises the question of preferring one creditor over another and whether the transfer made to the preferred creditors should be avoided. As we saw in that case, the debtor was in fact obligated to the creditor to whom the property was conveyed, and the value of the debtor's conveyance did not exceed the debt.

Ordinarily, such a preferential payment is not a fraudulent conveyance. For avoiding such a payment in favor of another creditor would merely work as substitution of one creditor for another. But in *Twyne's Case,* the preference was secretly made, the debtor retained possession of the property, and there were facts from which the preferred creditor's knowledge of, if not deliberate acquiescence for participation in, the debtor's fraudulent scheme could be inferred. Under present law, such circumstances may render a preference voidable.

The notion of "badges of fraud," and the various presumptions of fraudulent intent emanating from it, created uncertainty and conflict in the American jurisdictions; facts which created "prima facie" presumptions of intent to defraud in one jurisdiction created conclusive presumptions or perhaps no presumptions at all in others. In order to inject more consistency and predictability into the law of fraudulent conveyances, the Uniform Fraudulent Conveyance Act was drafted in 1919, with the hope that the states would quickly enact it. Roughly half the states have adopted the Act, and the law of fraudulent conveyances in states which have not adopted the Act remains comparatively unsettled.

Fraudulent Conveyances - In General

Fraudulent conveyance law in general is designed to protect creditors from debtors who transfer their assets in a form detrimental to creditors' claims. A creditor pursuing a delinquent debt or claim would as a first step reduce the claim against the debtor to a judgment. While enforcing the judgment, he may discover that the debtor has at some prior time disposed of his assets in a manner which now hinders, delays, or precludes altogether, satisfaction of the creditor's judgment. In such a case, creditor would have to rely upon the remedies available under various fraudulent conveyance statutes.

If a judgment creditor can show that the transfer or coveyance made by the debtor is fraudulent, the creditor may attach or levy execution directly upon the property in the hands of the debtor's grantee, or the creditor may simply annul the debtor's conveyance, and then proceed against the debtor or the property as if the conveyance had never been made.

Fraudulent conveyance law also provides provisional remedies for creditors whose claim against the debtor is not yet reduced to judgment, or whose claim is not even mature, fixed or liquidated. Under fraudulent conveyance law such persons nevertheless qualify as "creditors." When such a creditor notices or discovers that the debtor is conveying or has conveyed property in a manner which will hinder the creditor or frustrate collection efforts once the claim is mature or reduced to a judgment, that creditor may seek provisional relief in the nature of an injunction or restraining order, receivership, attachment or any other remedy which the circumstances of the case may require.

Every conveyance made by a debtor with intent to hinder, delay, or defraud creditors is fraudulent, as is every conveyance for less than fair consideration by a debtor who intends to incur debts beyond the ability to pay as they mature. In all these circumstances, creditors are entitled to the relief of setting aside the conveyance or levying on the property as if the conveyance had never been made.

Fraudulent Intent Not Necessary

Of course, there will be situations where the forbidden fraudulent intent of the debtor is not present or apparent and may be impossible to prove. For example, a debtor may simply give property to a friend, relative, or person in need for purely benign or charitable purposes. The debtor may make a "gift" of property or conduct a "bargain sale" of possessions to either raise ready cash, or with the hope or understanding that the property may be repurchased at a later date. Then again, a debtor may sell or otherwise convey property for less than fair value while engaged in an undercapitalized business or transaction.

All of these transfers, to describe a few, may be fraudulent conveyances subject to attack by creditors without regard to the debtor's subjective intent or belief. In other words, a fraudulent conveyance need not necessarily involve actual intent to defraud creditors.

In the United States, basically two types of fraudulent conveyance statutes have been adopted by the various states; one is the direct descendant of the Statute of Elizabeth; the other, adopted by about half the states, is the Uniform Fraudulent Conveyance Act.

"Statute of Elizabeth" Jurisdictions

In those jurisdictions that have not adopted the Uniform Fraudulent Conveyance Act, modernized versions of Statute of Elizabeth are in force which prohibit in general language every conveyance made with intent to hinder, delay or defraud creditors. We've examined above the basic evolution of the law of fraudulent conveyances based on the Statute of Elizabeth.

The language of such statutes seems to suggest that a debtor's actual fraudulent intent must affirmatively be proved. The courts nonetheless have developed categories of constructive fraud by creating so-called "badges of fraud" to assist creditors in proving debtor's actual fraudulent intent.

The courts have in practice recognized that fraud may be established without actual intent to defraud. For example, a debtor who makes a transfer for less than fair value, and thereby becomes insolvent in the sense of having insufficient assets to pay his debts would be presumed to have an intent to defraud[1].

The majority of the courts hold that the creditor must prove that the debtor did not receive fair value for the transfer or that the debtor as a result of the transfer was unable to pay his debts.[2]

Whether the debtor has received fair value for the transfer would hinge on whether he had received near equivalent property or an amount equivalent to the antecedent debt.[3] In many states if the debtor retains possession and use of the transferred property or retains rights in the property, the transfer may be prima facie or conclusively fraudulent.

We'll look in greater detail what constitutes fair consideration or reasonably equivalent exchange later in this chapter.

Many states require proof of actual fraudulent intent, although the "badges of fraud" may sometimes be used to support an inference of intent to defraud. These badges might include transfers pending litigation,[4] transfers for grossly inadequate consideration,[5] and transfers made outside the usual mode of business[6] or under unusually secretive circumstances.[7]

There is yet another situation that must be dealt with. What about the persons who become creditors of the debtor after the alleged fraudulent conveyance has occurred? It is possible that these creditors can also establish the requisite proof of intent to defraud if they can prove the transfer was made with the intent to defraud subsequent creditors.[8]

Of course, the creditor would face the much more difficult task of showing that the debtor anticipated or should have anticipated future obligations at the time of the conveyance.[9]

A third issue that must be considered under traditional fraudulent conveyance statutes is whether a good faith purchaser for value is protected as against the creditor of the transferor when the transferor made the conveyance with the intent to hinder, delay or defraud creditors. The law generally protects good faith purchasers for value who had no notice of the transferor's fraudulent intent. [10]

The purchaser is not made to investigate the transferor's business and motives, and the burden of establishing good faith is on the creditor.[11]

If the purchaser had actual knowledge or facts which would put a reasonable person sufficiently suspect and would lead him to the discovery of the fraud, then the transferee would not be considered to have entered into the transaction in good faith. The transferee who enters into the transaction in bad faith may not only lose the asset transferred but might also be liable for damages if, for example, the creditor can establish that a tort was committed as against the creditor by the transferee.[12]

Creditor's Recourse

What is the practical recourse for a creditor who faces a debtor who has made a fraudulent conveyance?

The creditor in such situations may simply ignore the transfer and go directly after the transferred asset in the hands of the transferee. In order to take this course of action the creditor must be certain that the transfer was a fraudulent conveyance. If his conclusion was incorrect he may face liability to the transferee. The more cautious route may be to have the transfer avoided and then levy upon the property. In that regard, the use of creditor's bill often serves as the procedural mechanism through which the conveyance is avoided.

Uniform Fraudulent Conveyance Act Jurisdictions

In the 1920's the commissioners on Uniform State Laws promulgated the Uniform Fraudulent Conveyance Act (UFCA). Approximately one-half of the jurisdictions have adopted the Uniform Fraudulent Conveyance Act.

The following jurisdictions have adopted the Uniform Fraudulent Conveyance Act: Arizona, California, Delaware, Idaho, Maryland, Massachusetts, Michigan, Minnesota, Montana, Nevada, New Hampshire, New Jersey, New Mexico, New York, North Dakota, Ohio, Oklahoma, Pennsylvania, South Dakota, Tennessee, Utah, Virgin Islands, Washington, Wisconsin, and Wyoming. The most recent adoption occured in 1969. In the above states, this is the basic state statutory law on fraudulent transfers.

(Recently the commissioners on the Uniform State Laws took another look at fraudulent conveyances. In 1984 they drafted what is now called the Uniform Fraudulent Transfer Act (UFTA), which is intended to repeal and replace the UFCA. However, as of late 1985, only three states - Hawaii, North Dakota, and Oregon - have adopted the UFTA. Therefore, the discussion in this chapter will be limited to various provisions of UFCA only; however, it is worth noting that results under the UFTA and the UFCA most often will be the same.)

There are two principal sections of UFCA that enable creditors to avoid fraudulent conveyances, one section is based upon actual fraud, and the other is based upon "constructive fraud."

Actual Fraudulent Transfers

The first major category of fraudulent transfers is that in which it can be established that the debtor had the actual intent to hinder, delay, or defraud its creditors.

Section 7 of UFCA deals with actual or intentional fraud as follows:

Every conveyance made and every obligation incurred with actual intent, as distinguished from intent presumed in law to hinder, delay or defraud either present or future creditors, is fraudulent as to both present and future creditors.

The language under this statute closely resembles the interpretation under the Statute of Elizabeth since both require a showing of actual intent.

Also note that both present and future creditors may avoid a conveyance as fraudulent under Section 7 of UFCA. Parties who become creditors after the transfer occurs need no t show that the debtors specifically intended to defraud subsequent creditors nor are they required to show an intent to defraud a particular subsequent creditor. In short, "a general actual intent to defraud existing creditors is sufficient to create rights in all subsequent creditors." A transfer intended to defraud present or future creditors is fraudulent as to both. [13]

Fraudulent Transfers in Real Life

An example of an actual fraudulent transfer would be when a debtor, with deliberate planning sells his property to someone and hides the proceeds from his creditors. He may, for example, put the proceeds in a secret Swiss bank account. The debtor's purpose is to keep it from his creditors, so that he can personally enjoy it later on. To add to the dilemma of creditors, such rather blatant and obvious fraudulent transfers are rarely seen in real life. More often, a debtor's attempts to defraud his creditors are typically far more subtle and sophisticated.

In most cases involving debtor's fraudulent conduct, direct evidence of fraudulent intent is often difficult, if not impossible, to produce. Modern science has not been able to come up with any technology to read a person's mind and tell us what he was thinking when he transferred away his property. Yet, it is necessary to prove that the debtor had the subjective evil intent to defeat, delay or defraud his creditors when he made the transfer. How can we do this?

For this, we fall back on the concept of badges of fraud that originated under the Statute of Elizabeth. Again, badges of fraud are really circumstantial evidence of fraud, the badges being those facts that commonly are associated with a fraudulent conveyance such as a general transfer of assets, intra-family transfers, transfers for less than fair consideration, and transfers with retention of use or possession. [14]

Phony Transfers

In a phony transfer a debtor formally transfers title to the transferee, but retains all economic and other benefits to the asset. In legal terms a phony transfer is labeled as a "transfer in trust" as described by Justice Brandeis, in the famous case of *Benedict v. Ratner*, 268 U.S.353 (925), which is in effect "a transfer with absolute dominion reserved"

In a phony transfer nothing changes in a realistic sense. Even though the debtor signs a title document that says title to his property has been transferred to somebody else, the facts thereafter show that the debtor continues to enjoy the use and benefit of the property just as if he were still its full owner. The law does not tolerate these phony transfers. If creditors or a trustee can show such a transfer in trust, then that is almost conclusive of the fact that a fraudulent transfer has taken place.

Other Badges of Fraud

Other badges of fraud are not conclusive in themselves, yet nonetheless point toward fraud. For example, where a debtor transfers title to an asset but retains possession of the asset without showing a legitimate commercial or business purpose for retaining possession, the debtor's action would be considered a badge of fraud.

A transfer of all or most of one's assets, leaving the transferor with little or nothing to his name also has been held to be a sign of fraudulent intent. Similarly, transfers during the pendency of a suit or intra-family transfers are also badges of fraud.

A transfer for unconscionably low consideration is also a sign of fraud. In fact, a transfer in which the transferee pays or purports to pay more for the asset than it is worth also has been listed as a mark, badge or evidence of fraud. Indeed, *Twyne's Case* even stated that language in the deed of transfer, stating that the transfer was legitimate, actually showed quite the opposite. As the court pointed out, there was no need for a really legitimate transaction to be so labeled. When one is trying to cheat his creditors however, then one is tempted to place into the document the self-serving statement that it is a legitimate transfer.

In assisting the creditor to prove actual intent, UFCA Section 4 (b) sets forth "factors" to be given consideration in the determination of actual intent. The factors are actually the type of facts that have been characterized as "badges of fraud" in the existing fraudulent conveyance law.

Section 4(b) of the UFCA lists the following factors:

"In determining actual intent under subsection (a)(1), consideration may be given, among other factors, to the fact that:

"(1) the relationship between the transferor and the transferee was close;

"(2) the transferor retained possession or dominion after the transfer;

"(3) the transfer was concealed;

"(4) prior to the transfer a creditor had sued, or was threatening to sue, the transferor;

"(5) the transfer was of substantially all the debtor's assets;

"(6) the debtor has absconded or has removed or changed the form of the assets remaining in his possession so as to make the assets less subject to creditor process;

"(7) the value of the consideration received by the debtor was not reasonably equivalent to the value of the asset transferred or the amount of the obligation incurred;

"(8) the debtor was insolvent or heavily indebted or reasonably should have expected to become so indebted;

"(9) the transfer occurred shortly before or after a substantial debt was incurred.

Proof of the existence of any one of the factors listed in this subsection does not in itself constitute prima facie proof that the debtor has made a fraudulent transfer or incurred a fraudulent obligation."

To recap, the litmus test of determining whether a transfer is fraudulent or not, is to ask yourself this question: How would someone act in an objective way if he were trying to cheat his creditors? If that is the way this particular transferor acted, then this, at least, is evidence, of a badge, or mark of his fraudulent intent.

Constructive Fraudulent Transfers

Proving actual fraudulent intent on the part of the transferor has never been easy. As we've seen above, it requires unearthing a number of so-called "badges of fraud." Thus, the law has always recognized a second major category of fraudulent transfers. These are transfers that are "deemed-in-law" to be fraudulent without regard to the actual intent of the transferor.

Section 4 of UFCA, which contains the principal constructive fraud provision, reads as follows:

> **Every conveyance made and every obligation incurred by a person who is or will be thereby rendered insolvent is fraudulent as to creditors without regard to his actual intent, if the conveyance is made or the obligation is incurred without a fair consideration.**

The classic example of a presumed-in-law fraudulent transfer is: When an insolvent simply gives away his property to his children, thereby getting nothing in return.

The theory behind constructive fraud is that property owned by an insolvent, although formally titled in the insolvent debtor's name, in equity really belongs to his creditors. Thus, if the debtor transfers away that property without getting a reasonably equivalent commercial exchange in return, then this is so prejudicial to creditors who in equity own the property that the law will give these creditors a remedy. The law will permit the creditors to get their property back, even though they cannot prove that the transferor had any evil intent to cheat them, but he made the transfer. The result would remain the same even if it can be shown that the transferor had benign or charitable motives in transferring the property.

The UFCA lists three of the so-called "deemed-in-law" fraudulent transfers, also called "presumed-in-law" or "constructive fraudulent transfers". The common thread running through the three constructive fraudulent transfers is that it involves a transfer by someone who is insolvent or near-insolvent, without getting in return fair consideration.

Categories of Constructive Fraudulent Transfers

The three categories of constructive fraudulent transfers are:

> **1. Transfer by an insolvent for less than fair consideration, or for less than a reasonably equivalent exchange;**

2. Transfer for less than fair consideration by a business person without retaining sufficient capital to meet the likely future needs of that business; and

3. Transfer for less than fair consideration by anyone - business person or consumer - without retaining enough property to meet his likely future debts as they become due.

Most fraudulent transfer litigation by creditors or a trustee in bankruptcy involves one of these presumed-in-law or constructively fraudulent transfers. The trustee makes out his case simply by showing the objective fact that a transfer was made by an insolvent or near-insolvent without getting the required fair consideration, or reasonably equivalent exchange in return. It is not necessary to establish that the transferor had any evil intent.

Fair Consideration or Reasonably Equivalent Exchange

The law of constructive fraudulent transfers establishes the standard of fair consideration or reasonably equivalent exchange. However, a transferor need not receive the exact market value of the property to satisfy this standard. Rather, something less than fair market value typically has been allowed. And this is for a good reason.

First of all, the law takes into account the fact that we live in a free market society where people are looking for "good deals" through fair and hard bargaining. Such free market mechanism cannot be ignored nor should it be discouraged.

Secondly, determining fair market value of an asset is not an easy task; a complex set of factors go into interplay in arriving at a fair market value. Therefore, courts are reluctant to upset transfers that have been fairly negotiated between the parties, simply because it can be shown at a later date that the transferor did not receive, in someone's opinion, then-fair market value of the property.

The appropriate question is: How far below the fair market value is acceptable to keep us within the "fair consideration" or the "reasonably equivalent exchange" concept and thus protect the transfer from a creditor's attack as a constructive fraudulent transfer?

The *Durrett* Decision

To answer the above question, we must look to the now-famous Durrett decision. *Durrett vs. Washington Nat'l. Ins. Co.,* 621 F. 2d (5th Cir. 1980): The court in this decision determined that fair consideration would be received as long as the debtor received at least 70% or more of the fair market value of the property. If the debtor did not receive at least that figure, the court reasoned that fair consideration had not been received.

Under the actual facts of the *Durrett* case, the parties had stipulated that only about 58% of the fair market value of the property had been received. Thus, the courts said that the case had failed to meet the standard of fair consideration.

Durrett decision has given us some general guidelines as to what might constitute a fair consideration. However, there might be instances where the market value of the property is so well-known and so easily attainable that even a small deviation from the fair market value might be considered less than a reasonably equivalent exchange.

Consider, for example, publicly-listed stock or securities. This can be sold on the public exchanges at a known and given price any day of the week. Thus, if a debtor does not get something pretty close to the listed market price on the day of his sale, then it could be successfully argued that a reasonably equivalent exchange had not taken place.

At the other end of the spectrum, there might be assets that are hard to market, have limited appeal and may be subject to distress sale. In such cases, if a debtor obtained, say, 50% of the fair market value, the courts may well be justified in accepting that as fair consideration under the circumstances.

In short, what constitutes a fair consideration or a reasonably equivalent exchange depends upon the peculiar circumstances of the case. The *Durrett* 70% rule should be used as a good rule of thumb with variations on the up side as well as down side acceptable depending upon the actual circumstances of the case.

Good Faith Purchaser

In order to successfully attack a fraudulent conveyance a creditor or trustee in bankruptcy has to cross two hurdles. First, he must prove the debtor's fraudulent intent - either actual or constructive. But this is not enough. He must also as a second step prove that the transferee is a "bad guy". In other words, the transferee lacked good faith in obtaining the property.

Under Section 9 of Uniform Fraudulent Conveyance Act a transferee is completely protected if he acts in good faith and pays equivalent value. In other words, no matter how fraudulent was the transfer by the debtor, there is nothing a creditor or trustee can do about it, if the transferee who now holds the property is a "good guy."

Good Faith Transferee

Now, precisely who is this good faith transferee who is protected from fraudulent transfer attack? A transferee who qualifies as a bona fide purchaser can keep the property free of the trustee's or creditor's claim to it, even though the transferor fraudulently transferred it to him.

Under the Uniform Fraudulent Conveyance Act, the good faith purchaser must meet three requirements:

• He takes the property in good faith;

• He takes the property without knowledge of the fraud on creditors that the transferor actually or constructively is seeking to perpetrate; and

• He himself gives fair consideration - that is, a reasonably equivalent exchange for the property received.

These are three essential elements for a transferee to qualify as a bona fide purchaser. If he fails on any one of these three elements, then he is not protected under the Fraudulent Conveyance Act and he will lose the property to creditors or the trustee in bankruptcy. Thus, a transferee may pay full and fair market value for the property, but if it can be established that he did so in bad faith or with knowledge that the transfer had the effect of hindering and delaying the transferor's creditors, then the transferee will lose the property to the trustee or creditors.

Less Than Fair Consideration

What if a transferee satisfies two of the three elements set forth above?

Say, a transferee acts in good faith and he acts without knowledge of the fraud being perpetrated on the transferor's creditors. He does, however, bargain too hard and ends up paying less than fair consideration.

As we observed above in the *Durrett* case, the transferee apparently acted in good faith and without knowledge that his purchase of the debtor's asset might be a transfer that had the effect of defrauding the transferor's creditors. But he only paid 58% of the fair market value which was less than acceptable to the court under its standard of reasonably equivalent exchange or fair consideration.

In such a case the transferee must give up the property to the creditors or trustee; he however, retains, a lien on the property to reimburse him for the consideration that he actually paid. In other words, a transferee who bargains too hard loses the benefit of his bargain. The court considers that bargain too unfair to the creditors to be tolerated even within the context of a free market society.

In a situation like this the court will order the property sold. From the sale proceeds the transferee will be given the amount needed to reimburse him for what he did pay - the 58% that the *Durrett* purchaser paid. The balance of the sale proceeds from the property will then be turned over to the trustee or creditors.

Fraudulent Conveyances in Bankruptcy

The Bankruptcy Code, like non-bankruptcy law, invalidates fraudulent conveyances. In fact, the provisions of Bankruptcy Code are very much like the non-bankruptcy fraudulent conveyance statutes. While the language in Section 548 of the Bankruptcy Code and the UFCA is not identical, there are, in fact, only a couple of substantive differences between them.

Section 548 of the Bankruptcy Code is based on the Uniform Fraudulent Conveyances Act. Section 548(a)(1) corresponds to Section 7 of the UFCA; it empowers the trustee to invalidate transfers made with actual intent to hinder, delay or defraud creditors. Section 548(b) is similar to the partnership provisions of Section 8(a) of the UFCA. And Section 548(a)(2) resembles UFCA Section 4-7.

It provides for avoidance of transfers where the debtor received less than a "reasonably equivalent value," and:

(i) was insolvent or became insolvent as a result of the transaction; or

(ii) was engaged in business or was about to engage in a business transaction with unreasonably small capital; or

(iii) intended to incur or believed that he would incur debts beyond his ability to pay.

Statute of Limitations

The UFCA does not have its own statute of limitation. States generally have a 3- to 6-year limitations period for actions to invalidate fraudulent conveyances. Under Section 548 of the Bankruptcy Code, the bankruptcy trustee may only reach transfers made within one year of the filing of the bankruptcy petition. This is one of the major differences between the provisions of the UFCA and the Bankruptcy Code.

Thus, a trustee in bankruptcy can attack a fraudulent transfer, either under Section 548 of the Code or under the applicable state law. In almost all cases, however, the substantive results will be the same under either statute, in spite of the fact that the language in the two statutes does not read exactly alike.

Illustration: Assume that Mr. Smith, on June 1, 1986, gives his daughter a new piano as an anniversary present. Mr. Smith is insolvent at the time of the gift. On July 19, 1987, more than a year later, Mr. Smith files a bankruptcy petition. Mr. Smith's bankruptcy trustee will not be able to recover the piano. Under Section 548, the transfer was a fraudulent conveyance (the transfer for less than "reasonably equivalent value" while insolvent) but it was made more than a year prior to the bankruptcy petition.

In reality, the trustee has greater powers. Section 548 is not the only provision in the Bankruptcy Code that invalidates fraudulent conveyances. The trustee may also use Section 548, 544(b) to invalidate fraudulent conveyances.

Under Section 544(b), the trustee can use applicable state laws to void any pre-bankruptcy transfer. Section 544(b) incorporates state fraudulent conveyance law into the Bankruptcy Code. In other words, if outside of bankruptcy the transfer would be governed by the Statute of Elizabeth fraudulent conveyance statute, then Section 544(b) corresponds with the Statute of Elizabeth; if the state statute is the UFCA, then Section 544(b) is the UFCA.

Additionally, the trustee would have the benefit of the state limitations period to set aside fraudulent conveyances. In the above example, although the trustee could not use the Bankruptcy Code Section 548 to set aside the fraudulent conveyance, he could nonetheless proceed under the state fraudulent conveyance statutes which would have longer limitations period.

---

[1]In re *Kassuba*, 10 Bankr. 309 (Sd Fla. 1981); *Tri-Star Cabinet & Top Co., v. Heatherwood Homes, Inc.*, 41 Ill. App. 3d 11, 354 NE2d 4 (1976); *Nelson v. Hansen*, 278 Ore. 571, 565 P2d 727 (1977); *Whipp v. Grider*, 330 Ill. App. 131, 70 NE2d 262 (1947).

[2]In re *Russo*, 1 Bankr. 369 (EDNY 1979); *Kailbab Indus., Inc. v. Family Ready Homes, Inc.*, 80 Ill. App. 3d 782, 372 NE2d 139 (1978); *Chambers v. Citizens & S. Nat'l Bank*, 242 Ga. 498, 249 SE2d 214 (1978).

[3]*Continental Bank v. Marcus*, 242 Pa. Super. 371, 363 A2d 1318 (1976); *West Gate Bank of Lincoln v. Eberhardt*, 202 Neb. 762, 277 NW2d 104 (1979); In re *Checkmate Stereo & Elecs. Ltd.*, 9 Bankr. 585 (Bankr. EDNY 1981); *John Ownben Co. Inc. v. Comm'r*, 645 F2d 540 (6th Cir. 1981).

[4]In re *Reed's Estate*, 566 P2d 587 (Wyo. 1977).

[5] *Arnold v. Dirrim*, 398 NE2d 442 (Ind. App. 1979).

[6]*Universal C.I.T. Credit Corp. v. Farmers Bank of Portageville*, 358 F. Supp. 317 (ED Mo. 1973).

[7] *Rees v. Craighead Inv. Co.*, 251 Ark. 336, 472 SW2d 92 (1971).

[8]Fla. Stat. Ann. § 726.07; Ill. Ann. Stat. ch. 59, § 4; Tex. Bus. & Com. Code § 24.02.

[9] *DeWest Realty Corp. v. Internal Revenue Service*, 418 F. Supp. 1274 (SDNY 1976); *Waukesha County Department of Social & Health Services v. Loper*, 53 Wis. 2d 713, 193 NW2d 679 (1974).

[10]*Wallin v. Scottsdale Plumbing Co., Inc.* 27 Ariz. App. 591, 557 P2d 190 (1976); *First S. Properties, Inc. v. Gregory*, 538 SW2d 454 (Tex. Civ. App. 1976).

[11] *Bank of Commerce v. Rosemary & Thyme Inc.*, 218 Va. 781, 239 SE2d 909 (1981).

[12]*Jahner v. Jacob*, 252 NW2d 1 (NE1977); *Alan Drey Co., Inc. v. Generation, Inc.*, 22 Ill. App. 3d 611, 317 NE2d 673 (1974).

[13]*Pettit v. North Am. Stock Exch.*, 217 F. Supp. 21 (DCNY 1963); *T.W.M. Homes Inc. v. Atherwood Realty & Inv. Co.*, 214 Cal. App. 2d 826, 29 Cal. Rptr. 887 (1963); *Yeiser v. Rogers*, 19 NJ 284, 116 A2d 3 (1955); *Masomi Sasaki v. Yana Kai*, 56 Cal. App. 2d 406, 133 P2d 18 (1943).

[14]*Arnold v. Dirrim*, 398 NE2d 442 (Ind. App. 1979); *U.S. v. Fernon*, 640 F2d 609 (11th Cir. 1981) For a summary of various badges of fraud under Section 7 of UFCA, see 5 Debtor-Creditor Law 22-57-22-58 (Matthew Bender 1982).

Specific Cases under Fraudulent Transfers 13

In the previous chapter we looked at several basic principles that characterize fraudulent transfers. In this chapter we will look at some actual cases decided by courts, and also look at some hypothetical examples of what may or may not be construed as fraudulent transfers.

Executory Promises of Support

This case involved an insolvent debtor who just prior to filing his bankruptcy transferred his house to his children in return for a promise from them to support him during his declining years. The court held that this was a presumed-in-law or constructive fraudulent transfer that could be set aside. *West Minister Savings Bank v. Saubler,* 39 A.2d 862 (Md. Ct.App.1944).

The court reasoned that an executory promise to furnish support does not constitute the fair consideration or reasonable equivalent exchange that the law demands. The consideration given for the transfer must be something that has recognized commercial value. What the court had in mind was something, such as money or salable property, that the creditors can use to make up for the original property that they lost by reason of the transfer. Note, however, that the law does not object to the satisfaction of a valid antecedent indebtedness owed by the transferor.

The court reasoned that if the creditors are going to lose property that in equity belonged to them and that, except for the transfer, they could have levied upon, then they ought to get in turn something that is equally useful to them. If the consideration received by the transferor is not of that kind, then the law declares that fair consideration was not received. In the instant case, of course, creditors cannot get their debts paid by a promise by children to furnish support to the parent.

The court then applied the remedy available in situations where less than fair consideration is furnished. The court ruled that the children transferees were protected to the extent that they already had actually furnished the support services prior to the filing of the suit to set aside the transfer. To that extent, the court ruled that they did qualify as bona fide good faith purchasers. The children were not, however, protected to the extent that their promise to furnish support, was executory and not yet performed.

The remedy in a case like this would be to order the sale of the property that was transferred and from the sale proceeds to reimburse the children for the sum already expended for the support of the insolvent parent and to turn over the balance of the sale proceeds to the creditors.

Other Executory Promises

The concept of executory promises as constituting the fair consideration or reasonable equivalent exchange as a necessary ingredient for a valid transfer has been rejected by courts on more than one occasion. In fact, Section 548(d) - (2)(a) of the Bankruptcy Code expressly codifies this principle by defining value as excluding "an unperformed promise to furnish support to the debtor or to a relative of the debtor."

Let's take a hypothetical case, where an insolvent debtor prior to his bankruptcy transfers his property to an attorney in return for a promise from that attorney to render future legal services. Of course, the Bankruptcy Code allows the creditors to examine the attorney fee arrangements and, to the extent that a fee arrangement is not reasonable, ask the court to modify it.

Suppose, however, that this arrangement was made more than one year before the bankruptcy and thus is outside the scope of Section 329 of the Code. Could the transfer of money to the attorney be attacked as a presumed-in-law fraudulent transfer? Did the insolvent debtor receive a reasonable equivalent exchange or fair consideration, when he received from the attorney only an executory promise to furnish personal legal services?

The truth of the matter is that the creditors derive no benefit from the transferee's executory promise to furnish legal services in the future. As we saw before, the children's promises to furnish support to their insolvent parent do not help creditors to pay their debts; an insolvent debtor's arrangement with an attorney to receive a promise of future legal services is equally of no value to the creditors. Thus, an executory promise of an attorney to render purely personal services to the transferor cannot qualify for fair consideration.

Inter-Corporate Transfers

Corporations, often owned by a single individual, are easy vehicles for fraudulent transfers for those so inclined. A typical scheme that may be fraudulent to the creditors may work like this:

Suppose a bank loans $100,000 to a parent corporation. In order to secure the loan, the bank takes back a security interest on the subsidiary corporation's assets. Unfortunately, the subsidiary corporation is heavily in debts and is forced into insolvency. The assets upon which the creditors can levy have been mortgaged away to the bank without the subsidiary corporation having received anything in return. All of the loan money went to the parent corporation, a separate legal entity.

Such a setup is clearly subject to fraudulent transfer attack. Although the bank gave fair consideration, the consideration all went to the parent corporation, which was not the actual debtor. The law requires fair consideration or reasonably equivalent exchange to be given to the debtor who actually transfers the property.

Here is the logic behind fair consideration theory. If an insolvent or a near-insolvent party gives away property that, in equity, belongs to the creditors, then this will be permitted only as long as the creditors get some reasonably equivalent property in return. In the above case, the parent corporation got the benefit of the money, upon which the creditors of the subsidiary corporation, a separate legal entity, cannot levy upon. Creditors or trustee in bankruptcy of the subsidiary corporation would have a prima facie case for setting aside the security interest as a presumed-in-law fraudulent transfer.

Leveraged Buyouts

In a typical leveraged buyout arrangement, management of the company obtains a loan secured by the assets of the corporation to pay off the existing shareholders. Taking a hypothetical case, assume a bank loans $100,000 to the sole shareholder of a corporation to allow him to buy the stock from the prior sole shareholder. The corporation in turn gives the mortgage on its assets to secure the loan to the new shareholder.

Such an arrangement is also a variation of a constructive fraudulent transfer. The corporation has transferred or mortgaged its assets but has received nothing in return, all of the loan money - or the consideration - went to the new sole shareholder. Thus, if the corporation is insolvent or made insolvent by reason of undertaking its stockholders' obligation, this is a prima facie case of a presumed-in-law fraudulent transfer.

Insolvency Test

In order to make a prima facie case for constructive fraudulent transfer, it is not necessary to show that the corporation was insolvent on its balance sheet. Under UFCA Section 5 it is only necessary to show that "the property remaining with the debtor after the mortgage is an unreasonably small capital" to meet the anticipated risks of that corporation. If, as a result of the mortgage, the corporation is left with insufficient capital to meet the future claims of trade creditors, then a prima facie case of presumed-in-law fraudulent transfer has been made out. See *United States v. Glen Eagles Inv. Co., Inc.,* 565F.Supp. 556 (M.D.P.A. 1983).

Appendix to Section V: Uniform Fraudulent Conveyance Act

Sec. 1. Definition of Terms. In this act "Assets" of a debtor means property not exempt from liability for his debts. To the extent that any property is liable for any debts of the debtor, such property shall be included in his assets.

"Conveyance" includes every payment of money, assignment, release, transfer, lease, mortgage or pledge of tangible or intangible property, and also the creation of any lien or incumbrance.

"Creditor" is a person having any claim, whether matured or unmatured, liquidated or unliquidated, absolute, fixed or contingent.

"Debt" includes any legal liability, whether matured or unmatured, liquidated or unliquidated, absolute, fixed or contingent.

Sec. 2. Insolvency.

(1) A person is insolvent when the present fair salable value of his assets is less than the amount that will be required to pay his probable liability on his existing debts as they become absolute and matured.

(2) In determining whether a partnership is insolvent there shall be added to the partnership property the present fair salable value of the separate assets of each general partner in excess of the amount probably sufficient to meet the claims of his separate creditors, and also the amount of any unpaid subscription to the partnership of each limited partner, provided the present fair salable value of the assets of such limited partner is probably sufficient to pay his debts, including such unpaid subscription.

Sec. 3. Fair Consideration. Fair consideration is given for property, or obligation,

(a) When in exchange for such property, or obligation, as a fair equivalent therefor, and in good faith, property is conveyed or an antecedent debt is satisfied, or

(b) When such property, or obligation is received in good faith to secure a present advance or antecedent debt in amount not disproportionately small as compared with the value of the property, or obligation obtained.

Sec. 4. Conveyances by Insolvent. Every conveyance made and every obligation incurred by a person who is or will be thereby rendered insolvent is fraudulent as to creditors without regard to his actual intent if the conveyance is made or the obligation is incurred without a fair consideration.

Sec. 5. Conveyances by Persons in Business. Every conveyance made without fair consideration when the person making it is engaged or is about to engage in a business or transaction for which the property remaining in his hands after the conveyance is an unreasonably small capital, is fraudulent as to creditors and as to other persons who become creditors during the continuance of such business or transaction without regard to his actual intent.

Sec. 6. Conveyances by a Person about to Incur Debts. Every conveyance made and every obligation incurred without fair consideration when the person making the conveyance or entering into the obligation intends or believes that he will incur debts beyond his ability to pay as they mature, is fraudulent as to both present and future creditors.

Sec. 7. Conveyance Made with Intent to Defraud. Every conveyance made and every obligation incurred with actual intent, as distinguished from intent presumed in law, to hinder, delay, or defraud either present or future creditors, is fraudulent as to both present and future creditors.

Sec. 8. Conveyance of Partnership Property. Every conveyance of partnership property and every partnership obligation incurred when the partnership is or will be thereby rendered insolvent, is fraudulent as to partnership creditors, if the conveyance is made or obligation is incurred.

(a) To a partner, whether with or without a promise by him to pay partnership debts, or

(b) To a person not a partner without fair consideration to the partnership as distinguished from consideration to the individual partners.

Sec. 9. Rights of Creditors Whose Claims Have Matured.

(1) Where a conveyance or obligation is fraudulent as to a creditor, such creditor, when his claim has matured, may, as against any person except a purchaser for fair consideration without knowledge of the fraud at the time of the purchase, or one who has derived title immediately from such a purchaser,

(a) Have the conveyance set aside or obligation annulled to the extent necessary to satisfy his claim, or

(b) Disregard the conveyance and attach or levy execution upon the property conveyed.

(2) A purchaser who without actual fraudulent intent has given less than a fair consideration for the conveyance or obligation, may retain the property or obligation as security for repayment.

Sec. 10. Rights of Creditors Whose Claims Have Not Matured. Where a conveyance made or obligation incurred is fraudulent as to a creditor whose claim has not matured he may proceed in a court of competent jurisdiction against any person against whom he could have proceeded had his claim matured, and the court may,

(a) Restrain the defendant from disposing of his property,

(b) Appoint a receiver to take charge of the property,

(c) Set aside the conveyance or annul the obligation, or

(d) Make any order which the circumstances of the case may require.

Sec. 11. Cases Not Provided for in Act. In any case not provided for in this Act the rules of law and equity including the law merchant, and in particular the rules relating to the law of principal and agent, and the effect of fraud, misrepresentation, duress or coercion, mistake, bankruptcy or other invalidating cause shall govern.

Sec. 12. Construction of Act. This Act shall be so interpreted and construed as to effectuate its general purpose to make uniform the law of those states which enact it.

Sec. 13. Name of Act. This Act may be cited as the Uniform Fraudulent Conveyance Act.

Sec. 14. Inconsistent Legislation Repealed. Section . . . . are hereby repealed, and all acts or parts of acts inconsistent with this Act are hereby repealed.

SECTION VI

Using Corporation to Protect Your Assets

14

Laughlin Associates, Inc. is a well-recognized Nevada firm that specializes in setting up Nevada corporations for businesses from every state. It has been doing this for over a decade and is easily the oldest and largest independent company of this nature in Nevada.

The services provided by Laughlin Associates are unique in that beyond setting up a Nevada corporation they provide a complete "staffed office package" that allows businesses from distant states to establish a legal base in the state. This package in essence fulfills the statutory requirements of being able to conduct business as a Nevada corporation. Laughlin Associates also provides business and management consulting services.

Laughlin Associates, Inc. can be reached at Capital Plaza, Suite 100, 1000 E. William Street, Carson City, NV 89701; Phone (800) 648-0966, in Nevada (702)883-8484.

The following material on corporations and their benefits and strategies to make your business judgment proof and reduce state taxes is reprinted with permission from the Corporation Manual published by Laughlin Associates, Inc.

What Is a Corporation?

In brevity, a corporation is a legal, artificial person: a person that is separate, distinct and apart from you. It is NOT you. You are NOT it. It is a distinct, different, and totally separate legal or artificial person.

Let's take a close look at what a corporation is. A corporation is a distinct, legal entity separate and apart from its members, stockholders, directors or officers. Although it is a separate entity, it can act only through its members, officers or agents and can have no knowledge or belief on any subject independent of the knowledge or belief of its people. A stockholder (owner or partial owner) is a holder of shares of stock in the corporation and is not in legal contemplation or danger. A stockholder is not the employer of those working for the corporation nor is he the owner of corporate property.

A corporation is an artificial person. Its rights, duties and liabilities do not differ from those of a natural person under similar conditions except, of course, where the exercise of duty would require the ability to comprehend or think. That's what the board of directors is for: they do the thinking. Proof that the directors thought on behalf of the corporation is evidenced by minutes or a resolution. For example, a corporation may become a debtor or trespasser. A corporation can buy, trade, sell and make loans; literally anything you as a person can do. Think it through. The possibilities become fascinating.

A corporation is a citizen of the state wherein it is created. (That is why you may want to incorporate in Nevada to take advantage of the best corporation and tax laws in the U.S.) A corporation does not cease to be a citizen of the state in which it is incorporated by engaging in business or acquiring property in another state.

Since corporations are solely creatures of statute, the powers of a corporation of another state are derived from the constitution and laws of the state in which it is incorporated.

A corporation is a legal person which has an existence separate and apart from the stockholders. As an artificial person, a corporation is considered to have its domicile or home in the state where it is incorporated and the place where it has its registered or statutory resident agent or home office in that state. When the corporation is actually in a different place, the site of its resident agent is sometimes said to be its "statutory domicile."

The existence of the corporation is not affected by the death or bankruptcy of a shareholder or by the transfer of its shares. It has a continuous existence. It is immortal as long as it complies with the annual requirements of the state in which it is incorporated.

It may be advantageous to use the corporate form of doing business to insulate the owner from the risks and liabilities of his businesses or to insulate a stable business from a risky business of the same owner.

Why You Should Incorporate: Limited Liability

There are a number of excellent reasons why you should be incorporated, plus many miscellaneous advantages and benefits. The foremost of them is, of course, the limited liability, protection of your personal assets from the creditors of the corporation.

When you create or form a corporation, you have created a legal entity, in effect a legal person. That entity is responsible for its own acts. You are NOT individually responsible (there are certain remote exceptions).

All you have to do is read the newspapers, listen to the radio, watch TV. It appears our nation is becoming more legalistic and our people more conversant with litigation. Everyone is either suing someone or being sued!

You read of malpractice suits, class action suits, discrimination suits, personal injury suits, antitrust suits, and on and on ad infinitum. You read of juries awarding fantastic amounts to plaintiffs.

IT CAN very easily and without warning HAPPEN TO YOU. One lawsuit can wipe you out and possibly destroy your life. You can prevent that risk. You can protect yourself. Be smart—INCORPORATE!

We suggest that you consider the wisdom of operating several corporations. Put separate activities in separate corporations with different names and then possibly set up a holding corporation that owns all the others.

Think about it! There are many variations and many strategies YOU may employ. Cut down and minimize the risk. Let the corporation take the risk; protect yourself. "An ounce of prevention is worth a pound of cure."

What Is a Holding or Parent Corporation?

The term "holding corporation" is reasonably self-explanatory. A holding corporation "holds" control of other corporations (subsidiaries).

"Control" as used in regard to a holding corporation usually means that the holding corporation owns at least 80% of the stock of the subsidiary corporation.

A holding corporation is often referred to as "the parent corporation." This is a somewhat self-explanatory term which pictures the holding corporation as the parent and, therefore, its subsidiary corporation or corporations as the holding corporation's children.

Do I Want a Holding Corporation?

There are good, valid and profitable reasons for utilizing a holding corporation. We will point out some of them. When these reasons exist or are in place, then, yes, you want a holding corporation.

However, when there are NO compelling reasons to utilize and operate a holding corporation, we recommend, as a general rule, a brother-sister relationship. Under the brother-sister relationship, the involved corporate entities are independent corporations, although under common control (the same control). In "tax terms" they are members of a controlled or affiliated group.

We believe it is usually more "comfortable" to have the corporations severed one from another, completely independent of each other, and therefore not having one or more owned by one another.

In either situation, most dealings between the corporations should be contractual in nature (reduced to writing in contract form). They should be natural transactions—not artificial. It usually only takes a little brain work to make them really happen. Each corporation involved should actually perform or deliver its duties or obligations under the contract. Each corporation should meticulously observe all corporate formalities.

What Is a Brother - Sister or Multiple Corporate Structure?

Often, instead of a holding company structure, a brother/sister or multiple corporate structure is preferable. The primary difference between a brother/sister structure and a holding company structure is that with a brother/sister structure or strategy, the stock of the corporations involved is owned by an individual stockholder or stockholders instead of being owned by a parent corporation. This brother/sister ownership is usually referred to as common control or common ownership. In tax talk they may be or become part of an affiliated or controlled group.

When all else is equal, we recommend the brother/sister structure as opposed to a holding corporation structure. We feel that it puts more distance between the involved corporations and better establishes the separateness and identities of the involved entities. Therefore, we refer to the structure as being more "comfortable." We feel that it may also assist in limiting liability to whichever entity might be attacked or at risk.

The little guy and/or privately held corporations can take advantage of and gain some great benefits from utilizing certain brother/sister corporate strategies that big brother, public corporations cannot because of their massive, public ownership. Although—make NO mistake about it, they would dearly love to. Yes—believe it or not—a sometimes advantage to the little guy that big brother cannot touch.

Reprinted with permission of Laughlin Associates, Inc.

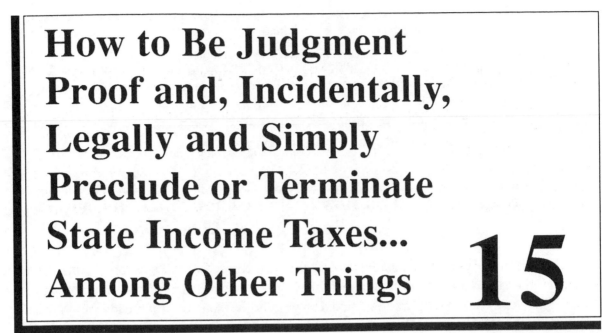

How to Be Judgment Proof and, Incidentally, Legally and Simply Preclude or Terminate State Income Taxes... Among Other Things

15

Some say "you can't be judgment proof and/or legally eliminate state income taxes." They're wrong because where there's a will, there's a way, and, after all, "Nothing is impossible." You can learn how by reading this. It works and is simple and legitimate.

This strategy is so simple that it usually takes a while for the impact of it to really soak in. It is so simple that many times it sends our lawyer friends digging and researching for weeks, playing the devil's advocate, trying to shoot it full of holes or tear it down. That's okay with us . . . we think that's the way it should be. We are convinced this strategy will stand up under any legal scrutiny or research and will further stand up in any court in the land if it is done properly.

Why? ? ? Because the principle of this strategy has been around since one business started doing business with another. There is nothing more tried and true in America than that principle. There is simply no law against two companies doing good, red blooded American business with each other. That is essentially what we are advocating here. That is the strategy.

So—how do two companies do business together so you can operate judgment proof and/or state income tax free? ? ? ? ?

Well, a lawyer friend once told me that the best liability insurance anybody could have was to be completely poverty stricken and destitute. That way you can be a turnip (you can't get blood out of a turnip) and, therefore, be judgment proof. I also know that if you never make a profit in your home state, you owe no income tax to your state provided your state income tax is based on net earnings, or profit, or taxable income as most states are. (The exception is an income tax based on gross income.)

But hey, wait a minute! Being judgment proof and not paying any state income taxes just isn't any fun if you are completely poverty stricken and never make a profit. No one wants to live in the street just so they won't get sued or have to pay state income tax. Rest easy . . with this strategy you'll be judgment proof. You'll eliminate your state income tax, live well, and have financial security, legitimacy, ease, efficiency and peace of mind.

Step-By-Step Blueprint on How to Do Business "State Income Tax Free" and Be Judgment Proof

---

(1) Incorporate your home state business that you currently derive income from. Make it a Nevada corporation and qualify it to do business in your home state. If you choose to use a corporation formed in your home state, or are already incorporated in your home state, that will generally work, too. For purposes of this example, we are going to call your home state corporation, **"Red, Inc."** That's because your home state operation will have a lot of red ink. It will try and try and try to make a profit but if it ends up with red ink (losing money), then there are no state income taxes to pay, now are there? Of course not . . .

NOTE: Elect a calendar year ending 12/31 as the tax year for **"Red Inc."**

(2) Next, set up a Nevada company — and make that company a Nevada corporation. For purposes of this example we will call this corporation, **"Warbucks Nevada, Inc."** Base that Nevada corporation in Nevada. This won't cost a lot of money because you can establish an economical, viable, provable operating base by utilizing the "Staffed Contract Office Package Service" provided by Laughlin Associates, Inc. By utilizing the Staffed Contract Office Package Service your **"Warbucks Nevada, Inc."** can have a Nevada office complete with its own telephone system, contract employees, Carson City, Nevada business license, Nevada bank account, complete mail service, and an all important one line advertisement in the Nevada yellow pages (providing what lawyers call a "public holding out to do business"— essential). All of this can be done for a very low price.

With the Office Package, **"Warbucks Nevada, Inc."** has its corporate base in tax free Nevada. It will operate only in tax free Nevada. It is going to earn a lot of money in Nevada. Therefore, any profit that **"Warbucks Nevada, Inc."** makes will be state tax free. Wow! Now what?

NOTE: Elect a fiscal tax year ending 6-30 for **"Warbucks Nevada, Inc."**

(3) Now **"Red, Inc."** enters the picture. Operating in your home state, **"Red, Inc."** decides it would be a fine idea to buy some products and/or services from **"Warbucks**

How to Be Judgment Proof and, Incidentally, Legally and Simply
Preclude or Terminate State Income Taxes...Among Other Things

151

Nevada, Inc." in Nevada. Remember that **"Red, Inc."** and **"Warbucks Nevada, Inc."** are separate corporations and are therefore separate persons. A corporation is an artificial person created by law. Corporations are separate from each other, and they are separate from you. Therefore, if **"Red, Inc."** writes a check to **"Warbucks Nevada, Inc."** money is spent by **"Red, Inc."** (your home state based person) and money is received by **"Warbucks Nevada, Inc."** (your Nevada based person). There is an expense in your home state to **"Red, Inc."**, and there is income in Nevada to **"Warbucks Nevada, Inc."** There was money earned in Nevada and an expense in your home state. If **"Red, Inc."** spends all its profit, it makes no money for your home state to tax...You even have an excellent judgment proofing tool...We'll explain how in a little bit.

This blue print puts the pieces in place to be judgment proof and to eliminate state income taxes. Now I'll explain in clear detail just how the blue print works...First, eliminating state income taxes...

Suppose that **"Red, Inc."** spends a lot of money with **"Warbucks Nevada, Inc."**, so much that when the end of its tax year rolls around, **"Red, Inc."** hasn't made any profit. That means **"Red, Inc."**, your home state company, according to its books and records, owes no state income taxes. The good news is that **"Warbucks Nevada, Inc."**, your Nevada company, has had a fantastic year and your profits are in tax free Nevada. Since you control both corporations, that is truly "The Happy Solution" for you.

Your home state income taxes have been eliminated and you're the proud owner of a Nevada corporation that is now making the profit and netting you up to 11.5% more profit for your labor. You save thousands or tens of thousands of dollars every year. Wow! You now have the great competitive edge.

It is said you don't have to be a lot smarter than the other guy—just a little edge will do. Think of what you can do with this kind of an advantage.

Oh yes . . .

Just what products and services can **"Warbucks Nevada, Inc."** sell to **"Red, Inc."** from Nevada while operating solely in the state of Nevada? First, we stress that the business conducted between the two entities should be legitimate, reasonable, and viable which is easily constructed. We are not suggesting this as a sham, and it would be subject to a calculated risk if done as a sham. We believe if it's worth doing, it's worth doing right. So, what are some products and services that **"Red, Inc."** buys from **"Warbucks Nevada, Inc."**?

Some ideas that can work, and are successfully used, are copyright material, research & development, and advertising. Turn on your creative juices — let your imagination serve your planning. Remember, "what the mind of man can conceive and believe, it can achieve." Prepare whatever you wish the corporation to sell, and ship what is to be sold to your **"Warbucks Nevada, Inc."** Nevada office. **"Red, Inc."** buys these products or services from **"Warbucks Nevada, Inc."** You can be anywhere in the world and supply those services or products to and through your Nevada corporation.

What we suggest as the most solid and workable option is that **"Warbucks Nevada, Inc."** simply loan money to **"Red, Inc." "Red, Inc."** would simply be buying the use of money from **"Warbucks Nevada, Inc."** When you borrow money, you generally pay interest. **"Red, Inc."** is no exception to that rule . . . Here's how it works...

Put money into **"Warbucks Nevada, Inc."** in exchange for stock. Maybe you supply **"Warbucks Nevada, Inc."** with a product or service that can be resold. Don't get me wrong, money is the best thing to put into **"Warbucks Nevada, Inc."** but many have successfully implemented this strategy by putting products (inventory) and services to be resold into the corporation...For the moment we'll talk about money and touch on other considerations later.

"Warbucks Nevada, Inc." uses the money that has been invested in it to make money. It does this by loaning that money to **"Red, Inc."** and possibly others. The condition of that loan to **"Red, Inc."** is that the money owed is due and payable when **"Warbucks Nevada, Inc."** asks for it (calls the note). The note (the piece of paper that is evidence of the loan terms) in this case is a demand promissory note which means that it's due when **"Warbucks Nevada, Inc."** demands payment.

Also, as any good business does, **"Warbucks Nevada, Inc."**, which you own charges **"Red, Inc."**, your home state operation, interest on the money that it loans to **"Red, Inc."** I remind you that **"Warbucks Nevada, Inc."** is located in and operating from Nevada. Nevada has no usury laws, so **"Warbucks Nevada, Inc."** charges **"Red, Inc."** whatever interest rate **Warbucks** thinks is fair. In our example, we'll say the rate is 26%. The interest is due each month or year. The interest may even be compounded monthly. This will get **"Red, Inc."** even further in debt to **"Warbucks Nevada, Inc."** which can be very beneficial as you'll see later.

To summarize so far, **"Red, Inc."** borrows money from **"Warbucks Nevada, Inc."** at 26% interest per year with the principal balance due upon demand (when **"Warbucks Nevada, Inc."** calls the note). The money owed to **"Warbucks Nevada, Inc."** is evidenced by a demand promissory note signed and executed by **"Red, Inc."** (the debtor) at the Nevada offices of **"Warbucks Nevada, Inc."** This shows that they money is borrowed in Nevada and, if worded correctly, that the note is governed by the laws of Nevada. (Sample notes are contained in the book, Corporation Forms and Explanations Made Easy, published by Laughlin Associates, Inc.)

How much does **"Red, Inc."** borrow from **"Warbucks Nevada, Inc."**? Well, at 26% simple interest (used only for example because with no usury laws in Nevada, **Warbucks** could charge more), if **"Red, Inc."** borrowed $100,000, this would mean a business interest expense to **"Red, Inc."** in your home state of at least $26,000 in one year . . . or the interest could be compounded monthly and interest charges would be even more . .

Do you see what profitable things are happening here?????

Depending upon the amount of money borrowed and the interest rate that the two companies (which you own) agree upon, the interest expense to **"Red, Inc."** in your home state could be as high or as low as you decide...

If the expense to **"Red, Inc."** in your home state is equal to or greater than the profit that your home state operation (**"Red, Inc."**) would have made if it had not borrowed from **"Warbucks Nevada, Inc."**, then **"Red, Inc."** in your home state has made no profit.

The result is that if **"Red, Inc."** makes no profit, then there are no state income taxes due. On the other hand, **"Warbucks Nevada, Inc."** in Nevada has made a state tax free profit. You have just legally precluded or terminated state income taxes.

Oh, yes...How does all this work if you put products (and services) into **"Warbucks Nevada, Inc."** for re-sale? Well, instead of just loaning money to **"Red, Inc."**, **"Warbucks Nevada, Inc."** would sell these products and services to **"Red, Inc."** and invoice the purchase. The purchase price is whatever the two companies, both of which you own, agree upon.

Everything works the same from there. **"Warbucks Nevada, Inc."** sells the products and services to **"Red, Inc."** and takes back a promissory note due and payable when **"Warbucks Nevada, Inc."** calls it. Interest on that note is due monthly (maybe with interest compounded monthly) or yearly. That interest is still an expense to **"Red, Inc."**, and the result can be the same: No profit for **"Red, Inc."** in your home state. The principal amount of the note may also be deductible to **"Red, Inc."** Again, we suggest the simple loaning of money from **"Warbucks Nevada, Inc."** to **"Red, Inc."**, but many use products (inventory) and services successfully.

So there you have it as far as state income tax is concerned. Your home state operation (**"Red, Inc."**) makes no profit, therefore there are no state income taxes due... So what about being judgment proof?

O.K. let's be judgment proof, too...

The stage is already set. . . and all that really remains is a few simple steps to make your business operation judgment proof. Let's analyze **"Red, Inc."** and **"Warbucks Nevada, Inc."** for just a second so this will be totally clear. . .

"Red, Inc." is busily conducting your current business. It's buying, selling, making deals. It's the corporation in the high exposure position. If a business deal goes sour, if something goes wrong, it's "Red, Inc." that will be sued.

"Warbucks Nevada, Inc." is based in Nevada and it maintains a low profile. It's merely financing a few things here and there for profit. Its main client is "Red, Inc." which you own. It's a totally separate corporation. "Warbucks Nevada, Inc." chances of getting sued are one in a million.

The idea is to make "Red, Inc." judgment proof, to turn "Red, Inc." into a turnip that no one can bleed and at the same time make sure it has the money, equipment, fixtures, land, buildings, etc. to conduct your business.

"Red, Inc." can also be transformed into your "liability lightning rod." I'm sure you're familiar with the concept of a lightning rod. When lightning strikes one, it doesn't do harm to the valuable things the lightning may otherwise destroy. The same is true here . . . When "Red, Inc." gets sued, the suit will not harm the valuable things you are trying to protect. Here is how it works:

We've already established the fact that "Red, Inc." is heavily indebted to "Warbucks Nevada, Inc." and the heavier in debt that "Red, Inc." is to "Warbucks Nevada, Inc." the better.

"Red, Inc." borrows money from "Warbucks Nevada, Inc." every time it gets a chance. It probably even finances part of its interest payments due to "Warbucks Nevada, Inc." because it can't quite make them all in cash. Therefore, each month or year the debt keeps increasing. It would not be hard to establish a debt so large to "Warbucks Nevada, Inc." that it eclipses the value of all the assets of "Red, Inc.".

Let's say "Red, Inc." has assets totaling $250,000.00 that you want to protect. "Red, Inc." borrows and borrows from "Warbucks Nevada, Inc.", getting deeper and deeper in debt. Finally, it's at least $250,000.00 or more in debt. The debt figure is limited only by the principal amount "Warbucks Nevada, Inc." and "Red, Inc." agree upon and the corresponding interest rate. Of course, owning those corporations you may have something to say about what they agree upon.

Well, "Warbucks Nevada, Inc." is no dummy — after all, you own it. When "Warbucks Nevada, Inc." loans money to anybody, "Warbucks Nevada, Inc." is going to make sure they get paid or else. So "Warbucks Nevada, Inc." will want some collateral on the loan to "Red, Inc." "Warbucks Nevada, Inc." and "Red, Inc." enter into a "security agreement." This is a common, powerful tool that is used to secure certain assets as collateral on a loan. With this security agreement they agree that the assets, receivables, inventory,

How to Be Judgment Proof and, Incidentally, Legally and Simply
Preclude or Terminate State Income Taxes...Among Other Things

155

everything belonging to **"Red, Inc."** is collateral for that loan. On any equity in real property **Red, Inc.** would issue a trust deed (mortgage) to **"Warbucks Nevada, Inc."** (Sample forms for such an agreement and trust deed may be found in Corporation Forms and Explanations Made Easy, published by Laughlin Associates, Inc.)

Then, as notice to the world that these assets are collateral for a debt owed to **"Warbucks Nevada, Inc."** in Nevada, **"Warbucks Nevada, Inc."** will record what is called a "UCC-1" financing statement with the Secretary of State's office in Nevada and with the Secretary of State's office and appropriate County Recorders in your home state. This UCC-1 form states that these assets are collateral for a note that is owed. It gives notice to the world that these assets are encumbered. It gives notice to the world that no one can touch these assets until the debt owed to **"Warbucks Nevada, Inc."** is paid.

Let me tell you something about UCC-1 filings and the security agreement that perfects a security interest in the assets of **"Red, Inc."** They come before everything else (except some tax claims). In other words, **"Warbucks Nevada, Inc."** is in a first position on all of the assets that **"Red, Inc."** owns and those assets can't be touched until **"Warbucks Nevada, Inc."** is paid.

In the case of a trust deed being used to secure equity in real property, that trust deed would be recorded in the county in which the property is located. This also has the effect of giving notice to the world that the property is encumbered by debt.

Now let's think about what happens if **"Red, Inc."** gets sued. The person suing you finds a dirty, mean and nasty attorney to sue **"Red, Inc."** One of the first things he asks the attorney is "what can we take this company for?" Of course, that is one of the big questions in the attorney's mind also, especially since many attorneys work on a percentage of what they can collect. That's how a lot of attorneys hope to get rich and that's how a lot of attorneys do actually get rich.

But in this case, that's when the lawyer and the person suing **"Red, Inc."** take a very cold shower. They do a search to see what **"Red, Inc."** is worth. That search includes looking for any real property the corporation owns along with any debt against it and any UCC-1 filings encumbering assets that **"Red, Inc."** may own. They find a big debt. . . they find that all of the assets of **"Red, Inc."** are encumbered. **"Red, Inc."** is worthless! It has nothing! My heavens, it's not even worth suing.

That's probably the end of the lawsuit against **"Red, Inc."** right there. On the other hand, let's say the person suing you just happened to pick a particularly sadistic lawyer. This person just wants to sue you anyway. So he files the lawsuit. He even gets a judgment. Now what happens?

Remember **"Warbucks Nevada, Inc."** is owed money by **"Red, Inc."** as evidenced by a promissory note due on demand. When **"Warbucks Nevada, Inc."** calls the note, **"Red, Inc."** has to pay. **"Warbucks Nevada, Inc."** decides it is time to get paid and calls the note. Oh heavens, **"Red, Inc."** can't pay such a large debt. **"Warbucks Nevada, Inc."** has no recourse except to execute on its security interest and/or trust deeds in the assets of **"Red, Inc."** In other words, **"Warbucks Nevada, Inc."** takes the assets of **"Red, Inc."** to satisfy the debt.

What happened? That's the same question the sadistic attorney who sued you is asking. He's got a judgment against **"Red, Inc."**, and **"Red, Inc."** has nothing to execute that judgment on. In fact, you could even call that attorney and tell him, "I'll just give you the whole corporation, come on down and get it." Because even though **"Warbucks Nevada, Inc."** has taken the assets of **"Red, Inc."** the debt that **"Red, Inc."** owed to **"Warbucks Nevada, Inc."** may have been so large that **"Red, Inc."** still owes money to **"Warbucks Nevada, Inc."** That being the case, the only thing a person suing the company would gain is a large debt owed to **"Warbucks Nevada, Inc."** that you own.

That's all there is to it. To summarize:

(1) **"Red, Inc."** owed **"Warbucks Nevada, Inc."** money.

(2) The money **"Red, Inc."** owes **"Warbucks Nevada, Inc."** is evidenced by a promissory note due when **"Warbucks Nevada, Inc."** says it's due.

(3) As security or collateral on that note **"Warbucks Nevada, Inc."** and **"Red, Inc."** have agreed that the assets of **"Red, Inc."** will be collateral and security for the note.

(4) As notice to the world and evidence of the fact that these assets are collateral on the loan, a UCC-1 filing is done in Nevada and in your home state, and a trust deed is executed on any real property and filed in the county in which the property is located (Sample trust deeds, and Nevada and California UCC-1 forms are available in Corporation Forms and Explanation Made Easy, published by Laughlin Associates, Inc.)

(5) **"Warbucks Nevada, Inc."** is in a first position on the assets of **"Red, Inc."** and no one suing **"Red, Inc."** can touch those assets until the debt to **"Warbucks Nevada, Inc."** (that you own) is paid.

(6) You are judgment proof, because even if there is a judgment against **"Red, Inc."**, there is nothing to take.

We believe this strategy is the best liability insurance you could find. Remember, a Nevada base for **"Warbucks Nevada, Inc."** is essential.

NOTE: It is imperative that to be truly judgment proof, whenever you do business, you do business as **"Red, Inc."** and not you. That means signing things as **"Red, Inc."** by: You, its President. You don't want anyone to have any cause of action against you personally.

What if "Red, Inc." needs institutional financing?

Is **"Red, Inc."** really broke? Well... yes and no. Perhaps it depends on how you want it. If **"Red, Inc."** desires bank financing or has similar needs, you can always prepare a consolidated financial statement for **"Red, Inc."** and **"Warbucks Nevada, Inc."** and present a very desirable position for **"Red, Inc."**

What is the real reason for doing This?

Never implement this strategy as a strategy to avoid taxes. Never state that as your primary purpose. The primary purpose is to open a company in Nevada and take advantage of Nevada's multiple pro-business benefits. The fact that you eliminated your home state taxes, and gained a great competitive advantage, super protection, and the best possible insurance is only an incidental happening or fringe benefit - it's only a happy result of the primary Nevada benefits . . . isn't it?

Is This Right? Of Course It Is...

Remember, what Federal Judge Learned Hand said in *Helvering v Gregory* 69 F(2d) 809 (2d Cir. 1934), "Any one may so arrange his affairs that his taxes shall be as low as possible: he is not bound to choose that pattern which will best pay the Treasury; there is not even a patriotic duty to increase one's taxes." This case was affirmed by the U.S. Supreme Court in *Gregory v Helvering*, 293 U.S. 454 (1935). The U.S. Supreme Court further agreed, "The legal right of a taxpayer to decrease the amount of what otherwise would be his taxes, or altogether avoid them, by means which the law permits, cannot be doubted."

What Do I Need to Do This????

Hopefully this special report has shown you how to do this but the best set of instructions in the world is useless without the tools to carry out the instructions.

Here are the tools you need:

(1) One Nevada corporation (**"Red, Inc."**) doing business in your home state.

(2) One Nevada corporation (**"Warbucks Nevada, Inc."**) based in and doing business in Nevada.

(3) Nevada officebase (to prove the corporation rents or has office space in Nevada.)

(4) People in the Nevada office to take care of business, answer the phone, greet and handle callers, customers, etc. (to prove that the corporation has operating base in Nevada).

(5) Telephone for the corporation in the Nevada office (proving operations are in Nevada with yellow page advertising showing the public this corporation does business there—what lawyers call a public holding out to do business.)

(6) A business license in the Nevada city where your corporate office is located.

(7) A bank account where its Nevada office base exists.

(8) Major service contracts, notes, exchanges of funds or any other major business transactions should be consummated, signed, notarized, and the money exchanged at your Nevada office or through the Nevada bank account.

The Estate Plan That Never Dies: "Long Term Corporate Planning Revisited"

Here is the "Long Term Corporate Planning" we suggest you consider. The sequence is important so follow it closely:

(1) Establish a corporation which when formed is what is called a "corporate shell." It has no assets, no liabilities, and its stock is worthless at this point.

(2) Cause the sale of its worthless (because it has no assets yet) stock from the corporation to your investors (heirs) at one cent ($.01) per share, divided by the prorated amounts you choose. Since the stock has been sold to them, it's not a gift. One object of all stock is to increase in value over a period of time. If the stock does increase in value, then nothing wrong, illegal, unethical, or strange has occurred.

(3) Form a limited partnership with you as general partner and your heirs as limited partners. The sole purpose of this limited partnership is to hold the stock of the corporation you just formed. In a limited partnership the general partner(s) manages the business and the limited partner(s) take no part in the running of it. Remember, the business of this limited partnership is to hold the stock of the new corporation. This means the general partner (you) will vote the stock at the annual stockholders meeting.

How to Be Judgment Proof and, Incidentally, Legally and Simply
Preclude or Terminate State Income Taxes...Among Other Things

159

All of the stockholders (you and your investors/heirs) put their newly acquired stock into the limited partnership. In return you become a 1% general partner and a 1% limited partner. Your investors/heirs become 98% limited partners. You, the general partner, manage the business. You vote the stock.

This limited partnership will have a set life. It will be in existence for a certain number of years. That number depends on you. Make the term of years long enough so that when the limited partnership ends, you either won't be around or if you are, you won't want to control the corporation. For example, the limited partnership may have a life of 30 or 40 or 50 years. You make that decision.

The limited partnership can be drawn up so that it ends upon the death of any of the general partners. So when you die, the limited partnership terminates and the other partners (your heirs) take their 98% of the stock in the corporation and go home. Only your 2% of the stock will go through probate and hopefully your estate will be small enough, because of your wise prior planning, to eliminate any problems.

Your heirs have the stock and they own the company, but you, by virtue of your general partnership, have complete control of the corporation, its assets, its money, real estate—everything. You can sell these assets and pay yourself the money, or add to the assets, pay for any and all expenses, travel, medical, and so forth. You can do anything you want for as long as you live.

But, wait a minute, the corporation doesn't have any assets or money. So . . .

(4) Put your assets and money into the corporation. Some suggested possibilities as to how you may accomplish this are as follows:

Sell the assets to the corporation in exchange for a demand promissory note to mature in 50 years or whatever term you deem appropriate. Take money out of the corporation any time you wish and mark it "to apply on promissory note." Word the note so that in the event of your demise, any sums remaining payable to you by the corporation under the note are automatically forgiven. We suggest the demand promissory note bear interest, probably at 12% simple interest per annum, and that the corporation pay you the interest when it becomes due. This will satisfy the IRS. Where does the corporation get the money to pay this interest? From the money or assets you sold to the corporation. You are simply taking money out of one pocket and putting it in another.

It's true the interest received by you may be taxable, depending on your adjusted gross income . . . that is on your "taxable" income or, stated another way, on how good a manager you are.

Explore the possibility of putting your assets into the corporation as a "Capital Contribution." With a little thought, innovation, and ingenuity you will discover many other ways to transfer your assets into the corporation successfully. There, so much for getting the assets into the corporation.

When you put your assets into the corporation, the value of its stock increases, but there are no taxes until such time as dividends are paid by the corporation or the stock is sold. In both cases this is a matter over which you have complete control and for which you can adequately plan in advance to legally avoid taxes.

The bottom line is this: When you pass on the Happy Haven in the Sky, your heirs already own all you want them to have. If you've ever thought of striking back from The Grave, here's your chance — This is almost like being The Executor or Executrix of your own will. Since your heirs already own your estate when you pass on, there's no transfer, no probate, no big taxes — no problems. It's all done, "The Happy Solution."

Also consider the possibility of taking from the corporation a contract in exchange for your services rendered: A life-time contract and guarantee that the corporation will provide for you, including all of your medical bills, convalescent care, and such other expenses and items as you may wish. (Be careful of possible tax consequences here - consult your tax advisor.)

With this plan you know what is going to happen to your loved ones when you pass on. Everything you have worked for, acquired, and have is going to the ones you wish it to go to. There won't be a long drawn-out probate case in court. You can have peace of mind. You don't have to worry about little or nothing existing for your heirs after all the legal fees, expenses, inheritance taxes, and so forth are paid. What can take years of legal delay, astronomical expenses, waste and agony for the ones you love is accomplished by them at their stockholders meeting through the election of directors and officers (probably prearranged). The transition is smooth. Everything continues without interruption. You have the peace, joy, satisfaction, and confidence of knowing that your loved ones have exactly what you intend for them to have.

What we're saying is this: Corporations never die, they just get a new president. Take advantage of this corporate immortality. Put what you have into a corporation and the corporation will live long past you to successfully distribute your assets to the people you wish to have them. This will eliminate the normal pitfalls of estate planning, probate and taxes.

Even though you utilize "Long Term Corporate Planning," have a simple will to handle any loose ends that, for one reason or another, might not have gotten into the corporation. You could will everything to the corporation which would make distribution consistent with your "Long Term Capital Planning."

Multiple Corporations

I have an acquaintance who owns a limousine service business. He has found a solution to the liability problem in multiple corporations. He formed several corporations each owning a limousine or two. He figures if one of his limousines was involved in an accident, in the worst-case scenario all he would lose would be the one corporation that owned the limousine, and the rest of his business would remain unaffected.

Apart from the protection from liability, multiple corporations have many tax and business advantages. Since total income of the enterprise is divided among several corporations, each corporation enjoys the benefits of lower tax brackets. A corporation is required to pay out excess income as dividends and is generally penalized on accumulated earnings over $250,000. With multiple corporations you are multiplying this credit several times, thereby generating significant tax savings. Corporations may adopt the accounting method, taxable period, and make elections such as depreciation, inventory valuation, installment sale, investment tax credit, etc. to suit their special needs. With multiple corporations you can increase the benefits by changing timing or methods among them. If you are planning to sell your business, sometimes it is easier to sell it in parts. Multiple corporations will come handy in such a situation.

There are also some disadvantages. If you are running a business as a single entity, you have the advantage of matching cash requirements of one operation with the cash generated by other operations. With multiple corporations, each corporation stands on its own and you lose the flexibility in the use of funds in your business. Of course, you can get around this problem by causing one corporation to loan funds to another. This disadvantage extends to the tax front. In a single business, profits from one part of the business are offset by the losses from other parts of the business. In multiple corporations, some will be profitable, some others not, and the profits and losses will not automatically be netted one against the other.

If you do decide that multiple corporations are for you, division of your business should be made along natural lines. Your objective is to own the property or business without incurring the liability arising from the hazards of operation. There can be a horizontal division of your business along different product lines or geographical regions, or you can have the functional division of the business, for example into sales and manufacturing operations.

Here are some examples of how certain businesses have used multiple corporations. A wholesale grocery business was divided into five corporations, one for each town in which it operated. The incorporation of 51 branches of a shoe chain into 21 corporations limited liability on leases. An owner of a chain of gas stations formed 24 separate corporations, one for each gas station. Multiple corporations are an ideal vehicle for limiting liability for real estate owners. You would need to work out tax angles to be sure.

Checklist -
Business Legal Exposure and Liability

Most business owners tend to minimize or entirely overlook the need to protect themselves and their business from potential lawsuits and liability. The importance of such protection cannot be over-emphasized. Years of hard work in building up a profitable business can be wiped out through a single lawsuit which could have been averted by proper planning.

The following checklist, by no means comprehensive, highlights those areas that pose the greatest danger to both businesses and individual owners and should be used to review the legal fitness of your business.

✓ **Accident, Liability, and Property Damage.** Assess various risks, formulate and implement a plan to minimize them and review the insurance protection available.

✓ **Anti-trust Violations.** Review corporate pricing policy, distribution, and licensing agreements. Define marketing policy, especially with reference to general sales and procurement procedures, guidelines for field representatives and contacts with competitors.

✓ **Inventions, Patents, Trademarks, and Trade Secrets.** Conduct a thorough analysis to ensure adequate protection.

✓ **Discrimination.** Guard against discrimination in employment hiring, promotion and firing. Watch out for age, sex, and race discrimination. Personnel policies should be periodically updated to reflect the latest changes in law and court decisions.

✓ **Libel and Slander.** Greatest potential for libel and slander lies in labor disputes, references for past employees, dealings with competitors, and customer collection activities.

✓ **Breach of Contract.** Areas to watch here are: employee hiring and firing and dealings with vendors and customers.

✓ **Product Liability.** Minimize exposure by taking the following steps:

(a) get products pre-tested by an independent laboratory;

(b) set up a quality control program;

(c) make sure instructions for proper use of the product are clear and prominently displayed on labels;

(d) make warranty definite - stating exactly what is being warranted and what is not; if the component parts or accessories are being warranted by others, see that these warranties are passed on;

(e) review product advertising and promotional literature to see that the claims are legitimate and reasonable;

(f) carry adequate product liability insurance; a policy with proper coverage can protect against claims, against defective or mislabeled products, products sold for improper use or under improper circumstances, negligence and breach of implied warranty.

Articles of Incorporation

16

The material in this chapter consists of forms of articles of incorporation, sometimes referred to as charters or certificates of incorporation, containing provisions concerning the name, purpose, place of business, names and addresses of directors and incorporators, and capitalization of the corporation.

Articles of incorporation may detail the operation of a business, but usually such details are spelled out in the corporation's bylaws.

Various state statutes prescribe the appropriate form and content of articles of incorporation. Generally, a standardized form of articles of incorporation is available in each state and you should use such a form and follow the required procedure for filing them with the appropriate state official.

Included in this chapter is a general form of articles of incorporation.

Checklist of Items to Be Considered in Drafting Articles of Incorporation

- Name of corporation.

- Purpose for which formed.

- Duration of corporate existence.

- Post office address of initial registered office and name of initial registered agent or place in which principal office for transacting business is located.

- Number of directors.

- Names and addresses of initial directors.

- Names and addresses of incorporators.

- Capital structure:

  - Class of stock to include both common and preferred.

  - Value of stock to be par or nonpar.

- Optional provisions.

- Signatures and acknowledgments.

Caution: Local statutes should, of course, be consulted to determine the applicability of a checkpoint in a particular jurisdiction.

Articles of Incorporation - General Form

State of _____)
)
County of _____)

To: Secretary of State

_____

_____

Article I

Name of Corporation

The name of the corporation hereby incorporated is _____.

[Note: Usually one of the following must be included as part of the corporation's name: "Corporation," "Company," "Corp.," "Co.," or "Inc."]

Article II

Registered Office and Agent

The address of the _____ Corporation's initial registered office in the State of _____ is: _____.

The initial registered agent at that registered office is: _____.

Article III

Duration of Corporation

The duration of the corporation is: _____ [e.g., perpetual, term of years].

Article IV

Purposes of Corporation

The purpose for which the corporation is organized is:

_____.

To do anything that may lawfully be done by a corporation organized under the
_____ Business Corporation Act, as that act may be amended or
supplemented from time to time.

Article V

Directors

The number of directors constituting the initial board of directors is _____,
and the names and addresses of the persons who are to serve as directors until the first annual
meeting of the shareholders or until their successors are elected and qualified are:

Name   Address

_____   _____

_____   _____

_____   _____

Article VI

Incorporators

The names and addresses of the incorporators are:

Name   Address

_____   _____

_____   _____

_____   _____

Article VII

Authorization of Shares

The aggregate number of shares that the corporation is authorized to issue is _____, divided into _____ classes. The designation of each class, the number of shares of each class, and the par value, if any, of the shares of each class or a statement that the shares of any class are without par value, are as follows:

Class	Series	Number of Shares	Par Value Per Share
_____	_____	_____	$_____
_____	_____	_____	$_____
_____	_____	_____	$_____

The preferences, qualifications, limitations, restrictions, and the special or relative rights in respect of the shares of each class are: _____.

Article VIII

Issuance of Shares

The class and number of shares that the corporation proposes to issue without further report to the Secretary of State and the consideration (expressed in dollars) to be received by the corporation are:

Class of Shares	Number of Shares	Total Consideration
_____	_____	$_____
_____	_____	$_____
_____	_____	$_____

Article IX

Commencement of Business

The corporation shall not commence business until it has received at least $_____ as consideration for the issuance of shares.

Article X

Indemnification of Officers and Directors

The corporation's board of directors is expressly authorized to indemnify its officers and directors to the full extent permitted by the laws of the State of _____. It is the corporation's policy to safeguard its officers and directors from liability for actions they take in good faith to further the interests of the corporation and its shareholders.

_____
Signatures

[Acknowledgments]

SECTION VII

Limited Partnership 17

The main attraction of limited partnership, as its name implies, is limited liability for its partners. In general, limited partners are not personally liable for partnership debts and obligations beyond the amount of their contributions.

This is the single most important characteristic that distinguishes a limited partnership from a general partnership and a limited partner from a general partner. The general partner in a limited partnership is personally liable for all debts and obligations of the limited partnership without limitation.

Role of Limited Partnership in Protecting Your Assets

Although limited partners ordinarily are not personally liable for partnership debts and obligations, they may incur such liability in a suit by partnership creditors to the extent of their contribution or interest in the partnership. For example, if the partnership and general partners become insolvent, the judgment creditor can sue to enforce the unpaid balance of a limited partner's agreed contribution or to collect part or all of his contribution which was withdrawn or repaid after the creditor's claim existed.

In this chapter we'll examine the rights of a partner in the partnership and specific property of the partnership vis-a-vis other partners and creditors of the partnership and also of individual partners. By understanding these rights, you'll be in a better position to evaluate the role of limited partnership in protecting your assets.

We'll first discuss the right of a partner in a specific partnership property and its status against the claims of creditors of individual partner and then contrast it with the right of a partner in the partnership. One is beyond the reach of creditors while the other can be reached, but only with great difficulty.

Requisites for Limited Liability

In order for a limited partner to preserve his or her limited liability, certain conditions must be fulfilled:

---

1. The limited partnership must be formed with substantial compliance in good faith with statutory requirements.

2. The limited partner's surname must not be used in the name of the limited partnership.

3. If the partnership certificate contains a false statement, and the limited partner has the knowledge of falsity and the statement was relied upon by a third party to his detriment, the limited liability may no longer be available.

4. A limited partner must not take part in control of the business.

Forming a Limited Partnership: Legal Overview

A limited partnership is a purely statutory creation in which individuals, upon complying with the statutory requirements, can contribute specified sums to the capital of a partnership firm and then limit their liability to the amount of their capital contribution.

Limited Partnership Defined

The Uniform Limited Partnership Act defines a limited partnership (and the Revised Uniform Limited Partnership Act adds to this a domestic limited partnership) as a partnership formed by two or more persons under the laws of a state and having one or more general partners and one or more limited or special partners. Limited partners are not bound by the obligations of the partnership.

The Uniform Limited Partnership Act does not specifically exclude corporations from such a partnership. The Revised Uniform Limited Partnership Act defines person as a natural person, partnership, limited partnership (domestic or foreign), trust, estate, association or corporation.

Partnership Business

The Uniform Limited Partnership Act, adopted by the majority of jurisdictions, and the Revised Uniform Limited Partnership Act adopted by a few jurisdictions, provide that a limited partnership may carry on any business that a partnership without limited partners could carry on, except those designated in the Act.

Statutory Compliance

A limited partnership is formed if there has been substantial compliance in good faith with the requirements of the enabling statute and by the filing of a certificate of affirmation, in compliance with the enabling statute. The partnership operates under a firm name. While the Uniform Limited Partnership Act does not require a limited partnership to identify itself as such in its name, the Revised Uniform Limited Partnership Act does require such identification.

General Partner

A general partner is a person whose rights, powers, and obligations are similar to those of partners in an ordinary partnership, while a limited partner is one who contributes capital primarily as a financial investment, with liability generally limited to an amount equal to the investment. A limited partner is one who is not bound by the obligations of the partnership.

A general partner in a limited partnership has rights and powers and knowledge comparable to those possessed by the members in an ordinary general partnership, and may become individually liable for all the debts of the firm. The general partner is accountable to other partners as a fiduciary.

Limited Partner

The rights of a limited partner are generally confined to the rights to have full information and to receive a share of the income, and the same rights as a general partner in reference to the dissolution and winding up by decree of a court.

A limited partner is liable for any losses of the partnership to the extent of the partner's investment in the assets of the business; however, a limited partner is not liable as a general partner unless, in addition to the exercise of the limited partner's rights and powers as a limited partner, the partner also takes part in the control of the business.

Under the Revised Uniform Limited Partnership Act a limited partner who knowingly permits the use of his name in the name of the limited partnership, except where the name is also the name of a general partner or the corporate name of the corporate general partner, would be liable to creditors who extend credit to the limited partnership without actual knowledge that the limited partner is not a general partner. Otherwise, a limited partner is not liable for the obligations of the partnership unless the limited partner is also a general partner or if the limited partner takes part in the control of the business.

Limited Partnership - At a Glance

Here are some of the characteristics of a limited partnership, including one that involves members of a family.

✓ Some partners can be general partners subject to the liabilities of the law as to general partners.

✓ Wife and/or children can be limited partners. Each limited partner can be entitled to a fixed percentage of the profits and losses from the operation of the business, or the liability of each limited partner can be expressed so as not to exceed the value of his capital contribution.

✓ Upon liquidation, the distributive shares of the partners can be in proportion to their partnership interest.

✓ General partners can be given complete management and control.

✓ Special or limited partners can be denied a voice in the management and operation of the business.

✓ General partners can be given limited authority to determine whether there is a need for additional working capital for enhancement of the business, or profits to be withheld for future expansion or development.

✓ With the death of a limited partner, his executor or personal representative may have all his rights just as if he had survived. Under these circumstances the partnership would continue to operate, but the continuation of the partnership after the death of a limited partner should be made contingent upon the consent of the general partners.

✓ The partnership agreement should provide either that the partnership terminates upon a general partner's death, bankruptcy, incompetency or transfer inter vivos of his general interest, or that the partnership may continue in such event only if all the partners agree to a continuation.

✓ The partnership would remain unaffected if a limited partner goes bankrupt or becomes incompetent.

✓ The agreement may set the duration of the partnership; at the end of the agreed term, there must be either dissolution or an agreement to continue.

✓ The partnership agreement may state the primary business activity of the partnership.

✓ In a limited partnership, the limited partner should not engage in the management of the business. If he does, he might be subject to liability as a general partner.

Partner's Right in Specific Partnership Property Is Not Assignable to Third Persons

There are several reasons why a partner cannot individually assign his rights in specific partnership property. Since the partnership relationship is a voluntary association one partner does not have the right to thrust a stranger upon the other partners without their consent. If a partner were permitted to assign his rights in specific partnership property, this would amount to imposing a new partner upon the rest of the partners.

The non-assignability of a partner's right in specific partnership property prevents interference by a third party with the conduct, management and disposition of partnership business and property. Even if there were no objections to an outsider taking part in the management of partnership affairs, it would often be a difficult, even an impossible, task to compute an individual partner's beneficial interest in a specific partnership asset.

The creditors of the partnership have the right to have all the firm assets applied to the payment of the partnership debts.

While a partner may not assign his interest in specific partnership property to a third person, the partner may nonetheless assign this right to other partners. It has been held that the Uniform Partnership Act does not prohibit a partner from assigning his interest in specific partnership property to his remaining partner or partners.

Partner Cannot Sell or Mortgage His Right in Specific Partnership Property

Since real ownership and legal title to partnership property is vested in the partnership, an individual partner cannot effectively sell or mortgage his right in specific partnership property. If a partner does attempt to sell or mortgage his interest in specific partnership property, title will not pass nor will a lien be created, and the vendee or mortgagee will take nothing thereunder except that partner's share of the profits and a share of the surplus after the settlement of the partnership business.

Tenancies in Partnership Are Not Subject to Partition

A limited partner cannot divide his interest in the partnership and transfer, sell, exchange, hypothecate or gift this divided interest to someone else.

Partner's Right in Specific Partnership Property Is Not Subject to Attachment, Execution or Garnishment

As mentioned above, one of the incidents of tenancy in partnership is that a partner's right in the property is not subject to attachment or execution by a judgment creditor, except on a claim against the partnership.

In one New York case, there was a dispute between the judgment creditor of one of the partners and the assignee for the benefit of the creditors of the partnership with regards to the ownership of certain property.

On October 27, 1950, the judgment creditor issued an execution to the sheriff and on the next day, October 28, the sheriff levied upon the property involved. Also, on the same date assignment of the property was made. Under New York law a judgment debtor's property becomes bound by the execution from the time of the delivery to the proper officer. Prior to actual levy under the execution, the title of the purchaser in good faith and without notice is protected, but an assignee for the benefit of creditors is not a bona fide purchaser. If the property belonged to the judgment debtor, the judgment creditor, by virtue of his execution, would have a superior title to that of the assignee. However, the property levied upon was a partnership property, and the partnership property is not available to satisfy a judgment against an individual partner. In other words, the assignee acquired title to the property by virtue of the assignment. The judgment creditor could not execute upon the partnership property.

Partnership funds cannot be garnished to satisfy the debts of an individual partner even where partners are husband and wife. *HILK vs. Bank of Washington*, 251 SW2d 963 (Mo App1952).

On Death of a Partner His Right in Specific Partnership Property Vests in Surviving Partner

As mentioned above, one of the incidents of tenancy in partnership is that upon the death of a partner his right in specific partnership property vests in the surviving partner or partners, except where the deceased was the last surviving partner, in which case his right in such property vests in his legal representative. Such surviving partner or partners or the legal representative of the last surviving partner has no right to possess a partnership property for any but a partnership purpose.

Partner's Interest in Partnership

Until now we have discussed partner's right in specific partnership property and, generally speaking, this right in specific partnership property cannot be levied upon by a judgment creditor.

In addition to a partner's right in specific partnership property, each partner has another type of property right - his interest in the partnership. Under the Uniform Partnership Act, a partner's interest in the partnership is defined as his share of the profits and surplus after the partnership debts are paid and after partnership accounts are settled and the rights of the partners' interest are adjusted. This interest under the Act is personal property regardless of the character of the partnership property.

Partner's Interest in Partnership Is Assignable

While a partner cannot assign his interest in specific partnership property he can make an assignment of his interest in the partnership. Such a conveyance to a partner or a third party does not of itself dissolve the partnership and free the partners from the terms and conditions of the partnership agreement.

Many assignments of a partnership interest are made merely as collateral security for a loan. The assigning party in such cases has no intention of terminating the partnership relationship.

In the absence of an agreement to the contrary during the continuance of the partnership, the assignee is not entitled to interfere in the management or administration of the partnership business or affairs, and is not entitled to any information or accounting of partnership transactions or to an inspection of the partnership books.

The assignee is merely entitled to receive in accordance with his contract the profits to which the assigning partner would otherwise be entitled. In the event of dissolution of the partnership the assignee is entitled to receive his assignor's interest and may require an account from the date of the last account agreed to by all the partners.

Partner's Interest in Partnership Vests in Executor

When a partner dies, his rights in specific partnership property, as mentioned above, vest in the surviving partner or partners. However, his interest in the partnership, which is considered personal property, vests in his executor.

The personal representative of the deceased partner has the duty to require that an accounting be made either by the surviving partner or by a receiver under court supervision. Where a complaint, alleging a cause of action for partnership accounting, was filed against the surviving partner by the beneficiaries under the will of the deceased partner, the court held it was subject to demurrer for defect of parties plaintiff in that deceased partner's personal representative was not a party plaintiff.

Rights of a Divorced Spouse

While we're on the subject of protecting a partner's interest in a partnership from the claims of a creditor, it's important to discuss the rights of a divorced a spouse of a partner.

The Uniform Partnership Act does not specifically address the issue of the rights of a divorced spouse of a partner. Can he or she assert a community property right in or obtain equitable distribution on account of the partner's property rights in the partnership? In at least one state, namely Texas, the divorced spouse is no more than the assignee of the partner's interest.

Specific Partnership Property

The divorced spouse is in a position analogous to the position of a partner's assignees, creditors and heirs. Thus, the divorced spouse has no interest in specific partnership property; it is not community property and is not subject to equitable distribution to a partner's divorced spouse.[1]

Interest in Partnership

Again by analogy to assignees, creditors, and heirs, the divorced spouse may have community property rights in or be entitled to equitable distribution on account of a partner's interest in the partnership.[2] So, although the divorced spouse cannot be awarded a specific partnership property, he or she would be entitled to share in the spouse's partnership interest.

In assessing the precise nature of the divorced spouse's interest, the courts have departed somewhat from the principles governing assignees and creditors. In the first place, it has been held that the spouse is entitled to share in the full value (including goodwill) of the partnership interest, rather than merely to share in distributions to the spouse by the partnership. It has been held that this value may be based on the buyout right fixed in the partnership agreement.

Although a partner's spouse may be entitled to share in the full value of the partner's interest, that does not necessarily mean that the spouse becomes an assignee of the interest. Rather, the spouse may be given a money judgment based on the value of the interest,[3] and this judgment may be enforced by a charging order.[4]

Right to Participate in Management

Even a spouse who obtains an interest in the partnership in a divorce is not a partner and consequently has no right to participate in management.[5]

Creditor of an Individual Partner

All of the above discussion now brings us to the $64,000 question:

How does a judgment creditor satisfy the individual debt of a partner?

As we've noted above, the creditors of a partnership have the first call upon the jointly-owned property of the partnership. Likewise, the personal creditor of an individual partner would look to the personal estate of the partner for the satisfaction of such individual obligations. As stated in *Virginia-Carolina Chemical Company vs. Walston,* 187 NC 817, 123 SE 196 (1924):

> "...Partnership creditors are entitled to have the partnership assets first applied to the payment of the debts of the partnership, and the separate and private creditors of the individual partners are entitled to have the separate and private estate of the partners with whom they have made individual contracts first applied to their debts."

This priority to attach the separate and private estate of the partner of the judgment debtor-partner is valid even in a case where the particular creditor happens also to be a partnership creditor.

Thus, when a bank, which was a creditor of the partnership had obtained a personal guarantee from an individual partner, this creditor could exhaust the individual member's assets to the exclusion of the other creditors of the partnership, and then share pro-rata with them in the assets of the insolvent firm. *Iowa: Simons vs. Simons,* 215 Iowa 654, 246 NW 597 (1933).

Partner's Interest According to the Uniform Partnership Act

In order to understand the extent of levy on a partner's interest in a partnership, it is important to understand precisely what that interest is. The Uniform Partnership Act provides a precise definition of a partner's interest in the partnership. The two relevant sections of this Act are reproduced below.

§25. Nature of a Partner's Right in Specific Partnership Property

"(1) A partner is co-owner with his partners of specific partnership property holding as a tenant in partnership.

"(2) The incidents of this tenancy are such that:

"(a) A partner, subject to the provisions of this Act and to any agreement between the partners, has an equal right with his partners to possess specific partnership property for partnership purposes; but he has no right to possess such property for any other purpose without the consent of his partners.

"(b) A partner's right in specific partnership property is not assignable except in connection with the assignment of rights of all the partners in the same property.

"(c) A partner's right in specific partnership property is not subject to attachment or execution, except on a claim against the partnership. When partnership property is attached for a partnership debt the partners, or any of them, or the representatives of a deceased partner, cannot claim any right under the homestead or exemption laws.

"(d) On the death of a partner his right in specific partnership property vests in the surviving partner or partners, except where the deceased was the last surviving partner, when his right in such property vests in his legal representative. Such surviving partner or partners, or the legal representative of the last surviving partner, has no right to possess the partnership property for any but a partnership purpose.

"(e) A partner's right in specific partnership property is not subject to dower, curtesy, or allowances to widows, heirs, or next of kin."

§ 26. Nature of Partner's Interest in the Partnership

"A partner's interest in the partnership is his share of profits and surplus, and the same is personal property."

The immediate result of the above provisions of the Uniform Partnership Act is first, to prevent the direct execution, attachment or garnishment against a partner's right in specific partnership property and second, to limit the claim of the creditor to whatever is remaining of the partner's interest.

Defining Partner's Right in Partnership

In practical terms the hapless creditor pursuing a debtor whose last remaining asset consists of an undivided interest in a partnership has to look to his share of the partnership after the partnership has been dissolved, the business has been wound up, debts of the partnership have been satisfied and then share pro-rata in the debtor-partner's profits of the firm.

The creditor, in other words, cannot collect from the firm anything in excess of the member's net equity therein. *First Nat'l Bank v. Schuetz,* 103 Kan 288, 173 P 288 (1918).

The essence of the rule was perhaps best stated by the District Court in *Maryland Cas. Co. v. Glassell-Taylor Co., Louisiana:* 63 F Supp 718 (WD La 1945), where it was held:

"The interest of the partner is residuary and can be made to respond to individual debts only after liquidation and satisfaction of partnership creditors."

Compare *Adler v. Nicholas,* 166 F2d 674 (10th Cir [Colo] 1948), where the court said in part:

"A partner's interest in the partnership property is his share of the surplus after all partnership debts have been paid, and that surplus alone is liable for the separate debts of each partner. It, therefore, must follow that the partnership creditors' claims must first be satisfied out of the partnership assets before there was any distributable surplus to the partners to which the Government could look for the satisfaction of the individual tax liability of the partners, and even then it would be limited in its attempt to collect the income taxes due from each partner to his interest in the remaining net proceeds of the partnership."

See also the following from *Claude v. Claude,* 191 Ore 308, 228 P2d 776 (1951):

"Our conclusions above with reference to the disposition of the personal property in the manner indicated are based primarily upon the well-known rule that partners do not, as individuals, own any specific part of the firm property. The interest of a partner in the firm assets is the share to which he is entitled after claims against the firm are satisfied and the equities and accounts, as between the partners, adjusted."

The judgment creditor has to wait not only till the process of dissolution is completed but he must also prove that winding up of the partnership affairs is completed.

Citizens' Nat'l Trust & Savings Bank v. McNeny, 10 Cal App2d 488, 52 P2d 492 (1935):

> "The partnership was not terminated by its dissolution, but continued during the winding up of the partnership affairs."

The most obvious effect of the rules immediately said above is, of course, to bar attachment and execution, as well as garnishment, of specific property belonging to the partnership, and to severely limit the reach of the creditors to a debtor-partner's interest in the partnership.

The above discussion should not lead to an erroneous conclusion that the creditor of a partner is entirely without recourse in reaching the debtor's interest in the partnership.

In a number of jurisdictions, the undivided interest of the member in his firm has been held to be a property right which is subject to levy in the same manner as other property.[6] In *Gaynes v. Conn,*[7] it was held that the court properly assessed the respective interests of all parties in a piece of partnership realty in a proceeding in aid of execution.

And where this remedy is not available, the enactment of the Uniform Partnership Act in a majority of jurisdictions results in the assurance that in those states at least, the creditor can resort to the "charging order," for which provision is made in Section 28 of the Uniform Act.

In the following chapter, we'll examine the remedy of charging order provided by the Uniform Partnership Act that allows a creditor to reach a debtor-partner's interest in the partnership, and then we'll look at the practical implications of the role played by the limited partnership in protecting an individual's assets against the claims of creditors. As it will become apparent, creditor of a limited partner is in a rather unenviable position, for he has to cross several hurdles before he can realize satisfaction of a debt held. In many cases, these hurdles may become insurmountable for many a creditor.

---

[1]*Riegler v. Riegler*, 243 Ark. 113, 419 S.W.2d 311 (1967) (chancellor erroneously awarded wife specific property owned by husband's medical partnership); *Warren v. Warren*, 12 Ark. App. 260, 675 S.W.2d 371 (1984) (divorce court should not have awarded partner's wife an undivided interest in partnership); *Dotson v. Grice*, 98 N.M. 207, 647 P.2d 409 (1982) (because spouse has no community interest in specific partnership property, need not join in conveyance); *McKnight v. McKnight*, 543 S.W.2d 863 (Tex. 1976). But *cf. Smoot v. Smoot*, 568 S.W.2d177 (Tex. Civ. App. 1978) (whether spouse had community property right in partner's interest in partnership held to depend on source of particular property acquired by partnership).

[2]*Wilen v. Wilen*, 61 Md. App. 337, 486 A.2d 775 (1985); *Bannen v. Bannen*, 286 S.C. 4, 331 S.E.2d 379 (S.C. App. 1985); *McKnight v. McKnight*, 543 S.W.2d 863 (Tex. 1976).

[3]*Bannen v. Bannen*, 286 S.C. 4, 331 S.E.2d 379 (S.C. App. 1985) (spouse precluded by statute from having a legal or equitable interest in medical partnership).

[4]*Riegler v. Riegler*, 243 Ark. 113, 419 S.W.2d 311 (1967).

[5]*Block v. Lea*, 688 P.2d 724 (Haw. App. 1984) (wife had no right to accounting).

[6]*Arkansas: Terral v. Terral*, 212 Ark 221, 205 SW2d 198 (1947), 1 ALR2d 1092 (1948).

Georgia: All Florida Sand v. Lawler Constr. Co., 209 Ga 720, 75 SE2d 559 (1953).

New York: Rhoades v. Robles, 1 Misc2d 43, 145 NYS2d 286 (1955).

Ohio: Mine Safety Appliances Co. v. Best, 49 Ohio L Abs 552, 36 Ohio Ops 361, 76 NE 2d 108 (1947).

Pennsylvania: Luick v. Luick, 164 Pa Super 378, 64 A2d 860 (1949).

Texas: O'Connor v. Gable, 298 SW2d 209 (Tex Civ App 1957).

[7]185 Kan 655, 347 P2d 458 (1959).

Charging Order: Creditor's Remedy to Reach Partner's Interest in Partnership

18

The Uniform Limited Partnership Act provides that a judgment creditor (or, in some jurisdictions, any creditor) of a limited partner may obtain a court order charging a limited partner's interest in the partnership with payment of any unsatisfied amount of a judgment debt. The statute further provides that such interest may be redeemed with the separate property of any general partner, but may not be redeemed with partnership property. It also expressly provides that the remedies conferred by the statute shall not be deemed exclusive of others which may exist and nothing in the act shall be held to deprive a limited partner of his statutory exemption.

Charging Order - Generally

Under the Uniform Partnership Act, the charging order has replaced the levy of execution as method by which a judgment creditor can reach the interest of an individual partner in the partnership. The judgment creditor does not acquire any greater rights than the debtor is entitled to for his own benefit.

The charging order remedy is intended to protect innocent partners of a partnership that have nothing to do with the claims of creditors of individual partners.

A judgment creditor of a partner may obtain a charging order by making due application to a competent court which then charges the interest of the debtor partner with payment of the unsatisfied amount of the judgment debt with interest thereon. The court may then or later appoint a receiver of the partner's share of the profits, and of any other money due or to fall due to him in respect of the partnership.

A receiver appointed on the application of a partner's judgment creditor and acting under a charging order is entitled to any relief necessary to conserve partnership assets for partnership purposes.

Rights of Creditors of Limited Partner

Section 22 of the Uniform Limited Partnership Act provides that:

"(1) On due application to a court of competent jurisdiction by any judgment creditor of a limited partner, the court may charge the interest of the indebted limited partner with payment of the unsatisfied amount of the judgment debt; and may appoint a receiver, and make all other orders, directions, and inquiries which the circumstances of the case may require.

(2) The interest may be redeemed with the separate property of any general partner, but may not be redeemed with partnership property.

(3) The remedies conferred by paragraph (1) shall not be deemed exclusive of others which may exist.

(4) Nothing in this act shall be held to deprive a limited partner of his statutory exemption."

Where the Uniform Limited Partnership Act has been adopted, the charging order is the exclusive remedy of the judgment creditor as respects the partner's interest in his firm. Where the judgment debtor fails to object to its entry, the co-partners, once they are found as a fact to be such, have no standing to oppose it.

Even under this statute, of course, the court may deny relief until settlement of the accounts of the partnership, thus establishing the entitlement of the judgment debtor, if any, to the assets of the firm.

Redeeming the Charged Interest

The Uniform Partnership Act provides two methods whereby the interest charged may be redeemed at any time before foreclosure or, in case of a sale being directed by the court, may be purchased without thereby causing a dissolution.

Any one or more of the partners may redeem or purchase the debtor partner's interest with their separate property. The alternative method is for any one or more of the partners, with the consent of all the partners, whose interests are not so charged or sold, to redeem or purchase the debtor partner's interest with partnership property.

Fraudulent Conveyance Voidable

If the transferee of partnership assets knew that a judgment creditor had obtained a charging order against a partner's interest in the partnership, if the transfer was without a fair consideration, and if the transferee knew that the transfer would diminish the value of the judgment creditor's lien, the judgment creditor will be entitled to recover from the transferee.

Here's a case in point.

Where the judgment creditors of the general partners of a limited partnership brought an action to set aside as fraudulent and void a conveyance by the limited partnership to a corporation shortly prior to the entry of judgments against the general partners, the court held that the record made out a prima facie case for a decree directing retransfer of title to the limited partnership. In its opinion, the court stated:

"Although the property of a partnership is not subject to attachment or execution except on a claim against the partnership, a judgment creditor of any general or limited partner has a statutory right to obtain an order charging his debtor's interest in the partnership with payment of the unsatisfied amount of the judgment with interest thereon . . . By conveying the hotel property from the limited partnership to G.C.H. Incorporated, the judgment debtors hindered, delayed and interfered with plaintiffs' ability to obtain the charging orders to which they were and are entitled. Until and unless the record title is retransferred to the limited partnership, plaintiffs are in no position to reach, through charging orders, the interests of the judgment debtors in the partnership property. . .The statutory right to charging orders against the judgment debtors' interests in a partnership is not broad enough to permit the obtaining of charging orders against the equitable interests of the judgment debtors under a declaration of trust executed by stockholders of a grantee corporation. It is to be noted that the declaration of trust is limited, in its reference to creditors, to creditors of the partnership, and that it does not purport to be for the benefit also of creditors of individual members of the partnership."

Creditor's Recourse against a Partner's Interest: Practical Implications

---

Although partnership property is shielded from the attack of a partner's individual creditor, the creditor does have recourse against the partner's interest in the firm.

As a first measure, the creditor may bring extra-legal pressures to induce the partner to assign his interest to the creditor, either absolutely or as security. Failing this, the creditor may employ the charging order remedy as specified in the Uniform Partnership Act §28, a device derived from the English Partnership Act. Although the UPA nowhere says that a charging order is the exclusive process available to the partner's individual creditor, the courts have generally interpreted it to be as such.[1]

Under UPA §28 (1), "the charging order remedy is available to any judgment creditor of a partner." In other words, the charging order is not a prejudgment remedy. Further, the charging order remedy has been granted to claimants who are not strictly judgment creditors, such as spouses seeking alimony or child support.[2]

The remedy is available even if the partnership agreement prohibits or limits assignments of partnership interests.[3]

Charging Order: Lien on the Partner's Interest

As we've seen in the earlier discussions, the charging order is a judicial proceeding in which the charging creditor must show that the debtor has an interest in the charged firm. If the non-debtor partners deny that the charged partner has such an interest, the question may have to be adjudicated under local court rules in a separate action.[4]

The order leads to a sort of lien on the partner's interest in the firm, but does not confer priority on the charging creditor over a partnership creditor.

Appointment of a Receiver

Moreover, the charging order alone is of little comfort to the charging creditor even vis-a-vis other creditors of the individual partner. In *Princeton Bank & Trust Co. v. Berley,*[5], the court held that a levying creditor of an individual partner had priority over an earlier charging creditor of the partner who had not obtained an order of receivership or any other order directing the delivery of property.

As suggested by the *Princeton Bank* case, the charging creditor should obtain one of the judicial orders ancillary to the charging order itself that are contemplated by U.P.A.§28. First, the creditor may request the court to order, pursuant to the last clause of §28(1), that payments, particularly distributions of earnings or withdrawals of capital,[6] that would otherwise go to the debtor partner should go to the creditor instead.[7]

The effect of such an order is quite similar to a garnishment and would, of course, depend on what the debtor partner was entitled to withdraw from the firm pursuant to the partnership agreement. U.P.A. §28(1) also authorizes the appointment of a receiver for the charged interest (as distinguished from the partnership or its property). The receiver is entitled to the judicial relief needed to conserve partnership property for payment to the creditors, but does not participate in management. The charging order and any ancillary orders should be made only upon giving full notice and opportunity to be heard to both debtor and non-debtor partners.[8]

After the charge and the entry of payment and other orders, the debtor continues to be a partner in all respects except distributions and withdrawals from the firm. Moreover, the charging creditor is not yet in the position even of an assignee of the interest.[9]

Foreclosure of Partner's Interest

This is apparent because U.P.A. §28(2) refers to the further step of foreclosure on the debtor partner's partnership interest, which would be necessary only if the interest had not already been assigned to the creditor. By foreclosing, the creditor can obtain a sale of the interest at which the interest is purchased by the creditor or a third party.[10]

Despite the reference to foreclosure in §28(2), there is some authority against a right of foreclosure on a partnership interest.[11]

Foreclosure would seem at least to be within the broad judicial power under the last clause of §28(1).[12]

However, because the foreclosing creditor threatens the continuity of the firm, foreclosure should be decreed only as a last resort - that is, if the charged interest is not likely to pay off the debt within a reasonable time.[13]

Even after foreclosure and sale, the creditor may be far from collecting the debt. At the foreclosure sale, only the partner's interest, not specific assets of the partnership, is sold.[14]

It is unlikely that the interest will bring a high price from third parties, because of the limited role to which the purchaser is relegated. If the creditor is the purchaser, it will still be entitled only to receive the charged partner's cash flow. Moreover, until dissolution the creditor has no right to an accounting.[15]

The principal change in the creditor's current status as a result of the foreclosure and sale is that the creditor now owns the partner's entire financial interest in the partnership, including all amounts ultimately due the partner on dissolution after settlement of liabilities.[16]

Often the only way the creditor can effectively obtain anything on account of the debtor partner's interest will be to exercise the assignee's power to seek a judicial dissolution under U.P.A. §32(2). On dissolution, the creditor can finally obtain whatever share would have come to the debtor partner after payment of all partnership creditors and claims of co-partners.

The rules concerning judicial foreclosure of a partnership interest are probably also applicable to non-judicial foreclosure of a consensual lien on a partnership under the Uniform Commercial Code insofar as the rights of debtor, creditor, and purchaser are concerned.

Non-Debtor Partners' Recourse

The non-debtor partners have a number of options in dealing with the threat to the continuity of the partnership posed by a charged interest. They may forestall the threat of foreclosure by redeeming the charged interest before foreclosure with their own property or, if they all consent, with partnership property.

There is no express statutory procedure for determining the redemption price. It may be the amount of the creditor's claim, which would make redemption uneconomic if the claim were greater than the value of the partner's interest. The court probably has general authority under the last clause of U.P.A. §28 (1) to value the interest and permit redemption at the value.

If the partners redeem the interest for the amount of the debt, and this is less than the value fixed by the court, the court may treat this as a loan to the debtor partner or order that the redeeming partners hold the interest in trust for the debtor partner. If the court decrees foreclosure, the non-debtor partners may buy the interest at the foreclosure sale.

The non-debtor partners (either before or after foreclosure) can remove the uncertainty created by the creditor's presence by dissolving the firm and buying the assets on liquidation. Pursuant to U.P.A. §27(2), the partners must account on dissolution to the charging creditor for the debtor partner's interest.[17]

If the partners do purchase the interest, a strong argument can be made that, as on redemption for less than value, the interest should be held in trust for the debtor partner, because of the fiduciary relation among the partners.

Distribution of Assets

Section 23 of the Uniform Limited Partnership Act provides that:

"1. In settling accounts after dissolution the liabilities of the partnership shall be entitled to payment in the following order:

a. Those to creditors, in the order of priority as provided by law, except those to limited partners on account of their contributions, and to general partners;

b. Those to limited partners in respect to their share of the profits and other compensation by way of income on their contributions;

c. Those to limited partners in respect to the capital of their contributions;

d. Those to general partners other than for capital and profits;

e. Those to general partners in respect to profits;

f. Those to general partners in respect to capital.

2. Subject to any statement in the certificate or to subsequent agreement, limited partners share in the partnership assets in respect to their claims for profits or for compensation by way of income on their contributions respectively, in proportion to the respective amounts of such claims."

The provisions of Section 23 concern both the rights of partners as between themselves and the rights of third persons. To the extent that they do govern the rights of the parties as between themselves they may be modified by agreement.

"The partners of either a general or limited partnership, as between themselves, may include in the partnership articles any agreement they wish concerning the sharing of profits and losses, priorities of distribution on winding up of the partnership affairs and other matters."

Subsection (1) (a) of Section 23 grants the first priority on dissolution to "creditors . . . except those to limited partners on account of their contributions, and to general partners."

This does not mean that limited partners, as to loans and other business transactions with the firm, are on a complete par with other creditors. Under Section 13 of the Uniform Act, no limited partner may receive any payment if the assets are not sufficient to pay outside creditors.

In the event of insolvency the provisions of Section 8 of the Uniform Fraudulent Conveyance Act and of Section 67 (d) (4) of the Bankruptcy Act also forbid any payment by the firm in satisfaction of any claim of a limited partner.

Conclusion

In general, the limited rights of a partner's individual creditor against partnership property mean that a partnership interest is a poor collateral for a loan. As a result, lenders seeking partnership property as collateral may be well-advised to structure the transaction as a loan to the partnership. It is important to keep in mind, however, that an agreement securing a loan to an individual partner with partnership assets may not bind the partnership without the consent of all the partners.

Looking from a debtor's point of view, limited partnership shields a debtor-partner's interest from the reach of all but the most-determined creditors. A creditor has to cross many hurdles before realizing any satisfaction on the debt held. More often than not, a creditor may hold nothing more than a charging order against the interest of the limited partner.

In the context of a family limited partnership, this would be an excellent asset protection device - if properly implemented. Consult a professional - someone who's thoroughly familiar with not only the legal aspects but also the financial implications - before proceeding.

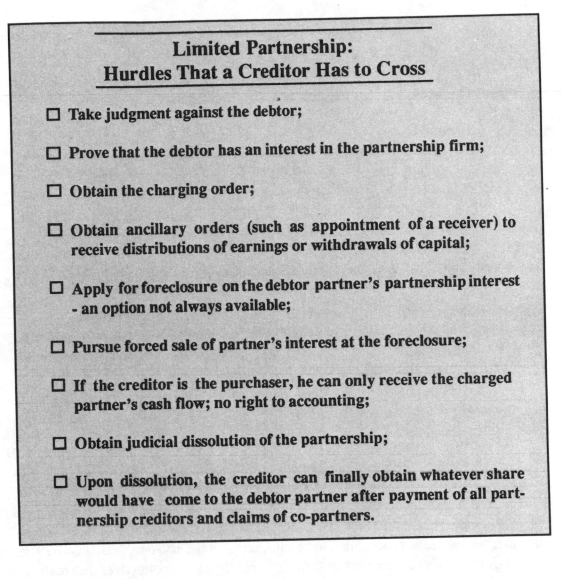

Limited Partnership:
Hurdles That a Creditor Has to Cross

☐ Take judgment against the debtor;

☐ Prove that the debtor has an interest in the partnership firm;

☐ Obtain the charging order;

☐ Obtain ancillary orders (such as appointment of a receiver) to receive distributions of earnings or withdrawals of capital;

☐ Apply for foreclosure on the debtor partner's partnership interest - an option not always available;

☐ Pursue forced sale of partner's interest at the foreclosure;

☐ If the creditor is the purchaser, he can only receive the charged partner's cash flow; no right to accounting;

☐ Obtain judicial dissolution of the partnership;

☐ Upon dissolution, the creditor can finally obtain whatever share would have come to the debtor partner after payment of all partnership creditors and claims of co-partners.

> **The following is a sample form of petition a judgment creditor can use to obtain a charging order against the interest of an individual partner of a partnership. For actual petition, consult a professional and follow local court procedure.**

Petition by Judgment Creditor of Individual Partner for Charging Order

Plaintiff says that in this court he recovered a judgment against the defendant, _____ for the sum of _____ dollars on the _____ day of _____, 19_____, being No. _____ upon the docket of this court; that said judgment is in full force and effect; that no part thereof has been paid; that there is also _____ dollars, comprising costs and interest on said judgment accrued and unpaid;

That said defendant is a partner of the firm known as _____ _____.

Wherefore, plaintiff prays that the defendant, _____ _____ be directed and required to make full disclosure of his ownership in said partnership; that the interest of the said defendant in said partnership be charged with the payment of plaintiff's said judgment, interest and costs, and that the said amount so found be declared and adjudged to be a lien upon the interest of the said defendant in all of the property, earnings and profits of said partnership; that a receiver be appointed for the share of the profits of said defendant in said partnership and of any other money due or to fall due to him in respect to the partnership; that if said profits and money due to the said defendant from said partnership are not sufficient to pay said judgment, then that his interest in said partnership be sold and the proceeds applied toward the payment of plaintiff's judgment, interest and costs and for such other and further relief as may be necessary and to which the plaintiff is entitled.

Defendant's Answer - Admission and General Denial

(a) Defendant admits that *(here specifically designate all matters stated in the petition, if any, which are admitted),* and denies each and every other material allegation contained in plaintiff's petition.

(b) The defendant denies each and every material allegation of plaintiff's complaint.

---

[1] *Matter of Pischke*, 11 B.R. 913 (E.D. Va. 1981); *Baum v. Baum*, 51 Cal. 2d 610, 335 P.2d 481 (1959); *Sherwood v. Jackson*, 121 Cal. App. 354, 8 P.2d 943 (1932); *Atlantic Mobile Homes v. LeFever*, 481 So. 2d 1002 (Fla, App. 1986); *Metropolitan Casualty Ins. Co. v. Cimino*, 108 N.J.L. 243, 157 A. 152 (1931); *Rader v. Goldoff*, 223 A.D. 455, 228 N.Y.S. 453 (1928); *Weisinger v. Rae*, 19 Misc. 2d 341, 188 N.Y.S.2d 10 (1959); *Northhampton Brewery Corp. v. Lande*, 133 Pa. Super. 181, 2 A.2d 553 (1938), noted 38 Mich. L. Rev. 421 (1940), 23 Minn. L. Rev. 538 (1939). But see *Grenada Bank v. Willey*, 694 F.2d 85 (5th Cir. 1983) (Mississippi law; although fieri facias clearly improper because requires physical possession of the interest, garnishment would be proper and not precluded by rule 69(a) of the Federal Rules of Civil Procedure); *Princeton Bank & Tr. Co. v. Berley*, 57 A.D.2d 348, 394 N.Y.S.2d 714 (1977) (garnishment remedy survives adoption of U.P.A. §28 where the garnishment statute specifically referred to garnishment of partnership interests).

[2] *Baum v. Baum*, 51 Cal. 2d 610, 335 P.2d 481 (1959). See Gose, The Charging Order under the Uniform Partnership Act, 28 Wash. L. Rev. 1, 21 (1953) (court can use powers other than under U.P.A. §28 to grant relief in such situations).

[3] *Tupper v. Kroc*, 88 Nev. 146, 494 P.2d 1275 (1972); *Jones v. Palermo*, 105 Misc. 2d 405, 432 N.Y.S. 2d 288 (1980).

[4] *Mitchell v. Superior Court for the County of Los Angeles*, 28 Cal. App. 3d 759, 104 Cal. Rptr. 921 (1973).

[5] 57 A.D.2d 348, 394 N.Y.S.2d 714 (1977).

[6] U.P.S. §28 permits the charging creditor to obtain only "money" due the partner. This has been broadened in some states to include other property and thus to permit the creditor to reach in-kind distributions. Ala. Code §10-8-42; Ga. Code Ann. §14-8-28.

[7] See *Grenada Bank v. Willey*, 694 F.2d 85 (5th Cir. 1983) (Mississippi law; creditor entitled only to cash flow due limited partner; not entitled to be made substituted limited partner and so to share in tax benefits).

[8] *First Natl. Bank of Denver v. District Court*, 652 P.2d 613 (1982) (notice to non-debtor partners required for order of sale of partner's interest because of possible adverse impact of sale, relying on "on due application" in §28(1)); Gose, n.2 above, at 19.

[9] *Taylor v. S&M Lamp Co.*, 190 Cal. App. 2d 700, 12 Cal. Rptr. 323 (1961). It follows, a fortiori, that, like an assignee, a charging creditor would have no right to participate in management of the firm.

[10] For a case in which the interest was sold to a third party, see *Beckley v. Speaks*, 39 Misc. 2d 241, 240 N.Y.S. 2d 553 (S. Ct. 1963), *affd.*, 21 A.D. 2d 759, 251 N.Y.S.2d 1015 (1964), *appeal dismissed*, 15 N.Y.2d 546, 254 N.Y.S.2d 362, 202 N.E.2d 906 (1964). In this case, the purchaser was denied the right to apply for renewal of the liquor license, which was the firm's only valuable asset, because it was partnership property and subject to management only by the partners.

[11] See *Buckman v. Goldblatt,* 39 Ohio App. 2d 1, 314 N.E.2d 188 (1974) (dictum; U.P.A. §28(2) must refer to foreclosure in support of a judgment against the partnership, because otherwise it would conflict with U.P.A. §25(2)(c), relying on a case (*Shirk v. Caterbone,* 201 Pa. Super. 544, 193 A.2d 664, 665 (1963)) dealing with a partnership creditor's levy on partnership property). Because of the threat posed by foreclosure to the coninuity of the firm, Georgia has modified its version of U.P.A. §28 to prohibit foreclosure. Ga. Code Ann. §14-8-28. See Ribstein, An Analysis of Georgia's New Partnership Law, 36 Mercer L. Rev. 443 490 (1985).

[12] *Tupper v. Kroc,* 88 Nev. 146, 494 P.2d 1275 (1972). See also *Taylor v. S&M Lamp Co.,* 190 Cal. App. 2d 700, 12 Cal. Rptr. 323 (1961), considering but not deciding whether a sheriff can hold an execution sale without a foreclosure order (that is, based only on the charging order and the debt judgment).

[13] See *City of New York v. Bencivenga,* 8 Misc. 2d 29, 169 N.Y.S.2d 515 (Sup. Ct. 1955) (granting charging order and appointing receiver, but denying authority to sell charged interest, without prejudice to a later application "upon a showing of the necessity for such foreclosure"); Gose, n.2 above, at 16.

[14] *Bohonus v. Amerco,* 124 Ariz. 88, 602 P.2d 469 (1979) (improper to sell partnership liquor license upon charging order and sale of partner's interest).

[15] *Tupper v. Kroc,* 88 Nev. 146, 494 P.2d 1275 (1972).

[16] As a result of this change in status, it has been held that there is no need for a receiver for the debtor partner's interest. *Tupper v. Kroc,* 88 Nev. 146, 494 P.2d 1275 (1972).

[17] *Cf. Spitzer v. Buten,* 306 Pa. 556, 160 A. 444 (1932), in which an attempted dissolution did not defeat the charging order.

Limited Partnership Agreement Forms   **19**

Introduction

A limited partnership agreement has many of the same elements and considerations included in a regular partnership agreement. There are some important differences. There are different classes of partners in a limited partnership, consisting of general partners and special or limited partners.

The contributions and liabilities of these different classes of partners vary. The general partner makes a contribution, is liable for partnership obligations to an unlimited degree, and actively engages in the management and business of the partnership. The limited partner contributes his capital primarily as a financial investment, his liability is generally limited to an amount equal to his investment, and he generally is not an active participant in the partnership management or business.

Rights of a Limited Partner

A limited partner has the same rights as a general partner to inspect and copy the partnership books and, when circumstances render his request just and reasonable, he is entitled to a full and accurate formal accounting of partnership affairs. He also has the right to seek dissolution of the partnership and winding up of its affairs by court decree.

A limited partner has the right to receive a share of partnership profits or other compensatory income, provided that after such payment is made the partnership assets are in excess of all liabilities of the partnership, except liabilities to limited partners on account of their contributions and to general partners. He also has the right to the return of his contribution to the partnership as provided by the Uniform Limited Partnership Act.

He may loan money to and transact other business with the partnership and, unless he is also a general partner, he may receive, with general creditors, and on account of resulting claims against the partnership, a pro rata share of the assets. However, no limited partner may, in respect to any such claim, receive or hold as collateral security any partnership property, nor receive from a general partner or from the partnership any payment, conveyance, or release from liability, if at that time the partnership assets are insufficient to discharge partnership liabilities to persons not claiming as general or limited partners.

It should be noted that a limited partner's interest in the partnership is personal property, and is assignable. The assignee of such an interest has the right to become a substituted limited partner if all the members of the partnership consent thereto, or if the assignor, having been previously empowered by the certificate of limited partnership, himself gives the assignee that right.

Rights and Liabilities of General Partner

A general partner in a limited partnership has all the rights and powers, and is subject to all the restrictions and liabilities of a partner in a general partnership, except that without the written consent or ratification of the specific act by all the limited partners, no general partner has the authority to:

1. Do any act in contravention of the certificate.

2. Do any act that would make it impossible to carry on the ordinary business of the partnership.

3. Confess a judgment against the partnership.

4. Possess partnership property, or assign his rights in specific partnership property, for other than a partnership purpose.

5. Admit a person as a general partner.

6. Admit a person as a limited partner, unless the right to do so is given in the certificate.

7. Continue the business with partnership property on the death, retirement, or insanity of a general partner, unless the right to do so is given in the certificate.

Checklist of Matters to Be Considered When Drafting a Limited Partnership Agreement

1. Name and place of residence of each member, general and limited partners being respectively designated.

2. Amount of cash, and description and agreed value of other property, contributed by each limited partner, and by each general partner.

3. Additional contributions, if any, agreed to be made by each limited partner, and the times at which, or events on the happening of which, they are to be made.

4. Time, if agreed on, when contribution of each limited partner is to be returned.

5. Share of profits, or other compensation by way of income, that each limited partner is to receive by reason of his contribution.

6. Right, if given, of limited partner to substitute assignee as contributor in his place, and terms and conditions of such substitution.

7. Right, if given, of partners to admit additional limited partners:

    a. With consent of all partners
    b. With consent of all general partners
    c. Other

8. Right, if given, of one or more limited partners to priority over other limited partners, as to contributions or as to compensation by way of income, and nature of such priority.

9. Right, if given, of limited partner to demand and receive property other than cash in return for his contribution.

10. Right, if given, of limited partner to vote on matters affecting basic structure of partnership, including election or removal of general partners, termination of partnership, amendment of partnership agreement, sale of all or substantially all partnership assets, and other matters of similar nature.

Limited Partnership Agreement - General Form

Agreement of limited partnership made _____, 19_____, between _____ of _____ _____[address], City of _____, County of _____, State of _____, herein referred to as general partner, and _____ _____ of _____[address], City of _____, County of _____, State of _____, and _____ of _____ _____[address], City of _____, County of _____, State of _____, both herein referred to as limited partners.

RECITALS

1. General and limited partners desire to enter into the business of _____ _____.

2. General partner desires to manage and operate the business.

3. Limited partners desire to invest in the business and limit their liabilities.

AGREEMENT

In consideration of the mutual covenants contained herein, the parties agree as follows:

1. General Provisions. The limited partnership is organized pursuant to the provisions of _____ *[cite statute]* of the State of _____, and the rights and liabilities of the general and limited partners shall be as provided therein, except as herein otherwise expressly stated.

2. Name of Partnership. The name of the partnership shall be _____, herein referred to as the partnership.

3. Business of Partnership. The purpose of the partnership is to engage in the business of _____, and in such other related business as may be agreed on by the partners.

4. Principal Place of Business. The principal place of business of the partnership shall be at _____ *[address]*, City of _____, County of _____, State of _____. The partnership shall also have other places of business as from time to time shall be determined by general partner.

5. Capital Contribution of General Partner. General partner shall contribute _____ dollars ($_____) to the original capital of the partnership. The contribution of general partner shall be made on or before _____, 19_____. If general partner does not make his entire contribution to the capital of the partnership on or before that date, this agreement shall be void. Any contributions to the capital of the partnership made at that time shall be returned to the partners who have made the contributions.

6. Capital Contributions of Limited Partners. The capital contributions of limited partners shall be as follows:

Name	Amount	Other Property	Agreed Value of Other Property
_____	$_____	_____	_____
_____	$_____	_____	_____

Receipt of the capital contribution from each limited partner as specified above is acknowledged by the partnership. No limited partner has agreed to contribute any additional cash or property as capital for use of the partnership.

7. Duties and Rights of Partners. General partner shall diligently and exclusively apply himself in and about the business of the partnership to the utmost of his skill and on a full-time basis.

General partner shall not engage directly or indirectly in any business in conflict with the business of the partnership at any time during the term hereof without obtaining the written approval of all other partners.

General partner shall be entitled to _____ days of vacation and _____ days of sick leave in each calendar year, commencing with the calendar year 19_____. If general partner uses sick leave or vacation days in a calendar year in excess of the number specified above, the effect on his capital interest and share of the profits and losses of the partnership for that year shall be determined by a majority vote of limited partners.

No limited partner shall have any right to be active in the conduct of the partnership's business, nor have power to bind the partnership in any contract, agreement, promise, or undertaking.

8. Salary of General Partner. General partner shall be entitled to a monthly salary of _____ dollars ($_____) for the services rendered by him. The salary shall commence on _____, 19_____, and be payable on the _____ day of each month thereafter. The salary shall be treated as an expense of the operation of the partnership business and shall be payable irrespective of whether or not the partnership shall operate at a profit. The payment of such salaries shall be an obligation of the partnership only to the extent that there are partnership assets available for them, and shall not be an obligation of the partners individually.

9. Limitations on Distribution of Profits. General partner shall have the right, except as hereinafter provided, to determine whether from time to time partnership profits shall be distributed in cash or shall be left in the business, in which event the capital account of all partners shall be increased.

In no event shall any profits be payable for a period of _____ months until _____ percent (_____%) of those profits have been deducted to accumulate a reserve fund of _____ dollars ($_____) over and above the normal monthly requirements of working capital. This accumulation is to enable the partnership to maintain a sound financial operation.

10. Profits and Losses for Limited Partners. Limited partners shall be entitled to receive a share of the annual net profits equivalent to their share in the capitalization of the partnership.

Limited partners shall each bear a share of the losses of the partnership equal to the share of profits to which each limited partner is entitled. The share of losses of each limited partner shall be charged against the limited partner's capital contribution.

Limited partners shall at no time become liable for any obligations or losses of the partnership beyond the amounts of their respective capital contributions.

11. Profits and Losses for General Partner. After provisions have been made for the shares of profits of limited partners, all remaining profits of the partnership shall be paid to general partner. After giving effect to the share of losses chargeable against the capital contributions of limited partners, the remaining partnership losses shall be borne by general partner.

12. Books of Accounts. There shall be maintained during the continuance of this partnership an accurate set of books of accounts of all transactions, assets, and liabilities of the partnership. The books shall be balanced and closed at the end of each year, and at any other time on reasonable request of the general partner. The books are to be kept at the principal place of business of the partnership and are to be open for inspection by any partner at all reasonable times. The profits and losses of the partnership and its books of accounts shall be maintained on a calendar year basis, unless otherwise determined by general partner.

13. Accounting. *Capital Accounts.* A capital account shall be maintained on the partnership books on behalf of each partner. Such account shall be credited with that partner's contributions to the capital of the partnership and shall be debited and credited in the manner prescribed herein.

Income Accounts. An income account shall be maintained on the partnership books on behalf of each partner. Such account shall be closed to the capital account of each partner at the close of each fiscal year.

As soon as practicable after the close of each fiscal year, and at such other times as the partners may decide, the income account of each partner shall be credited with that partner's distributive share of profits or debited with his share of losses.

Any losses to be debited to a partner's income account that exceed the credit balance of such account shall be debited to the partner's individual capital account. If, as a result of debiting a partner's individual capital account with the excess losses, his capital account is depleted, future profits of that partner shall be credited to his capital account until such depletion has been eliminated.

Drawing Accounts. A drawing account, to which withdrawals shall be debited, shall be maintained on the partnership books on behalf of each general partner. Withdrawals may be made subject to such limitations as the partners may from time to time adopt. The drawing account shall be closed to the income account at the close of each fiscal year.

14. Substitutions, Assignments and Admission of Additional Partners.

General partner shall not substitute a partner in his place, or sell or assign all or any part of his interest in the partnership business without the written consent of limited partners.

Additional limited partners may be admitted to this partnership on terms that may be agreed on in writing between general partner and the new limited partners. The terms so stipulated shall constitute an amendment to this partnership agreement.

No limited partner may substitute an assignee as a limited partner in his place; but the person or persons entitled by rule or by intestate laws, as the case may be, shall succeed to all the rights of limited partner as a substituted limited partner.

15. Termination of Interest of Limited Partner; Return of Capital Contribution. The interest of any limited partner may be terminated by (a) dissolution of the partnership for any reason as provided herein, (b) the agreement of all partners, or (c) the consent of the personal representative of a deceased limited partner and the partnership.

On the termination of the interest of a limited partner, there shall be payable to such limited partner, or to his estate, the value of his interest, as determined by the next paragraph, as of the date of termination. Such payment shall be made within _____ *[number]* _____ [months] of the termination of the limited partner's interest.

The value of a limited partner's interest in the partnership shall be computed by (1) adding the totals of (a) his capital account, (b) his income account, and (c) any other amounts owed to him by the partnership; and (2) subtracting from the sum of the above totals the sum of the totals of all amounts owed by him to the partnership. For the purposes of valuation, it is agreed that the good will of the partnership business, as well as other intangible items, shall not be valued.

16. Borrowing by Partner. In case of necessity as determined by a majority vote of all partners, a partner may borrow up to _____ dollars ($_____) from the partnership. Any such loan shall be repayable at _____ percent (_____%) per year, together with interest thereon at the rate of _____ percent (_____%) per year.

17. Term of Partnership and Dissolution. The partnership term commences _____, 19_____, and shall end on (a) the dissolution of the partnership by operation of law, (b) dissolution at any time designated by general partner, or (c) dissolution at the close of the month following the qualification and appointment of the personal representative of deceased general partner.

18. Payment for Interest of Deceased General Partner. In the event of the death of general partner there shall be paid out of the partnership's assets to decedent's personal representative for decedent's interest in the partnership, a sum computed by (1) adding the totals of (a) his capital account, (b) his income account and (c) any other amounts owed to him by the partnership, and (2) subtracting from the sum of the above totals the sum of the totals of (a) his drawing account and (b) any amount owed by him to the partnership.

19. Amendments. This agreement, except with respect to vested rights of partners, may be amended at any time by a majority vote as measured by the interest and the sharing of profits and losses.

20. Binding Effect of Agreement. This agreement shall be binding on the parties hereto and their respective heirs, executors, administrators, successors, and assigns.

    In witness whereof, the parties have executed this agreement at _____ _____ *[designate place of execution]* the day and year first above written.

_____

_____

[Signatures]

Certificate of Limited Partnership

Introduction

Partnership certificates and partnership agreements are not identical. Certificates are required to be filed at a designated state governmental office. The partnership agreement may be express or implied and clarifies the relations among the partners.

To form a limited partnership, two or more persons must execute a certificate of limited partnership. The certificate is intended to place creditors on notice of the facts concerning the capital of the partnership and the rules regarding additional contributions to and withdrawals from the partnership. It must also clearly delineate the time at which the persons become general and limited partners. The certificate must be amended upon the occurrence of any statutorily enumerated event.

Filing Requirement

The Uniform Limited Partnership Act requires that two or more persons desiring to form a limited partnership sign, acknowledge, and file in the office of the recorder of the county (or other designated state official) in which the partnership's principal place of business is situated a certificate, the contents of which are designated by statute. Only when the requirements as to the certificate are substantially complied with in good faith is a limited partnership formed.

If the partnership has places of business situated in, or holds title to real property in, different counties, it must cause either such recorded certificate or a copy of such recorded certificate, certified by the recorder in whose office it is recorded, to be recorded in the office of the recorder of each such different county. Recording the certificate in accordance with the statutory requirements creates the same conclusive presumptions in favor of any bona fide purchaser for value of partnership real property as are provided by the signing, acknowledgement, and verification of a statement of partnership.

Liability for False Statement

If the certificate of limited partnership, amendment, or certificate of cancellation contains a false statement, one who suffers loss by reliance on the statement may recover damages for the loss from the person who executed the statement if they knew it was false at the time it was executed, or if there were a general partner who knew or should have known that the statement was false.

Dissolution of the Partnership

The certificate of formation is required to state the period for which the partnership is to exist. Dissolution of the partnership under the Uniform Limited Partnership Act occurs on the retirement, death, or insanity of a general partner unless the business is continued by the remaining general partners under a right to do so stated in the certificate, or with the consent of all members.

Under the Revised Uniform Limited Partnership Act, a limited partnership is dissolved and its affairs must be wound up upon the happening of or at the time of events specified in the certificate of limited partnership, upon written consent of all partners, upon withdrawal of a general partner, unless there is at least one other general partner and the certificate permits business to be carried on, or upon entry of decree of judicial dissolution. The revised act further provides the general partners who have not wrongfully dissolved the partnership, or, if none, the limited partners, may wind up the partnership's affairs except as otherwise provided in the partnership agreement.

Checklist of Items Included in a Certificate of Limited Partnership

A. Mandatory items

1. Name of partnership.

2. Statement of character of the business.

3. Location of principal place of business.

4. Name and place of residence of each member, general and limited partners being respectively designated.

5. Term for which partnership is to exist.

6. Amount of cash, and description and agreed value of other property, contributed by each limited partner.

7. Additional contributions, if any, agreed to be made by each limited partner, and times at which or events on happening of which they shall be made.

8. Time, if agreed on, when contribution of each limited partner is to be returned.

9. Share of profits or other compensation by way of income that each limited partner is to receive by reason of his contribution.

B. Items that may or may not be mandatory

1. Statement of right of limited partner to substitute assignee as contributor in his place, and terms and conditions of such substitution.

2. Statement of right of partners to admit additional limited partners.

3. Statement of right of one or more limited partners to priority over other limited partners, as to contributions or as to compensation by way of income, and nature of such priority.

4. Statement of right of remaining general partner(s) to continue business on death, retirement, or insanity of a general partner.

5. Statement of right of limited partner to demand and receive property other than cash in return for his contribution.

6. Statement of right of limited partner to vote on certain partnership matters and vote required for election or removal of general partners or to cause other action to be effective as to partnership.

Certificate of Limited Partnership under Uniform Limited Partnership Act

CERTIFICATE OF LIMITED PARTNERSHIP
OF

_____*[name]*

We, the undersigned, desiring to form a limited partnership pursuant to the Uniform Limited Partnership Act as set forth in _____ *[cite statute]* of the State of _____, do hereby certify:

1. The name of the firm under which the partnership is to be conducted is _____.

2. The character of the business intended to be transacted by the partnership shall be as follows: _____.

3. The location of the principal place of business shall be at _____ _____ *[address]*, City of _____, County of _____, State of _____.

4. The name and place of residence of each general partner interested in the partnership are as follows:

Name	Place of Residence
_____	_____
_____	_____

The name and place of residence of each limited partner interested in the partnership are as follows:

Name	Place of Residence
_____	_____
_____	_____

5. The partnership shall exist for _____ *[specify period or* an indefinite period*]* commencing_____, 19_____.

6. The amount of cash and a description and the agreed value of the other property contributed by each limited partner are as follows:

Name	Cash Contributed	Property Contributed	Value of Other Property
_____	$_____	_____	_____
_____	$_____	_____	_____

7. The _____ *[additional contributions agreed to be made by each limited partner and the time at which or the events on the happening of which they shall be made are as follows: or* limited partners may make such additional contributions to the capital of the partnership as may from time to time be agreed by all the partners*]*.

8. The contribution of each limited partner shall be returned as follows: _____.

9. The share of the profits or other compensation by way of income that each limited partner shall receive by reason of his contribution is as follows: _____
_____ shall receive _____ [_____percent (_____%) of the profits of the partnership *or* _____ dollars ($_____) per year *or as the case may be]*. _____
_____*[Repeat the above clause as necessary for each limited partner.]*

10. The right of a limited partner to substitute an assignee as limited partner in his place, and the terms and conditions of the substitution, are as follows: _____
_____.

11. The right of the partners to admit additional limited partners is as follows: _____.

12. The right of one or more of the limited partners to priority over other limited partners, as to contributions or as to compensation by way of income, and the nature of such priority, are as follows: _____.

13. The right of the remaining general partner or partners to continue the business on the death, retirement, or incapacity of a general partner is as follows: _____.

14. The right of a limited partner to demand and receive property other than cash in return for his contribution is as follows: _____.

In witness whereof, the undersigned have executed this certificate this _____ day of _____, 19_____.

_____

[Signatures of General Partners]

_____

[Signatures of Limited Partners]

Certificate of Limited Partnership - Amendment

A certificate of limited partnership must, by statute, be amended if:

1. There is a change in the name of the partnership or in the amount or character of the contribution of any limited partner.

2. A person is substituted as a limited partner.

3. An additional limited partner is admitted.

4. A person is admitted as a general partner.

5. A general partner retires, dies, or becomes insane, and the business is continued.

6. There is a change in the character of the business of the partnership.

7. There is a false or erroneous statement in the certificate.

8. There is a change in the time as stated in the certificate for dissolution of the partnership or for the return of a contribution.

9. A time is fixed for the dissolution of the partnership, or the return of a contribution, no time having been specified in the certificate.

10. The members desire to make a change in any other statement in the certificate in order that it accurately represents the agreement between them.

11. There is a change in the right to vote on certain matters.

A writing amending a certificate must conform to the requirement of an original certificate so far as necessary to set forth clearly the change in the certificate, and it must be signed and acknowledged by all members of the partnership and, if the amendment adds a partner, by the person being added. The amendment becomes effective when it is filed for record as provided by statute.

Amendment to Certificate of Limited Partnership

_____ *[Name of limited partnership]*, a limited partnership existing under the laws of the State of _____, pursuant to the provisions of _____, *[cite statute]*, hereby amends its certificate of limited partnership now filed in the office of _____, *[designate official]*, as follows:

_____ *[When a new provision is to be added to the certificate, state:* The certificate of limited partnership now on file is hereby amended by the addition of a new provision thereto as follows: _____ _____ *(set out new provision in full).]*

_____ *[When a provision of the certificate is to be deleted, state:* The certificate of limited partnership now on file is hereby amended by the deletion therefrom of _____ *((identify portion to be deleted by paragraph), is hereby amended to read as follows:* _____ *(set out exactly portion to be deleted).]*

_____ *[When the language of a provision of the certificate is to be changed, state:* _____ *(identify provision to be changed, such as:* Paragraph _____ of the certificate), which now reads as follows: _____ *(set out exactly unamended provision),* is hereby amended to read as follows: _____ *(set out exactly provision as amended).]*

The foregoing amendment to the certificate of limited partnership now on file is hereby adopted by all of the members of the limited partnership, including, where appropriate, added, substituted, and assigning members, to be effective on the filing of this amendment for record in the office of _____*[designate official]*, and on the filing to become a provision of the partnership agreement and of the certificate of limited partnership.

In witness whereof, the undersigned have executed this certificate of amendment at _____ *[designate place of execution]* on _____, 19_____.

_____

_____

[Signatures]

Certificate of Limited Partnership - Cancellation

A certificate of limited partnership must be canceled when the partnership is dissolved or all limited partners cease to be such. A writing effecting cancellation of the certificate must be signed by all members of the partnership, and it must be filed for record in the appropriate office in order for cancellation to be effective.

Cancellation of Certificate of Limited Partnership

The undersigned, partners in the firm of _____ _____ [name], a limited partnership organized under the [Uniform Limited Partnership Act or Revised Uniform Limited Partnership Act] of the State of _____, hereby cancel, pursuant to the provisions of _____ _____ [cite statute], the _____ [original or amended] certificate of limited partnership executed by the undersigned, dated _____, 19_____, and now of record in the office of _____ _____, State of _____, for the reason that _____ [state condition requiring cancellation].

In witness whereof, the parties hereto have duly executed this document on _____, 19_____.

_____

_____

                                                            [Signatures]

Family Partnership 20

A family partnership is one of many types of partnership arrangements. It is generally similar in construction to any other partnership, formed for either commercial or non-commercial purposes, except the partners are all related by familial ties.

The family partnership is a technique frequently utilized as a means of shifting the income tax burden from parents to children or other members of the family. Typically, an interest in the business is given to a child or other relative, either by admitting the member of the family into an existing partnership or by creating a partnership as a result of a gift of part of an unincorporated business. A well-structured family partnership can shift future appreciation and income to the younger members while allowing the older members to retain significant controls.

A family limited partnership can also be an excellent asset protection device. A properly-structured family limited partnership can protect the business or other family assets of the prime wage-earner (husband or wife, in most cases.) As a general rule, a limited partnership may not be broken up or dissolved simply because one limited partner is sued. Under most limited partnership statutes, the assets of the partnership are protected from the individual creditors of a limited partner.

Definition of a Family

Under the Internal Revenue Service Code, the "family" of any individual shall include only his spouse, ancestors, and lineal descendants, and any trust for the primary benefit of such persons. ((Section 704(e)(3); Reg. §1.704-1(e)(3) (i)(a)).

The term "spouse" includes the husband or wife of the transferor. The term "ancestor" includes parents, grandparents, etc. of the transferor, but does not include in-laws, aunts, uncles, great-aunts or great-uncles. The term "lineal descendants" includes children, grand-children and great-grand-children, but does not include a son-in-law or daughter-in-law, niece, nephew, grand-niece, or grand-nephew.

Impact of Tax Reform on Family Partnership

Before we discuss various benefits of family partnerships, we should look at the way the tax reform acts of 1986 and 1987 have impacted the family partnerships.

The Tax Reform Act of 1986 has substantially eliminated the benefit of income shifting to children under age 14. For children under age 14, unearned income in excess of $1,000 generally will be taxed at the parents' top marginal rate. Although family partnerships have sometimes been attacked by IRS as being mere tax avoidance schemes that should not be recognized for tax purposes, if the rules for establishing and operating such partnerships are carefully followed, the IRS will recognize the validity of this income shifting device.

In the past the family partnership was also used as a method for "freezing" the value of a person's estate for federal estate tax purposes. This benefit was substantially eliminated by the Revenue Act of 1987, for property transfers after December 17, 1987.

Advantages of Family Partnership

Family partnerships have several advantages as a means of making gifts of large assets.

1. They are relatively simple, requiring a partnership agreement, a deed of gift, and a certificate of limited partnership in the case of limited family partnerships. Only one transfer of the property is required, since subsequent changes of the donor and donee interests require only an amendment to the partnership agreement and the certificate. Even on a gift of real estate, only a single transfer needs to be recorded, although if state law requires recording of a certificate of partnership, the operation becomes somewhat more complicated.

2. A family partnership can eliminate ancillary probates when used to make gifts of real estate located in a state in which the donor does not reside. Real estate must be probated in the state where it is located, regardless of the residence of the deceased owner; but most states treat a partnership interest as personal property for probate purposes, even if the partnership owns real estate.

It may take many years of annual gifts before a donor has given away all of a parcel of real estate, and any retained interest in real estate would continue to be subject to ancillary probate if the donor dies before completing the gifts. However, a gift of real property through a family partnership eliminates the need for an ancillary probate, even as to the donor's retained partnership interest.

3. A family partnership enables a donor to retain substantial control over the property being given away, until the entire transfer is completed. The donor can be designated managing partner of a general partnership, or sole general partner of a limited partnership. In either case, the donor retains most or all of the managerial controls over the property being given away, until all of it has been transferred to the donee/partners.

4. A partnership is not a taxable entity for income tax purposes, so making gifts through a family partnership entirely avoids the problem of the double taxation of net income of an ordinary (non-S) family corporation.

Disadvantages of Family Partnership

1. Using family partnerships as a means of making large gifts has relatively few disadvantages. One is that the donor's annual gifts of partnership interests are valued on the date of each individual gift. The donor cannot usually freeze the gift tax value of the partnership asset at the time it is given to the partnership. Thus, if the underlying asset continues to increase in value, the donor is credited with the appreciation on the retained interest, making even more gifts necessary to give away the entire interest.

This same problem exists in outright gifts of partial interests and in gifts of stock in a family corporation, but it does not exist with an installment gift. Therefore, tax-free gifts of large assets through a family partnership may take somewhat longer to complete than tax-free gifts through an installment gift.

2. Family partnerships are subject to several special tests that must be met for interests created by gift to be treated as partnership interests for income tax purposes. Specifically, capital must be a material income-producing factor for the partnership, and the donee must be the real owner of an interest in that capital. Unless these tests are met, partnership income will be taxed solely to the donor and others who invested their own capital or services, depriving the donor of all income-shifting advantages otherwise sought from the family partnership.

Example: Mother created a family partnership for her five children. She transferred equipment to the partnership, which leased it to a corporation controlled by Mother. Mother retained the actual control over this partnership assets, in violation of the family partnership rules. Thus, the children were not treated as the real partners and Mother was taxed personally on all of partnership income. Additionally, because Mother retained the actual control over the partnership assets and the children were not real partners, Mother still owns all of the partnership assets for estate tax purposes.

Where Can You Use Family Partnership?

A family partnership can be used advantageously in at least three situations.

1. The tool of family partnership can be used when it is desired to shift the income tax burden from the parent who is in a high income tax bracket to a child or other relative who is in a lower income tax bracket, this providing for intra-family income splitting and resultant tax saving.

However, after 1986, under the Tax Reform Act of 1986, the "net unearned income" (generally unearned income in excess of $1,000) of a child under the age of 14 is taxed at his parents' top tax rate. This applies to unearned income from any source including gifts made before 1987. As a result, income shifting to children under age 14 will be of limited benefit.

Keep in mind, however, that the above limitation applies to children under age 14, leaving open the possibility of tax planning, where there are minors over 14 in the family. Even with children under 14, you can shift assets that produce income up to $1,000 and be taxed at no more than 15%. For instance, transfer of an asset worth $12,500 generating income at 8% will still allow you to reap the benefits of income splitting.

2. A family partnership can also be utilized where it is desired to conduct a family business in a form other than the corporate form. For example, operating a business in a corporate form may cause tax problems, which otherwise would not be present if the business were to be conducted in a partnership form. Specifically, partnerships are not subject to personal holding company rules, accumulated earnings restrictions and unreasonable compensation problems.

A family limited partnership allows the transferor (parent, in most instances) to run the family business and preserve control over it, whereas in a corporation control is centralized in a board of directors and voting power generally shifts with any transfer of stock.

3. A family partnership is an excellent estate planning tool; it allows you to transfer ownership interest to the younger generation without loss of control. It may also help you lower the taxes. A partnership agreement may have restrictions on the transfer, assignment or liquidation of partnership interest, and this may allow you to claim a substantial discount in the value of the estate transferred.

4. Of course, a family limited partnership can be used with proper planning to insulate the family wealth from the attacks of creditors. Courts are likely to give closer scrutiny to family arrangements than other non-family limited partnerships to make sure that the transactions meet the standards of fairness and arms-length conduct, but in all other respects the rules applicable are no different than those applied to other partnerships.

Family Partnership - Illustrations

Here are two applications of family partnerships in two different situations.

Illustration: A businessman, sole proprietor of an unincorporated manufacturing and distribution concern, wishes to use family partnership to split income among his family and realize tax savings. In his business, both personal services and capital are material income-producing factors. He's married and has two adult children, over the age of 14. He files a joint return with his wife; his wife and his children do not have any income of their own.

The net income from the business for last year was approximately $200,000. The businessman pays himself a salary of $52,000 annually. Since the business is run as a sole proprietorship, the businessman is taxed on the net profit of the business, which in this case is $200,000.

The businessman can minimize his income tax burden by splitting the income with his children. He would form a partnership with his children and make a gift of 30% of his business to his children, each child receiving a 15% interest. (If his children were minor, their interest could be placed in trust.)

The businessman would continue to draw a salary of $52,000 a year for the services rendered. The balance of the partnership income would be split 70% to the father and 15% to each of the two children.

Thus, the father would receive $103,600 (in addition to his salary) and each of the two children would receive $22,200. Father would be taxed on $52,000 of salary and $103,600 of partnership income. Each of the two children would be taxed on $22,200 of partnership profit. By creating a family partnership and putting the business in the partnership in this manner, the businessman has transferred $44,400 of business income which was previously taxed at father's higher income tax bracket to his children who would be taxed at their lower tax rate.

There's also an estate planning angle to this arrangement. If the business continues to appreciate in value, 30% of that appreciation may be shifted out of father's estate, thereby reducing future estate taxes.

Illustration: John and Mary Smith own several parcels of real property, mainly apartment buildings, worth several million dollars. They decide to form a family partnership between themselves and their two children. The partnership would allow them to transfer a significant portion of their estate to their children, especially if the real properties continue to appreciate in value during their lifetime.

If the partnership contains language similar to a recent Tax Court case, which limits the rights of a partner to liquidate the partnership after his death, a substantial discount may be available. In that case, the court reasoned that the value of a partnership interest is reduced where you must find someone to buy an interest in the partnership with multiple properties. *Estate of Watts v. Comm'r.*, 51 TCM (CCH) 60 (1985). See also *Estate of Daniel J. Harrison, Jr. v. Comm'r.*, 52 TCM 1306 (1987).

Rules Applicable to Family Partnerships

Family partnerships are subject to all the partnership rules applicable to other partnerships. Thus, even though a partnership consists only of the members of a single family, it must satisfy the general definition of a partnership.

If two or more persons agree to carry on a trade or business as a partnership and each contributes his own services to the enterprise or his own capital, where capital is a material income-producing factor, there is little question that a valid partnership exists. And this is true even though some or all of the partners belong to the same family.

The validity of family partnerships has been questioned chiefly where a child, or other related individual, who contributes little or no services and whose interest in the enterprise was acquired by gift from the related active partner, is claimed as a partner. In this situation, if the business is a personal service business in which capital is not a material income-producing factor, IRS and the courts will not recognize the partnership for tax purposes.

On the other hand, where capital is a material income-producing factor of the enterprise, recognition will be given to a partner who receives his interest by gift if certain requirements of the Code are satisfied.

The Supreme Court stated that a family partnership can exist even if a wife, child, etc., did not contribute vital services (*Culbertson*, 337 U.S. 733 (1949)). The basic test is whether the "partners really and truly intended to join together and share in the profits and losses for both."

Code Section 704(e) confirms a taxpayer's right to transfer an interest in a partnership to a member of his family, whether by gift or by purchase. If the partnership is of the personal service type, the Code requires the donee-partner to have an active role in the business. Thus, a professional firm generally cannot use the limited partnership as an effective estate planning tool, at least if the donee is a minor.

But, if capital is a material income-producing factor, under §704(e)(i) income may be attributable to a minor partner even though he may not participate actively in the business. In such cases, tax benefits are limited to the portion of partnership income attributable to the capital interest transferred, and the partnership income must be reduced by a reasonable allowance for services rendered to the partnership by the donor.

Note : A husband and wife, or parents and children may conduct an enterprise, such as a farm, as a partnership. To be recognized as such, the legal relationship of a partnership must be established; merely doing the chores, helping with the harvest, or keeping house and cooking for the family and employees does not establish a partnership.

Donee's Interest

The limited partnership must be organized and conducted under the applicable state limited partnership law. It isn't necessary for the donee of a limited partnership interest to render services or participate in management. A donee's interest as a limited partner will have to meet the same tests of real ownership which apply to other partnerships.

If the limited partner's right to transfer or liquidate his interest is subject to substantial restrictions, or if the general partner retains any other control which substantially limits any of the rights which would ordinarily be exercisable by an unrelated limited partner in normal business relationships, the restrictions on the right to transfer or liquidate may be considered to show a lack of reality to the donee's ownership.

Examples of substantial restrictions would be where the interest of the limited partner is not assignable in a real sense, or where the interest may be required to be left in the business for a long term of years.

We'll examine in greater detail the legal requirements of a valid family partnership later in this chapter.

Using Family Partnerships in Estate Planning

A family partnership can be an effective estate planning tool. It allows you to transfer a large asset from the older members of the family to the younger members while retaining significant controls.

General or Limited Partnership

A family partnership may either be a general or limited partnership. In a general partnership, all partners have unlimited liability for partnership debts and all are legally entitled to participate in the management of the partnership business. In a limited partnership, only the general partner is fully liable for partnership recourse debts and may participate in the partnership business. The limited partners are liable on partnership debts, only to the extent of their investment and may not participate in the partnership business.

Whether you should use a general partnership or limited partnership depends on your peculiar circumstances. A family limited partnership would be more attractive to a donor who does not want to surrender or share the managerial control over the partnership assets.

Partnership Interest Transferred in Piecemeal Fashion

In a typical estate planning move, the donor would create a family partnership in which the donor and other members of the family would be partners and the donor would transfer a property to the partnership. The objective of such a move would be to divide a large asset into smaller parts for tax-free transfer to the other members of the family.

The partners who receive their interest without contributing there own capital or services automatically receive a proportionate share of any property transferred to the partnership. Additional gifts may be made merely by amending the partnership agreement to increase the donee/partner's relative interest.

Illustration: In 1987, Mother wishes to give Daughter and Son interests in an office building worth $700,000. Mother creates a general partnership to which she transfers the office building. The partnership agreement makes Mother a 11.5 percent partner and Son and Daughter each 44.25 percent partners. Thus, Mother gives away 88.5 percent of the building ($619,500), one-half to each of her children. This gift is sheltered from tax by Mother's unified credit and annual exclusions.

In 1988, the property increases in value by 6 percent and is worth $742,000. Mother amends the partnership agreement to increase Son and Daughter's interests from 44.25 percent each ($328,335) to 45.5 percent each ($337,610), decreasing her own interest from 11.5 percent ($85,330) to 9 percent ($66,780).

This procedure is followed annually until Mother has given away her entire interest in the partnership. Each gift is kept within Mother's annual exclusion and unified credit, but the total time required to transfer the property is greater than a single outright gift, since appreciation during the transfer period also had to be given away.

Partnership Compared with Corporation

The use of a family partnership to divide a large asset into smaller units for annual tax-free gifts is similar to the use of a family corporation. In either case (corporation or partnership) a separate legal entity is created and the property transferred to it. The interest in the entity in the form of stock or partnership interest is given away to designated beneficiaries over a number of years.

Also, like in an S corporation, the character of items of income, deduction, gain and loss recognized at the partnership level is preserved and then passed to the partners directly for tax purposes.

However, a family partnership offers far more flexibility in estate planning than a regular C or S corporation:

1. The partners in their partnership agreement can define their respective rights and interests with far greater precision.

2. Contributed property can be withdrawn from a partnership with far fewer tax problems than with a corporation.

3. The limitations on the number and type of stockholders that restricts the use of S corporations do not apply to family partnerships.

Helpful Hints in Forming a Family Partnership

1. There should be a written formal partnership agreement, whether general or limited, that spells out the rights and obligations of the partners.

2. A meticulous record of all agreements, filings, and transactions should be kept.

3. The donor (or managing partner) should be paid a reasonable compensation.

4. Transfers to the donee partner should not be used to discharge parental support obligations, such as medical care, education, etc.

5. If a minor is involved and his interest his held in trust, the trustee should be an independent trustee and not subject to the direct or indirect control of the donor.

6. Assets should actually be transferred to the partnership and all official records should reflect partnership as the true owner of the assets.

Dangers of Family Limited Partnership

Here, at a glance, are some of the dangers of the family limited partnership that may subject it to an attack by the IRS.

What can you do to make it less vulnerable to such an attack?

✓ Avoid making the interest of limited partners assignable.

✓ Avoid forcing investments by limited partners to be left in the business for a long period of time subject only to the right of the limited partner to bring about dissolution of the partnership and an accounting of his interest by court decree, upon proof of wrongdoing or unfitness of the general partners, or special circumstances.

✓ Avoid giving the general partners total discretion as to distributions of income to limited partners.

✓ Where a trust is a limited partner, be sure that the trustee's right to receive his distributive share of the income isn't restricted, either by the partnership agreement or the conduct of the partnership affairs. His right to periodic drawings cannot be subject to the controlled dictates of the grantor in his capacity as a general partner.

✓ There are special problems involved in setting up a family limited partnership. A limited partner may not engage in the management of the business without subjecting himself to liability as a general partner. Therefore, it is important that a limited partner does not participate in the management of the business nor contribute services to the business.

✓ In some cases, retention of so much control in the hands of a general partner may make the interest of a limited partner seem more nominal than real. This would particularly be the case if the general partner has sole discretion as to distribution of income to the limited partners.

✓ In a typical family limited partnership, the donor (husband in most cases) will make himself a general partner and his children or wife, limited partners; he will retain all the substantial incidents of ownership. There is a danger that the Treasury may treat such a group as an association and tax it as a corporation (REG. §301.7701-3(b) (1)).

✓ IRS will closely scrutinize any attempts to split family income through the use of a limited partnership. For example, when a limited partner buys in or gets his interest in return for services, IRS may hold that the intent to form a partnership is lacking. Where a limited partner receives his interest through a gift, IRS may claim that a completed gift was never made.

Basic Requirements for a Bona Fide Family Partnership

A partnership interest acquired by gift is recognized by the IRS for income tax purposes only if capital is a material income-producing factor in the partnership business and the donee is the real owner of an interest in partnership capital.

For this purpose, a donee is deemed to have acquired a partnership interest by gift if it is actually given to the donee, if it is given to the donee through another person or entity (a gift to a third person, who gives it to the donee), or if the donee buys it from a parent, ancestor, lineal descendant, or a trust for the benefit of any such person. With careful planning, a family partnership can be structured that would avoid these problems.

Capital Must Be a Material Income-Producing Factor

Capital must be a material income-producing factor for a family partnership. Capital is a material income-producing factor if, considering all of the relevant facts and circumstances:

(1) "a substantial portion of the gross income of the business is attributable to the employment of capital in the business conducted by the partnership," and

(2) "fees, commissions, or other compensation for personal services" are not the principal source of partnership income.

Thus, a family partnership will not be recognized for income tax purposes if its income stems from the performance of services; if its income is from both capital and services, the partnership must reasonably compensate the partners for their personal services to the partnership.

In general, capital is not a material income-producing factor where the income of the business consists primarily of fees, commissions, or other compensation for personal services performed by members or employees of the partnership. For example, in law firms, accounting firms, advertising agencies, and sales organizations operating on the commission basis, capital is not considered a material income-producing factor.

Capital is ordinarily a material income-producing factor, if the operation of the business requires substantial inventories or a substantial investment in plant, machinery or other equipment. Thus, for example, capital would be a material income-producing factor for companies that take title to the property they sell, manufacturing companies, and transportation businesses.

The determination as to whether capital is a material income-producing factor is made by reference to all the facts of each case. The regulations do not indicate the facts to be considered. However, it appears that it would be appropriate to measure the interest that would be earned on the capital and then to compare the deemed interest amount to the gross income of the partnership.

Case: In one Tax Court case, a limited partnership was created with $5,550 of contributed capital. Five thousand dollars came from five trusts set up through effort of a controlling shareholder of the corporation that became the general partner (and which contributed $550.)

Large sums were borrowed by the partnership on the personal guarantee of the controlling shareholder of the general partner and by the general partner. However, 90% of the profits were allocated to the five trusts (based on the ratio of original contributed capital.)

The majority of the Tax Court found that capital was not a material income-producing factor in this partnership and thus did not recognize the five limited partners, causing all of the income to be allocated to the taxpayer in this case (the corporation that was the general partner.) *(Carriage Square, Inc., 69 TC 119 (1977))*

Ordinarily, capital is a material income-producing factor in family partnerships that are used to make tax-free gifts of a large asset. The gift asset typically constitutes the capital that is a material factor in producing the partnership's income, although the partnership must still be careful to compensate the partners adequately for services rendered in making the capital productive.

Illustration I: Father gives an office building to a partnership in which Son and Daughter are partners. The office building is the partnership's sole asset and all of its income is from rents. Capital is clearly a material income-producing factor to the partnership.

Illustration II: The facts are the same as in Illustration I, except that Father also is the manager of the office building. He works for four or five hours a day at the building, keeping the machinery in repair, negotiating leases, and generally managing the property. Son and Daughter will not be recognized as partners with respect to the partnership rental income unless Father is adequately compensated for his special services to the partnership.

In the following types of businesses, courts have determined whether capital is a material income-producing factor for the reasons stated:

. . . Practice of medicine. The Tax Court approved a husband-wife family partnership involving the practice of medicine which was set up to use a fiscal year where the doctor and his wife bought a medical practice with borrowed money. The notes were signed by both and guaranteed by doctor friends of theirs. The wife worked with her husband as his secretary and office manager. A partnership was orally entered into between the doctor and his wife providing for a 75-25 division of profits.

While a medical practice would normally be considered a personal service business in which capital is not a material income-producing factor, the X-ray equipment and supplies were necessary to perform this particular service. Capital was therefore a material income-producing factor.

. . . Engineering and technical services partnership was held to require capital as a material income-producing factor where the firm had to carry large accounts receivable.

. . . CPA practice. A partnership, consisting of trusts set up by a CPA for his minor children and employing accountants and other personnel formerly employed by the CPA as an individual practitioner, is not one in which capital is a material income-producing factor. The Second Circuit recognized a family partnership involving CPAs and their wives where the wives contributed capital.

. . . Sales partnership. The daughter of the dominant partner of a sales partnership was not recognized as a valid partner despite her contribution of $5,000 in capital and assumption of liability for partnership debts. The court found that capital was not a material income-producing factor since the firm had functioned for 15 years on nominal capital of $500. There was no showing that the daughter's investment affected operations. This was basically a personal services partnership without capital investment for inventories or fixtures.

But in another sales partnership, capital was a material income-producing factor because the partnership granted credit to customers, had substantial operating expenses, in many cases paid commissions to salesmen before customers' payments were received, and for some taxable years carried inventories.

. . . Ranching. While the partners contributed valuable services, the quality of the land, the efficiency of the machinery, and the development of the land were critical to success. Therefore, capital was a material factor.

. . . Farming. IRS conceded that capital was a material income-producing factor where a farm's income principally was derived from rents paid with crop shares. In addition, water from irrigation wells was furnished to neighboring farmers for a share of their crops. Finally, some income was derived from the sale of calves.

Donee Must Be the Real Owner of an Interest in Partnership Capital

An interest acquired by gift is recognized for income tax purposes only if the donee is the real owner of an interest in the partnership capital. This requirement should not present a problem for family partnerships used as vehicles for making tax-free gifts of large assets, since the donor wants to remove part of the partnership capital from his or her estate to that of the donee. However, this requirement makes a family partnership unfeasible if the donor wants to shift income to a donee without giving the donee a genuine interest in the partnership, or if the donor insists on retaining excessive personal control over the donee's partnership interests.

Donee's Interest Must Be in Partnership Capital

Generally, a donee owns an interest in the partnership capital if the donee will receive a portion of the partnership assets upon withdrawal from or liquidation of the partnership. Thus, a donee's interest in partnership profits and losses alone will not be respected for income tax purposes.

Illustration: Father creates a partnership and conveys an office building to it. Son and Daughter are made partners, but neither contributes any money or property to the partnership. Under the partnership agreement, Son and Daughter will receive a share of the net partnership income annually. However, when the partnership is terminated or when it sells its assets, all of the proceeds will go to Father. Under the family partnership rules, Son and Daughter lack an interest in partnership capital, since they will not share in the capital features of the partnership.

Gift Must Be Legally Effective

The donee will not be viewed as the real owner of a partnership interest unless the gift is legally effective to vest complete dominion over the interest in the donee. If a minor donee cannot hold title personally, it must be held through a Uniform Gifts to Minors Act custodianship or a trust. Also, it is important that any documents required to transfer property to the partnership or to delineate the donee's interest in the partnership, such as a certificate of partnership, be properly executed and recorded, according to state law requirements.

Illustration: If a son is given 20% of the capital, while the father retains 80%, a provision in the partnership agreement providing for an equal split after allowances for services will not be recognized. The son will be taxed on 20% of the profits, the father, on 80%.

Powers the Donor Should Not Retain

The validity of a family partnership is dependent upon the partners "owning" a capital interest. The Code does not spell out what this means. However, the regulations state that the transferee of a partnership interest must be the "real owner" of the capital interest and have dominion and control over that interest.

The regulations spell out four retained controls (i.e., powers retained by a donor of a family partnership interest) which are of particular significance in showing that a donee lacks true ownership of his interest. These controls include:

1. Retaining control of the distribution of income or restricting the amount of such distributions.

2. Limiting the right of a donee partnership to sell or liquidate his interest in his discretion and without financial detriment.

3. Retaining control of assets essential to the partnership business.

4. Retaining management powers inconsistent with normal relationships among partners.

However, retention of control of the business management or of the voting control of the partnership in a manner that is common in ordinary business relationships will not of itself invalidate the partnership if the donee is free to liquidate his or her interest in the partnership at his discretion and without financial detriment. In addition, it is important that the donee have sufficient maturity and understanding so as to be capable of exercising that discretion.

Illustration: Mother creates a partnership with Son and Daughter, both of whom are minors. Mother conveys a shopping center to the partnership. Because Son and Daughter are minors, Mother transfers their interests to a trust of which she is the sole trustee. As trustee, Mother holds broad managerial powers, exercisable in her sole and absolute discretion. These broad powers, although held as a trustee, may prevent recognition of Son and Daughter as genuine partners for tax purposes.

Illustration: Father creates a general partnership with Son and Daughter, both of whom are adults. Under the agreement, Father is the "Managing General Partner," but in that capacity he can deal with the partnership assets virtually without limitation or restriction. Son and Daughter's combined interests in the partnership are not sufficient to oust Father, even if they wanted to do so. Father's total control over the partnership may cause Son and Daughter not to be recognized as partners for tax purposes.

Illustration: Father and Mother create a family partnership in which Son and Daughter receive interests as gifts. One provision in the partnership agreement says that Son or Daughter (but not Father or Mother) may require the partnership to redeem their interest at any time, if the partnership fails for two consecutive taxable years to make a cash distribution in a year in which the partnership has at least $50,000 in taxable income. The agreement says that an independent appraiser will value the interest being redeemed, and that the partnership and the partners agree to abide by that appraisal. This provision gives special credibility to Son's and Daughter's ownership of their partnership interest, since they can easily realize on its value under certain situations.

Powers the Donee Should Have

1. Participation in Management of Partnership Business

The test of real ownership of a general partnership interest by a donee is his or her participation in the management of the partnership business.

Illustration: Father creates a partnership with Son. Father conveys a rental house to the partnership. Father and Son are both general partners, according to their agreement. However, without consulting Son, Father negotiates all leases, decides on the rental rate, arranges for repairs, and even lists the house for sale. The IRS will probably not consider Son a valid partner for income tax purposes.

2. Actual Income Distributions

According to the regulations, the actual distribution to the donee of all or a major share of debt partnership income is "substantial evidence of reality of the donee's interest, provided the donor has not retained controls inconsistent with" the donee's real ownership.

3. Recognition of the Donee in the Conduct of the Partnership Business

The donee should act as the real owner of a partnership interest in form as well as substance.

Acquisition of Partnership Interest Must Be in Bona Fide Transaction

A donee or purchaser will not be recognized as a partner unless the interest is acquired in a bona fide transaction, not a mere sham for tax avoidance or evasion purposes, and the donee is the real owner of the interest.

The following illustrations will give you some guidance as to whether a real partnership was formed.

A partnership was found to exist in the following case:

. . . Taxpayer promised his brother and sister that he would make it up to them for not contributing his share of support for their widowed mother by giving each of them a 10% interest in the net profits of his real estate ventures. Although there was no formal written partnership agreement, taxpayer wrote numerous letters to them asking for their advice and referring to their 10% interests. Also, when taxpayer sold a parcel of land for use as a shopping center, he directed the purchaser to give his brother and sister 10% of the down payment each and 10% each of the proceeds of promissory notes given in payment of the balance of the purchase price.

No partnership was found to exist in the following cases:

. . . A father furnished the necessary capital to his daughter and son-in-law to go into the used car business. He never entered into a partnership agreement with them or showed himself as a partner on his tax returns. The father had merely made a gift to his daughter and her husband to help set them up in business.

. . . No accounting of business profits was ever made to the wife by her husband; they never filed a partnership tax return or signed any document or entered into any agreement with anyone in which the wife was represented as being a partner; and the wife had no control over the income that the husband received. At most, the wife permitted some of the husband's business enterprises to be conducted on property in which she had an interest as joint owner, and she performed some services that assisted him in the business, but these services were such as any devoted wife might perform for her husband.

. . . A partnership agreement had been signed and a bank account maintained. Property was allegedly contributed to the partnership for development, but ownership of the office building constructed on the property was taken by two brothers individually after they obtained, in their individual capacities, a mortgage loan. From this, the Tax Court concluded that the property was never contributed to the partnership. Without use of or title to the property there was no showing of intent to have the partnership operate as a viable partnership.

... Taxpayer owned a construction business and formed a partnership of his five children, age 7 to 20, to own equipment and lease it to the construction business. Taxpayer determined what equipment to acquire and what rental would be charged. Taxpayer sometimes acquired equipment for the partnership without consulting the partners (his children). Taxpayer, who wasn't a partner, signed partnership checks (from '72 to '75, he was the only one authorized to do so) and his secretary kept the partnership's check ledger. Taxpayer's total control led the court to deny partnership status.

Partnership Formalities Must Be Met

The regs place heavy emphasis on whether the donee is actually treated as a partner in the operation of business. Unless he is held out publicly as a partner in the conduct of the business, in relations with customers or with creditors and other sources of financing, it will be difficult to obtain recognition. Other factors considered significant in this connection are:

(a) Compliance with local partnership, fictitious names, and business registration statutes;

(b) Control of business bank accounts;

(c) Recognition of the donee's rights in distributions of partnership property and profits;

(d) Recognition of the donee's interest in insurance policies, leases, and other business contracts and in litigation affecting business;

(e) The existence of written agreements, records, or memoranda, contemporaneous with the taxable year or years concerned, establishing the nature of the partnership agreement and the rights and liabilities of the respective partners;

(f) Filing of partnership tax returns as required by law;

But while lack of compliance with all the formalities may cause a nonrecognition of the partner's interest, a faithful compliance with all formalities doesn't guarantee recognition if the donor has retained substantial ownership of the interest transferred.

Minor Children as Partners

Minor children are generally not recognized as partners. However, they may be recognized as partners in two specific circumstances:

---

1. When there is another person who controls the property for the minor. Control over the property of a minor child can be exercised by another person, such as a guardian acting as fiduciary for the sole benefit of the child, if the fiduciary's conduct is subject to judicial supervision.

It is almost always a bad idea for a minor to be given a partnership interest outright. A minor who owns such an interest outright will be recognized as the real owner of the interest for tax purposes only if it is shown that the minor has "sufficient maturity and experience to be treated by disinterested persons as competent to enter business dealings and otherwise conduct his affairs on a basis of equality with adult persons, notwithstanding legal disabilities of the minor under State law." Thus, as a practical matter, only in the most extraordinary situations should a minor serve as a partner without a fiduciary.

---

2. When the minor has sufficient experience and maturity. If a minor child is shown to be competent to manage his own property and participate in the partnership activities in accordance with his interest in the partnership, the minor child can be recognized as a partner.

An independent or unrelated trustee of an irrevocable trust who receives actual income distributions may hold a donee's interest in a family partnership on behalf of a donee. The IRS will look at the trustee rather than the donee to see whether trustee is the real owner of an interest of a capital of a partnership in which capital is a material income-producing factor.

Where a child is a purported partner, the courts will carefully scrutinize such transactions, determine the bona fides thereof, and determine whether the transaction was merely a sham for tax purposes, or whether the donor had in fact relinquished dominion and control over the purported gifts.

A district court in the Ninth Circuit sustained a family partnership despite the inclusion of two minor children who had no business experience where there was absolute and unlimited vesting of interests in the partnership in each of the donee children and the donor did not exercise any control over those interests or the income therefrom. The court was satisfied that the partnership was bona fide and that the donor's impelling motive was to give the children business experience and not tax avoidance.

On the other hand, children were not recognized as partners where the oldest was 3 1/2 at the time of the transfer and no trustee was appointed for them. A similar result was reached where there was no binding agreement transferring any interest and the father maintained complete control, supervision and dominion of all the activities of the business.

Under the Tax Reform Act of 1986, very little tax advantage can be obtained by making a child a member of a family partnership unless he or she will reach the age of 14 before the end of the taxable year. If the child is younger than this, virtually all of his or her unearned income (essentially, any income that is not compensation for personal services) will be taxed at the parents' top rate.

Trust as Partner

A trustee can qualify as either a general or a limited partner in a family partnership. If the trustee is unrelated to and independent of the grantor, he will be treated as a partner if he participates as a partner and receives income distributions, unless the grantor of the trust retains controls inconsistent with the trustee's ownership of a partnership interest.

If the trustee is either the grantor or a person subject to his control, the partnership may still be valid. But there will be a closer scrutiny of both the trust instrument and the partnership agreement to determine whether the trustee is acting in a fiduciary capacity. He must actively represent the interest of the beneficiary and not subordinate them to the interests of the grantor.

In addition, it is important that: (1) the trust is recognized as a partner in business dealings with customers and creditors; and (2) any part of the trust's share of income that exceeds the reasonable needs of the business is distributed to the trust annually and either paid to the beneficiaries or reinvested solely for their benefit.

Trusts will not be treated as valid family partners where the facts indicate that the trust arrangement is a sham.

In the following cases trusts were recognized as partners in family partnerships:

... Ceramic ware business. The managing partner created the trusts for minor children with gifts of interests in the capital of the partnership, naming an attorney and the children's mother and uncle as trustees. The uncle, who was the trusts' chief representative in partnership affairs, was not subservient to the managing partner and sometimes prevailed over him in disagreements. The trusts were not used to support the children and their investments weren't limited to the partnership. The trusts were real owners of partnership interests.

...Residential building business. Mr. Peterson formed two trusts for his two infant daughters, with his wife as trustee. He contributed $10,000 to each trust. The same day each trust contributed its $10,000 for a limited partnership interest in his business. Gift tax returns were filed and all necessary formalities were carried out.

The court held that the trusts were valid partners because the transfers were real and bona fide and not a mere pretense or sham. Where there is a valid transfer of ownership, recognition is required regardless of the donor's motive in creating the partnership.

...Wholesale shoe distributing company. Mr. Smith and his wife each created a trust for one of their minor children, making the other spouse trustee. They put $30,000 in bonds in each trust. On the same day, the trusts used these assets to buy a 15% interest in the existing partnership of Mr. and Mrs. Smith. All the necessary formalities were carried out. The trusts were valid partners and their share of the firm's income was taxable to them, not to Mr. and Mrs. Smith.

Tax Implications of Family Partnership

1. A reasonable allocation of partnership income must be made to the donor partner in recognition of his other services to the partnership.

Where the interests of family members are acquired by gift and/or intra-family sale, a mandatory allocation of the partnership profits in proportion to capital contributed after due allowance has been made for the compensation for services of the donor general partners must be made.

For example, if father and son are each 50% partners in a family partnership whose net income for the year is $100,000 and reasonable services for the donor father would be $20,000, the remaining $80,000 would be taxed $40,000 each to the son and the father. This should be in addition to the $20,000 taxed to the father as compensation for services rendered.

2. The partnership itself does not pay federal income taxes. However, a partnership return must be filed. Each partner pays taxes individually based upon his or her share of partnership income.

3. Generally, no gain or loss will be realized when property is transferred to the family partnership. The basis of the partnership in the contributed property is the same basis the property had in the hands of the contributing partners.

4. Gifts of a partnership interest are subject to gift tax and will likely raise questions regarding the value of the transferred interest similar to those raised by gifts of stock in closely held corporations. The regulations state that the same principles of valuation should apply. The fair market value at the date of the gift is the value for gift tax purposes.

5. A partnership interest owned by a decedent at his or her death is valued in his or her estate at the fair market value at the date of death or the alternate valuation date.

To the extent a partnership interest was given away by a donor, the appreciation from the date of the gift should not be includible in the donor's estate.

6. If at the time of formation of the partnership the value of a child's partnership interest exceeds the child's contribution to the partnership or amounts paid by the child for the partnership interest, there will be a gift from parent to child subject to the gift tax.

7. To avoid inclusion of a partnership interest in the older family member/donor's estate, the IRS regulations require that the decedent may not retain either the enjoyment of or the right of the income from the property or the power to designate who would receive the right to the income. If the donor retains control over the family partnership property and all incomes from the property, any transferred income in the partnership will be included in the gross estate of the donor under §2036.

8. For gift tax purposes a taxable gift is considered to have been made by the amount by which the value of property contributed by an older member to the partnership exceeds the older member's capital account.

Family Limited Partnership Form

21

The following is a general form for forming a family limited partnership with parents as general partners and minor children represented by trustees as limited partners. Of course, you should seek the services of a competent professional to help you form such a partnership.

Certificate and Agreement of Family Limited Partnership - Parents, Minor Children and Trustees - General Form

This is a Certificate and Agreement of Limited Partnership dated as of _____, 19_____, made and entered into by and between _____ _____, herein referred to as husband, _____ _____, herein referred to as wife, both as general partners, and _____ _____ and _____, herein referred to as children, as limited partners, all of _____ *[address]*, City of _____, County of _____, State of _____, and _____, as trustee of Trust "A" and _____ _____, as trustee of Trust "B", both of _____ _____ *[address]*, City of _____, County of _____, State of _____, both referred to herein as trustees, and all herein collectively referred to as partners.

RECITALS

1. Husband and wife desire to create a family limited partnership for the purpose of _____.

2. Husband and wife desire to include their children, both of whom are minors, as limited partners in the business.

3. Husband and wife desire to establish trust agreements for the benefit of their children as limited partners.

4. The children desire to become limited partners.

5. Trustees desire to serve as managers of the trusts established for the children.

In consideration of the mutual covenants contained herein, the parties agree as follows:

SECTION 1
FORMATION OF LIMITED PARTNERSHIP

The parties hereby form a Limited Partnership pursuant to the_____
[name of state] Uniform Limited Partnership Act. The rights and duties of the partners shall be as provided in that Act except as modified by this agreement.

The general partners shall timely file this agreement as a certificate of limited partnership in the _____ *[insert place required to be filed]* Office and shall take the steps as are necessary to allow the partnership to legally conduct business in any jurisdiction where the partnership conducts business.

SECTION 2
NAME

The business of the partnership shall be conducted under the name _____
_____ *[insert name]* or that other name as the general partners shall hereafter designate in writing to the limited partners.

SECTION 3
BUSINESS OF THE PARTNERSHIP

The business of the partnership is _____
and such other related business as may be agreed on by the partners.

SECTION 4
NAMES AND ADDRESSES OF PARTNERS

The names and addresses of the partners are: *[insert names and addresses where partners wish to be contacted about partnership related affairs]*.

SECTION 5
TERM

The term of the partnership shall commence on the date this agreement is filed and shall continue until _____, 19_____, unless sooner dissolved by an act or event specified in this agreement or by the law as one effecting dissolution, or until both children attain majority, become self-supporting, are deceased, or marry, whichever occurs first.

SECTION 6
BUSINESS OFFICES

The principal place of business of the partnership shall be _____
_____. The general partners may from time to time change the principal place of business or establish additional offices of the partnership, and in such event the general partners shall notify the limited partners in writing within thirty days of the effective date of the change or addition.

SECTION 7
CAPITAL AND CONTRIBUTIONS

Contribution to Capital. Each general partner, as his respective share, shall contribute to the capital of the partnership as follows:

Name	Cash	Services or other property	Agreed value of services or other property
_____	$_____	_____	$_____
_____	$_____	_____	$_____

Each limited partner, as his respective share, shall contribute to the capital of the partnership as follows:

Name	Cash	Other property	Agreed value of other property
_____	$_____	_____	$_____
_____	$_____	_____	$_____

Interest on Capital Contributions. No partner shall be paid interest on any capital contribution.

Withdrawal and Return of Capital Contributions. No partner shall be entitled to withdraw any part of his capital contribution or to receive any distributions from the partnership except as provided by this agreement. No partner shall have the right to demand or receive property other than cash in return for his capital contribution.

SECTION 8
DISTRIBUTIONS

Determination. The general partners or a surviving general partner shall have the right, except as hereinafter provided, to determine whether partnership profits from time to time shall be distributed in cash or shall be left in the business, in which latter event the capital account of all partners shall be increased.

Profit and Loss Sharing by Limited Partners. The limited partners shall receive the following shares of the net profits of the partnership:

Name   Share

_____   _____%

_____   _____%

Each limited partner shall bear a share of the losses of the partnership equal to the share of the profits to which he is entitled. The share of the losses of each limited partner shall be charged against his contribution to the capital of the partnership.

No limited partner shall at any time become liable for any obligations or losses of the partnership beyond the amount of his respective capital contribution.

Profit and Loss Sharing by General Partners. After provision has been made for the shares of profits of the limited partners as hereinabove provided, all remaining profits of the partnership business shall be divided between the general partners in the following proportions:

Name   Share

_____   _____%

_____   _____%

After giving effect to the share of losses shareable against the capital contributions of limited partners, the remaining partnership losses shall be borne by the general partners in the same proportions in which, as between themselves, they are to share profits.

SECTION 9
BOOKS OF ACCOUNT, RECORDS, AND REPORTS

Responsibility for Books and Records. Proper and complete records and books of account shall be kept by the general partners in which shall be entered fully and accurately all transactions and other matters relative to the partnership's business as are usually entered into records and books of account maintained by persons engaged in businesses of a like character. The partnership books and records shall be kept on the basis of accounting determined to be in the best interests of the partnership by the general partners. The books and records shall at all times be maintained at the principal place of business of the partnership and shall be open to the inspection and examination of the partners during reasonable business hours, and any partner may, at his own expense, examine and make copies of the books of account and records of the partnership.

Capital Accounts. A capital account shall be maintained on the partnership books on behalf of each partner. Such account shall be credited with that partner's contributions to the capital of the partnership and shall be debited and credited in the manner prescribed herein.

Income Accounts. An income account shall be maintained on the partnership books on behalf of each partner. Such account shall be closed to the capital account of each partner at the close of each fiscal year.

As soon as practicable after the close of each fiscal year, and at such other times as the partners may decide, the income account of each partner shall be credited with that partner's distributive share of profits or debited with his share of losses.

Any losses to be debited to a partner's income account that exceed the credit balance of such account shall be debited to that partner's individual capital account. If, as a result of debiting a partner's individual capital account with the excess losses, his capital account is depleted, future profits of that partner shall be credited to his capital account until such depletion has been eliminated.

Drawing Accounts. A drawing account, to which withdrawals shall be debited, shall be maintained on the partnership books on behalf of each general partner. Withdrawals may be made subject to such limitations as the partners may from time to time adopt. The drawing account shall be closed to the income account at the close of each fiscal year.

Reports to Partners. As soon as practicable in the particular case, the general partners shall deliver to every other partner:

(1) Information concerning the partnership after the end of each fiscal year as shall be necessary for the preparation by a partner of his income or other tax returns;

(2) An unaudited statement prepared by the general partners setting forth, as of the end of and for each fiscal year, a profit and loss statement, a balance sheet of the partnership, and a statement showing the amounts allocated to or against each partner during that year;

(3) Other information as in the judgment of the general partners shall be reasonably necessary for the other partners to be advised of the results of operations of the partnership.

SECTION 10
PARTNERSHIP FUNDS

The funds of the partnership shall be deposited in such bank account or accounts, or invested in such interest-bearing and non-interest-bearing investments, as shall be designated by the general partners. All withdrawals from any such bank accounts shall be made by the duly authorized agent or agents of the partnership. Partnership funds shall be held in the name of the partnership and shall not be commingled with those of any other person.

SECTION 11
FISCAL YEAR

The fiscal year of the partnership shall end on the thirty-first day of December in each year.

SECTION 12
DEATH OF PARTNER

On the death of husband, wife, or minor children, the operation of the partnership business shall be continued by the surviving partners and the decedent's legal representative.

If either husband or wife should die, the survivor shall become the sole active partner in the business. If both husband and wife should die during the term of this agreement, the representatives of both husband and wife shall continue the partnership and shall be the active partners in the business. The share of a decedent spouse shall go into the estate of the decedent on distribution of partnership assets.

If either child should die, the partnership shall continue and the decedent child's interests shall be transferred to the surviving child. If both children should die, the partnership shall terminate and the interest of each child shall be paid to that child's estate.

SECTION 13
POWERS, RIGHTS, AND DUTIES
OF THE LIMITED PARTNERS

Limitations. The limited partners shall not participate in the management or control of the partnership's business nor shall they transact any business for the partnership, nor shall they have the power to act for or bind the partnership, these powers being vested solely and exclusively in the general partners.

Liability. No limited partner shall have any personal liability whatsoever to the creditors of the partnership for the debts of the partnership or any of its losses beyond his capital contribution.

SECTION 14
POWERS, RIGHTS, AND DUTIES
OF THE GENERAL PARTNERS

Authority. The general partners shall have exclusive authority to manage the operations and affairs of the partnership and to make all decisions regarding the business of the partnership. Pursuant to the foregoing, it is understood and agreed that the general partners shall have all of the rights and powers of a general partner as provided in the Uniform Limited Partnership Act and as otherwise provided by law, and any action taken by the general partners shall constitute the act of and serve to bind the partnership. Persons dealing with the partnership are entitled to rely conclusively on the power and authority of each general partner as set forth in this agreement.

Powers and Duties. The general partners are hereby granted the right, power, and authority to do on behalf of the partnership all things that, in their sole judgment, are necessary, proper, or desirable to carry out these duties and responsibilities, including but not limited to the right, power, and authority:

(a) To incur all reasonable expenditures; to employ and dismiss from employment any and all managers, employees, agents, independent contractors, real estate managers, brokers, attorneys, and accountants.

(b) To let or lease all or any portion of any property for any purpose and without limit as to the term thereof, whether or not the term (including renewal terms) shall extend beyond the date of the termination of the partnership and whether or not the portion so leased is to be occupied by the lessee or, in turn, subleased in whole or in part to others.

(c) To create, by grant or otherwise, easements and servitudes relating to the partnership's property.

(d) To borrow money and as security therefor to mortgage all or any part of any property.

(e) To construct, alter, improve, repair, raze, replace, or rebuild any property.

(f) To obtain replacements of any mortgage or mortgages related in any way to the property owned by the partnership, and to prepay in whole or in part, refinance, recast, modify, consolidate, or extend any mortgages affecting any such property.

(g) To do any and all of the foregoing at such a price, rental or amount, for cash, securities, or other property and upon such terms as the general partners deem proper.

(h) To place record title to any property in the name of a nominee or a trustee for the purpose of mortgage financing or any other convenience or benefit of the partnership.

(i) To sell all, or substantially all of the assets of the partnership, without the consent of the limited partners.

(j) To keep, or cause to be kept, full and accurate records of all transactions of the partnership.

(k) To prepare, or cause to be prepared, and delivered to each limited partner the necessary reports and other information.

(l) To deposit partnership funds in an account or accounts established and authorize withdrawals of such funds by such persons, at such times, and in such amounts as the general partners may designate, and to pay out of partnership funds any expenses necessary to discharge the partnership's obligations.

(m) To secure the necessary goods and services required in performing the general partner's duties for the partnership.

(n) To determine the amount of distributable cash and make distributions when distributable cash is available and when distributions are advisable but no less frequently than annually.

(o) To set aside funds as reserves for contingencies and working capital.

(p) To cause the partnership to carry such indemnification insurance as the general partners deem necessary to protect themselves and any other persons entitled to indemnification by the partnership.

(q) To cause the partnership to carry such general liability insurance in such forms and limits (including deductibles) as the general partners shall deem appropriate.

(r) To be reimbursed for expenses incurred in discharging their responsibilities as general partners, including but not limited to (i) all legal, accounting, and other professional services rendered to the partnership, including all professional services necessary to furnish reports and tax information to the limited partners; (ii) expenses connected directly with the acquisition, ownership, maintenance, or disposition of the partnership property; (iii) compensation and expenses of any employees or agents of the partnership; (iv) travel expenses of partnership employees and of the general partners in connection with the partnership's business; (v) insurance; and (vi) taxes on property of the partnership.

(s) To execute, acknowledge, and deliver any and all instruments to effectuate any and all of the foregoing.

Time to Be Devoted to Business. The general partners shall devote such time to the partnership business as they, in their sole discretion, shall deem to be necessary to manage and supervise the partnership business and affairs in an efficient manner; but nothing in this agreement shall preclude the employment, at the expense of the partnership, of any agent or third party to manage or provide other services in respect of the partnership business, subject to the control of the general partners.

Liability. The general partners shall not be liable, responsible, or accountable in damages or otherwise to the partnership or any limited partner for any action taken or failure to act on behalf of the partnership within the scope of the authority conferred on any partner by this agreement or by law unless the act or omission was performed or omitted fraudulently or in bad faith or constituted negligence.

Indemnification. The partnership shall indemnify and hold harmless the general partners and persons claiming through the general partners from and against any loss, expense, damage, or injury suffered or sustained by him by reason of any acts, omissions, or alleged acts or omissions arising out of their activities on behalf of the partnership or in furtherance of the interests of the partnership, including but not limited to any judgment, award, settlement, reasonable attorney's fees, and other costs or expenses incurred in connection with the defense of any actual or threatened action, proceeding or claim, if the acts, omissions, or alleged acts or omissions upon which the actual or threatened action, proceeding, or claims are based were for a purpose reasonably believed to be in the best interests of the partnership and were not performed or omitted fraudulently or in bad faith and were not in violation of the general partners' fiduciary obligation to the partnership. Any such indemnification shall only be from the assets of the partnership.

SECTION 15
RESTRICTIONS ON TRANSFERS OF INTERESTS

Limited Partner Assignment. No limited partner may assign the whole or any part of his interest, without the prior written consent of the general partners or until he has complied with all of the following conditions:

(a) He has delivered to the general partner an irrevocable written offer to sell his interest to the general partners at the price stated in the offer at any time within 60 days after delivery of the offer.

(b) The general partners have failed to accept the offer.

(c) An instrument of transfer executed by both the assignor and assignee of the interest shall be delivered to the general partners within 30 days after expiration of the offer to the general partners, stating a purchase price no less than that offered to the general partners.

(d) The assignment will not in the opinion of the general partners (who may require the opinion of counsel of the limited partner) result in the termination of the partnership for purposes of the then-applicable provisions of the Uniform Limited Partnership Act or violate the provisions of any applicable federal or state securities law.

(e) The assignment is not to a minor or incompetent, except that this limitation shall not apply to a transfer in trust for the benefit of a minor or in custodianship under the Uniform Gift to Minors Act or similar legislation.

This assignment shall confer upon the assignee the right to become a substituted limited partner. Any purported assignment of an interest that is not made in compliance with this agreement is hereby declared to be null and void and of no force or effect whatsoever.

Unless an assignee becomes a substituted limited partner, the assignee shall have no right to require any information or account of partnership transactions, or to inspect the partnership's books. Such an assignment merely entitles the assignee to receive the share of distributions, income, and losses to which the assigning limited partner would otherwise be entitled. Each limited partner agrees that he will, upon request of the general partners, execute such certificates or other documents and perform such acts as the general partners deem appropriate after an assignment of his interest (whether or not the assignee becomes a substituted limited partner) to preserve the limited liability of the limited partners under the laws of the jurisdictions in which the partnership is doing business. Each limited partner further agrees that he will, prior to the time the general partners consent to an assignment of an interest by that limited partner, pay all reasonable expenses, including attorneys' fees, incurred by the partnership in connection with the assignment.

Transferees Bound by Agreement. Any person admitted to the partnership as a substituted limited partner shall be subject to and bound by all the provisions of this agreement as if originally a party to this agreement.

SECTION 16
DISSOLUTION OF THE PARTNERSHIP

The happening of any one of the following events shall work an immediate dissolution of the partnership:

(a) The retirement, withdrawal, death, adjudication, or bankruptcy of a general partner, or the occurrence of any other event causing dissolution of a limited partnership under state law. However, if, within six (6) months from the retirement, withdrawal, adjudication of insanity or incompetency, adjudication of bankruptcy, or death of a general partner, any remaining general partner or, if there is none, the other partners elect to continue the partnership, then: (i) the partnership will not be dissolved; (ii) the partnership will continue under this agreement, and if there is no remaining general partner the remaining partners will elect a new general partner (and the agreement and certificate will be amended); and (iii) the interest of the deceased, adjudged insane, incompetent, or bankrupt general partner will be converted into a limited partnership interest, and such partner (or his or her trustee in bankruptcy, executors or administrators, successors or assigns, or other personal or legal representatives) will be a limited partner.

(b) The sale or other disposition of all or substantially all of the assets of the partnership.

(c) The agreement by a vote of a majority in interest of the limited partners to dissolve the partnership.

(d) The expiration of the term of the partnership as provided in this agreement.

SECTION 17
ESTABLISHMENT AND TERMINATION OF TRUST

Trust "A" shall be established with _____
[name] as trustee for the benefit of minor child _____,
and Trust "B" shall be established with _____
[name] as trustee for the benefit of minor child _____.
Both trusts are established for the purposes of securing and managing the partnership interests of the respective minor children. Copies of the two trust agreements are attached hereto as Exhibits "_____" and "_____". These trusts shall terminate on each child's attaining majority, becoming self-supporting, or marrying.

The partnership shall continue on the termination of the first of the two trusts, but shall terminate when both trusts have terminated, as provided herein.

On the termination of each trust, the proceeds contained therein shall be distributed to the respective beneficiary, or to the beneficiary's estate if the beneficiary is deceased.

SECTION 18
WINDING UP, TERMINATION,
AND LIQUIDATING DISTRIBUTIONS

Upon Dissolution. Upon its dissolution, the partnership will terminate and immediately commence to wind up its affairs. The partners shall continue to share in profits and losses during liquidation in the same manner and proportions as they did before dissolution. The partnership's assets may be sold, if a price deemed reasonable by the partners may be obtained. The proceeds from liquidation of partnership assets shall be applied as follows:

First, all of the partnership's debts and liabilities to persons other than partners shall be paid and discharged in the order of priority as provided by law.

Second, all debts and liabilities to partners shall be paid and discharged in the order of priority as provided by law.

Third, all remaining assets shall be distributed proportionately among the partners in the ratios of their respective partnership interests.

Gain or Loss. Any gain or loss on the disposition of partnership properties in the process of liquidation shall be credited or charged to the partners in proportion to their partnership interests. Any property distributed in kind in the liquidation shall be valued and treated as though it were sold and the cash proceeds distributed. The difference between the value of property distributed in kind and its book value shall be treated as a gain or loss on the sale of property and shall be credited or charged to the partners accordingly.

Partnership Assets Sole Source. The partners shall look solely to the partnership's assets for the payment of any debts or liabilities owed by the partnership to the partners and for the return of their capital contributions and liquidation amounts. If the partnership property remaining after the payment or discharge of all of its debts and liabilities to persons other than partners is insufficient to return the partners' capital contribution, they shall have no recourse therefor against the partnership or any other partners, except to the extent that such other partners may have outstanding debts or obligations owing to the partnership.

Winding Up. The winding up of partnership affairs and the liquidation and distribution of its assets shall be conducted by the partners, who are hereby authorized to do any and all acts and things authorized by law in order to effect such liquidation and distribution of the partnership's assets.

SECTION 19
MISCELLANEOUS

Power of Attorney. Each limited partner, including each substituted limited partner, by the execution or adoption of this agreement (as the case may be), irrevocably constitutes and appoints the general partners his true and lawful attorneys-in-fact with full power and authority in his name, place, and stead to execute, acknowledge, deliver, swear to, file, and record at the appropriate public offices such documents as may be necessary or appropriate to carry out the provisions of the agreement.

This power of attorney may be exercised by the general partners, acting alone for each limited partner, or by listing all of the limited partners and executing any instrument with a single signature of the general partners as attorneys-in-fact for all of them.

Power with an Interest. The power of attorney granted under this section (a) is a power coupled with an interest, (b) is irrevocable and survives the partner's incompetency, (c) may be exercised by any general partner by a facsimile signature or by listing all of the limited partners executing the instrument with a signature of the general partner as the attorneys-in-fact for all of them, (d) survives the assignment of a limited partner's interest, and (e) empowers the general partner to act to the same extent for such successor limited partner.

Notices. All notices and demands required or permitted under this agreement shall be in writing and may be sent by certified or registered mail, postage prepaid, to the partners at their addresses as shown from time to time on the records of the partnership and shall be deemed given when mailed. Any partner may specify a different address by notifying the general partners in writing of the different address.

Amendments. This agreement may not be amended or modified in any respect except by an instrument in writing signed by the general partners and a majority in interest of the limited partners.

Entire Agreement. This agreement constitutes the entire agreement among the parties. It supersedes any prior agreement or understandings among them, and it may not be modified or amended in any manner other than as set forth herein.

Governing Law. This agreement and the rights of the parties hereunder shall be governed by and interpreted in accordance with the laws of _____*[name of state].*

Effect. Except as herein otherwise specifically provided, this agreement shall be binding upon and inure to the benefit of the parties and their legal representatives, heirs, administrators, executors, successors, and assigns.

Pronouns and Number. Wherever from the context it appears appropriate, each term stated in either the singular or the plural shall include the singular and the plural, and pronouns stated in either the masculine, feminine, or neuter gender shall include the masculine, feminine, and neuter.

Captions. Captions and section headings contained in this agreement are inserted only as a matter of convenience and in no way define, limit, or extend the scope or intent of this agreement or any provision hereof.

Partial Enforceability. If any provision of this agreement, or the application of the provision to any person or circumstance shall be held invalid, the remainder of this agreement, or the application of that provision to person or circumstances other than those with respect to which it is held invalid, shall not be affected thereby.

Counterparts. This agreement may be executed in several counterparts, each of which shall be deemed an original, but all of which shall constitute one and the same instrument.

IN WITNESS WHEREOF, the undersigned have executed this agreement as of this _____ day of _____, 19_____.

LIMITED PARTNERS: GENERAL PARTNERS:

_____   _____

_____   _____

Acknowledgment

STATE OF _____

COUNTY OF _____

      The foregoing instrument was signed and sworn to before me on _____, 19_____, by _____, the general partners.

_____
Notary Public

My commission expires: _____

STATE OF _____

COUNTY OF _____

      The foregoing instrument was signed and sworn to before me on _____, 19_____, by _____, the limited partners.

_____
Notary Public

My commission expires: _____

Appendix to Section VII: Jurisdictions Where the Uniform Partnership Act Has Been Adopted

Jurisdiction	Statutory Citation
Alabama	Ala Code §§10-8-1 to -103 (1975)
Alaska	Alaska Stat §§32.05.101-.430 (1974)
Arizona	Ariz Rev Stat Ann §§29-201 to -244 (1956)
California	Cal Corp Code §§15001-15045 (West 1949)
Colorado	Colo Rev Stat §§7-60-101 to -143 (1973)
Connecticut	Conn Gen Stat Ann §§34-39 to -82 (West 1958)
Delaware	Del Code Ann tit 6, §§1501-1543 (1974)
District of Columbia	DC Code Ann §§41-101 to -142 (1981)
Florida	Fla Stat Ann §§620.56-.77 (West 1973)
Hawaii	Hawaii Rev Stat §§425-101 to -143 (1968)
Idaho	Idaho Code §§53-301 to -343 (1947)
Illinois	Ill Ann Stat ch 106 1/2, §§1-43 (Smith-Hurd 1973)
Indiana	Ind Code Ann §§23-4-1-1 to -43 (West 1971)
Iowa	Iowa Code Ann §§544.1-.43 (West 1975)
Kansas	Kan Stat Ann §§56-301 to -343 (1975)
Kentucky	Ky Rev Stat §§362.150-.360 (1951)
Maine	Me Rev Stat Ann tit 31, §§281-323 (1964)
Maryland	Md Corps & Assns Code Ann §§9-101 to -703 (1973)
Massachusetts	Mass Gen Laws Ann ch 108A, §§1-44 (West 1932)
Michigan	Mich Comp Laws Ann §§449.1-43n (West 1979)
Minnesota	Minn Stat Ann §§323.01-.43 (West 1975)
Mississippi	Miss Code Ann §§79-12-1 to -85 (1972)
Missouri	Mo Ann Stat §§358.010-.430 (Vernon 1969)
Montana	Mont Code Ann §§35-10-101 to -615 (1947)
Nebraska	Neb Rev Stat §§67-301 to -343 (1943)
Nevada	Nev Rev Stat §§87.010 to .430 (1975)
New Hampshire	NH Rev Stat Ann §§304-A:1 to :43 (1955)

New Jersey	NJ Stat Ann §§42:1-1 to -43 (West 1947)
New Mexico	NM Stat Ann §§54-1-1 to -43 (1978)
New York	NY Partnership Law
	§§1-74 (McKinney 1940)
North Carolina	NC Gen Stat §§59-31 to -73 (1979)
North Dakota	ND Cent Code §§45-05-01 to -09-15 (1981)
Ohio	Ohio Rev Code §§1775.01 to .42 (Baldwin 1953)
Oklahoma	Okla Stat Ann tit 54, §§201-244 (West 1971)
Oregon	Or Rev Stat §§68.010-.650 (1953)
Pennsylvania	59 Pa Cons Stat Ann §§301-356 (1975)
Rhode Island	RI Gen Laws §§7-12-12 to -55 (1956)
South Carolina	SC Code Ann §§33-41-10 to -1090 (Law Co-op 1976)
South Dakota	SD Comp Laws Ann §§48-1-1 to 48-5-56 (1967)
Tennessee	Tenn Code Ann §§61-1-101 to -142 (1956)
Texas	Tex Rev Civ Stat Ann art
	6132b (Vernon 1925)
Utah	Utah Code Ann §§48-1-1 to -40 (1953)
Vermont	Vt Stat Ann tit 11, §§1121-1335 (1947)
Virginia	Va Code §§50-1 to -43 (1950)
Washington	Wash Rev Code Ann §§25.04.010 to .430 (West 1975)
West Virginia	W Va Code §§47-8A-1 to -45 (1966)

SECTION VIII

Irrevocable Trusts

Introduction

Trusts are either inter vivos or testamentary. Inter vivos trusts (or living trusts) may be revocable or irrevocable. The testamentary trust is created by the decedent's will and becomes irrevocable at the time of decedent's death.

The irrevocable living trust is the mainstay of estate planning and asset protection strategies. Recent changes in law have made it possible to realize significant federal income and estate tax savings through the use of an irrevocable living trust.

Application of Irrevocable Trusts

A trust can be used for many purposes. For example, a trust can be set up to manage investments or to conserve property for beneficiaries.

The principal reasons for setting up an inter vivos irrevocable trust is to obtain:

- significant estate and income tax savings,
- protection of grantor's assets against the claims of creditors,
- flexibility in the dispositive pattern to suit varying needs of members of the family.

Thus, a trust can provide for the long-term security of relatives who do not have the inclination or financial acumen to manage a large, complex estate, thereby protecting substantial assets from dissipation by imprudent investments.

The vehicle of trust allows you to meet special family needs, too. For example, the creation of a life estate and the remainder can be coupled with accumulation, sprinkling and invasion powers.

When it comes to minors, property can be transferred to the trust for their benefit and managed and invested without the legal complications created by guardianships, and without the necessity of having to distribute the assets at age 21 or earlier, as the case would be in custodianships.

Disadvantages of Trusts

Trusts also have disadvantages; they involve start-up and operating expenses generally not incurred with outright gifts. Annual income tax returns must be filed for the trust and periodic accountings to courts or beneficiaries may be required. In some situations, the income and estate tax savings provided by the trust may be partially offset by the gift tax incurred on the creation of the trust.

Relinquishing the Property

Most important, the irrevocable living trust, by its very definition, means that you're parting with your property on a permanent basis. In other words, you lose control and ownership of the asset. This may be dangerous unless you have sufficient assets outside the proposed trust to provide for your future anticipated needs. Needless to say, an irrevocable trust should be undertaken only after careful analysis of your needs and resources.

An irrevocable trust is an outright gift of property to keep the trust property out of the estate, and also out of the reach of creditors. The trust must be properly structured, i.e., the grantor must not have any strings attached to the trust that may indicate that he has not really parted with the trust property. Thus, he cannot reserve the right to revoke the trust, to receive the income therefrom, to designate the beneficiaries of the trust income or trust property (except by the original instructions contained in the trust instrument itself), or to determine how the trust property or income will be distributed (except again as provided in the trust instrument originally.)

Irrevocable Trusts for the Protection of Grantor's Family against Financially Hazardous Business Ventures

Irrevocable trust, as we have noted above, offers the ultimate in asset protection; since you no longer own the asset transferred to the trust, your creditors cannot reach it in an action against you. An irrevocable trust can be used in many situations; here is one example:

Let's say, you're about to undertake a business venture that is fraught with uncertainties and you wish to provide for your family so that they will not suffer in the event the business is unsuccessful. A revocable inter vivos trust will not accomplish your objective because by reserving the power to revoke the trust you've made the trust estate reachable by your creditors.

If, however, the trust is not revocable, creditors of the business venture may not be able to reach the property placed in trust. The transfer of the property in trust, of course, must be such that it cannot be set aside as a transfer in fraud of creditors. Or you would fail in your objective in protecting the property from creditor claims.

Income Shifting after 1986 Tax Reform

The Tax Reform Act of 1986 ended most intra-family income-splitting techniques, including the Clifford trust and spousal remainder trust. The rules of the game have changed, still certain strategies are available to an estate planner that could result in significant tax savings. If the grantor is willing to make a nonreversionary transfer (i.e., relinquish irrevocably the control and ownership of the property,) savings in income tax are available.

Example: A parent transfers in 1989 property generating $10,000 a year of income to an irrevocable trust, which in turn pays out the income to a child 14 years or older. The family, as a whole, would find its tax bracket fall from 33% (parents' top bracket) to 15% (child's bracket) on the transferred income under certain circumstances. The tax bill for the family could be cut by 18%.

For the family described above, the tax saving would be $1,875 a year. The additional $75 in saving comes because of the standard deduction the child receives, which eliminates the tax on the first $500 of unearned income. The illustration below shows the effect of this saving compounded over a 4-year period and then over two succeeding 5-year periods.

Actually, the tax saving could be increased substantially, if the income could be split among more than one child. Under the law, each child could receive up to $500 of unearned income and pay no tax. If the $10,000 income was divided among, say, four children so that $2,500 was paid to each child, only $8,000 ($2,000 times 4, after the $500 deduction) would be subject to tax in the 15% tax bracket. This results in a tax of only $1,200 instead of the $3,300 that probably would have been paid by the parents at their 33% rate. The annual saving would be $2,100 as a result of the intra-family transfer.

Intra-Family Transfer to Child 14 or Over

Property transferred to an irrevocable trust	$100,000
Rate of return on investment	10%
Interest income	$10,000
Parents' tax bracket	33%
Child's tax bracket	15%
Trust's tax bracket	15%

	Parent	Child	Trust
Interest income	$10,000	$10,000	$10,000
Tax	3,300	1,425	1,485
After-tax income	6,700	8,575	8,515
Tax saving per year	-	1,875	1,815
Tax saving compounded over:			
4 years	-	9,572	9,266
9 years	-	28,008	28,917
14 years	-	57,698	57,653

Irrevocable Trusts

By transferring property irrevocably to other members of the family, you would

- put the property out of the reach of creditors;
- remove the property from your gross estate, thereby reducing tax on it;
- possibly save on income tax.

Caution: Be sure you can afford to relinquish the property permanently. And, you must not have any strings attached to the transfer, nor should you do it in fraud of the creditors. Your trust should have an independent trustee.

Conclusion: An excellent asset protection device, especially for a large estate owner in a high-risk profession or business. Seek competent professional counsel before proceeding.

Irrevocable Trust Agreement - General Form

Trust agreement made _____, 19_____, between _____ _____, of _____ *[address]*, City of _____, County of _____, State of _____, referred to as trustor, and _____, of _____ _____ *[address]*, City of _____, County of _____, State of _____, referred to as trustee.

In consideration of the mutual covenants and promises set forth herein, trustor and trustee agree:

SECTION ONE
TRUST ESTATE

Trustor hereby assigns transfers and delivers to trustee the property shown on Schedule A (attached hereto and made a part hereof) receipt of which is hereby acknowledged by trustee to have and to hold, the same, together with all other property which trustee may hereby receive subject to the trust, in trust for the uses and purposes and subject to the terms, conditions, and provisions hereinafter set forth.

SECTION TWO
ADDITIONS TO TRUST

Trustor and any other person shall have the right at any time to add property acceptable to trustee to this trust. Such property, when received and accepted by trustee, shall become part of the trust estate.

SECTION THREE
IRREVOCABILITY OF TRUST

This trust shall be irrevocable and shall not be revoked or terminated by trustor or any other person, nor shall it be amended or altered by trustor or any other person.

In no event shall any portion of the income or principal of the trust be used to satisfy any obligation of trustor or of his estate.

SECTION FOUR
DISPOSITION OF PRINCIPAL AND INCOME

Trustee shall hold, manage, invest, and receive the trust estate in the manner hereinafter provided, shall collect the income thereof, and shall dispose of the net income and principal as follows:

(a) Pay the net income in quarterly installments to _____
_____, wife of trustor, for the term of her life, and upon her death to trustor's children, in equal shares per capita.

(b) Upon the death of the last to die of trustor's children, pay the principal of the trust estate together with any undistributed income to the then-living issue of trustor, in equal shares, per stirpes, or in default of such issue to such persons as would have inherited the same, and in the same proportions as they would have taken, if trustor had died intestate immediately after such last deceased child, the absolute owner of the trust estate, owning no other property, and a resident of the State of _____.

SECTION FIVE
INVASION OF PRINCIPAL

In the event that the net income of this trust is at any time insufficient to provide for the care, comfort, maintenance, and support of _____
[appropriate beneficiary or beneficiaries], trustee, in its uncontrolled discretion, may pay or apply for such purposes such sums from the principal of the trust estate as trustee may deem proper, considering any other sources of income of such _____
_____ [beneficiary *or* beneficiaries].

SECTION SIX
PAYMENTS TO MINORS

If any principal of the trust estate shall become distributable to a minor, trustee may in its absolute discretion either pay such principal at any time to the parent or guardian of the property of such minor, to a person having care or custody of such minor, or to a custodian under the Uniform Gifts to Minors Act, or retain the same for such minor during minority. In case of such retention, trustee may apply such principal and any income received to the support, maintenance, and education of such minor, irrespective of the other resources of such minor or his or her parents, either directly or by payments to any of the persons specified above, in any case without requiring any bond, and the receipt of any such person shall be a complete discharge to trustee, which shall not be bound to see to the application of any such payment. Any such principal retained and income received which is not so applied shall be paid to such minor upon his or her attaining majority, or, if he or she shall sooner die, to his or her estate. In holding any property for any minor, trustee shall have all the powers and discretions hereinafter conferred upon it.

SECTION SEVEN
PAYMENT OF DEATH TAXES

Trustee is authorized and directed to pay out of the principal of the trust estate the proportionate share of any succession, legacy, inheritance, death, transfer or estate taxes, including any interest and penalties thereof, that may be assessed by reason of the death of trustor. In making such payment, trustee may rely on the written statement of the executor or administrator of the estate of trustor as to the proportionate share of such taxes chargeable to the trust estate.

SECTION EIGHT
ACCOUNTING

Trustee at any time shall be entitled to render to the current income beneficiary or beneficiaries of the trust estate an account of the acts of trustee and transactions with respect to the income and principal of the trust estate from the date of the creation of the trust or from the date of the last previous account of trustee, and such beneficiary or beneficiaries shall have full power and authority on behalf of all persons now or hereafter interested in the trust to finally settle and adjust such account. Approval of such account by such beneficiary or beneficiaries shall constitute a full and complete discharge and release of trustee from all further liability, responsibility, and accountability for or with respect to the acts and transactions of trustee as set forth in such account, both as to income and principal.

SECTION NINE
SUCCESSOR TRUSTEE

(a) If _____ shall, for any reason, cease to act as trustee hereunder, then his successor or successors shall be such person or persons (individual or corporate) as he may designate in a writing acknowledged by him; and if he shall fail to make such designation, then _____, shall act as successor trustee. If the said _____ shall, for any reason, fail or cease to act as trustee hereunder, then such person or persons shall act as successor trustee or trustees as the last surviving trustee shall appoint in writing duly acknowledged by him.

(b) The successor trustee shall be qualified by executing a written instrument, duly acknowledged by such successor trustee, by which he or she shall agree to assume the trust created hereunder and faithfully to carry out the provisions thereof.

(c) No bond or security shall be required of any trustee acting hereunder, whether original or successor.

SECTION TEN
POWERS OF TRUSTEE

In addition to any powers granted under applicable law or otherwise, and not in limitation of such powers, but subject to any rights and powers which may be reserved expressly by trustor in this agreement, trustee of each trust established hereunder are authorized and empowered to exercise the following powers in their sole and absolute discretion:

a. To hold and retain any or all property, real, personal, or mixed, received from trustor's estate, or from any other source, regardless of any law or rule of court relating to diversification, or non-productivity, for such time as trustee shall deem best, and to dispose of such property by sale, exchange, or otherwise, as and when they shall deem advisable; notwithstanding this provision or any other contained herein, trustees shall stand without power to sell or otherwise dispose of any interest in a closely-held business unless they shall have consulted with all of the adult beneficiaries and the legal representatives of all the minor beneficiaries of this trust, and they shall have agreed to such sale or other disposition by an affirmative vote of a majority of such beneficiaries and representatives.

b. To sell, assign, exchange, transfer, partition and convey, or otherwise dispose of, any property, real, personal or mixed, which may be included in or may at any time become part of the trust estate, upon such terms and conditions as deemed advisable, at either public or private sale, including options and sales on credit and for the purpose of selling, assigning, exchanging, transferring, partitioning, or conveying the same, to make, execute, acknowledge, and deliver any and all instruments of conveyance, deeds of trust, and assignments in such form and with such warranties and covenants as they may deem expedient and proper; and in the event of any sale, conveyance or other disposition of any of the trust estate, the purchaser shall not be obligated in any way to see the application of the purchase money or other consideration passing in connection therewith.

c. To invest and reinvest or leave temporarily uninvested any or all of the funds of the trust estate as said trustees in their sole discretion may deem best, including investments in stocks, common and preferred, and common trust fund, without being restricted to those investments expressly approved by statute for investment by fiduciaries, and to change investments from realty to personality, and vice versa.

d. To lease any or all of the real estate, which may be included in or at any time become a part of the trust estate, upon such terms and conditions deemed advisable, irrespective of whether the term of the lease shall exceed the period permitted by law or the probable period of any trust created hereby, and to review and modify such leases; and for the purpose of leasing said real estate, to make, execute, acknowledge and deliver any and all instruments in such form and with such covenants and warranties as they may deem expedient and proper; and to make any repairs, replacements, and improvements, structural and otherwise, of any property, and to charge the expense thereof in an equitable manner to principal or income, as deemed proper.

e. To vote any stock, bonds, or other securities held by the trust at any meetings of stockholders, bondholders, or other security holders and to delegate the power so to vote to attorneys-in-fact or proxies under power of attorney, restricted or unrestricted, and to join in or become a party to any organization, readjustment, voting trust, consideration or exchange, and to deposit securities with any persons, and to pay any fees incurred in connection therewith, and to charge the same to principal or income, as deemed proper, and to exercise all of the rights with regard to such securities as could be done by the absolute owner.

f. To borrow money for any purpose in connection with the administration of any trust created hereby, and to execute promissory notes or other obligation for amounts so borrowed, and to secure the payment of any such amounts by mortgage or pledge or any real or personal property, and to renew or extend the time of payment of any obligation, secured or unsecured, payable to or by any trust created hereby, for such periods of time as deemed advisable.

g. To compromise, adjust, arbitrate, sue or defend, abandon, or otherwise deal with and settle claims, in favor of or against the trust estate as trustees shall deem best and their decision shall be conclusive. Trustees, however, shall not be required to take any action until indemnified to their satisfaction.

h. To make distributions in cash or in kind, or partly in each, at valuations to be determined by trustee, whose decision as to values shall be conclusive.

i. To determine in a fair and reasonable manner whether any part of the trust estate, or any addition or increment thereto be income or principal, or whether any cost, charge, expense, tax, or assessment shall be charged against income or principal, or partially against income and partially against principal.

j. To engage and compensate, out of principal or income or both, as equitably determined, agents, accountants, brokers, attorneys-in-fact, attorneys-at-law, tax specialists, realtors, clerks, custodians, investment counsel, and other assistants and advisors, to delegate to such persons any discretion deemed proper, and to do so without liability for any neglect, omission, misconduct, or default of any such agent or such agent or professional representative, provided he or she was selected and retained with reasonable care.

k. To apportion extraordinary stock and liquidating dividends between the income and principal in such manner as shall fairly take into account the relative interests of the beneficiaries and to determine what constitutes such dividends.

i. To hold and administer the trusts created hereby in one or more consolidated funds, in whole or in part, in which the separate trusts shall have undivided interests.

m. To rely upon any affidavit, certificate, letter, note, telegraph or other paper, or on any telephone conversation, believed by them to be sufficient and to be protected and held harmless in all payments or distributions required to be made hereunder, if made in good faith and without actual notice or knowledge of the changed condition or status of any person receiving payments or other distributions upon a condition.

n. To purchase securities, real estate, or other property from the executor or other personal representative of trustor's estate, the executor or other personal representative of trustor's husband's/wife's estate, and trustees of any agreement or declaration executed by trustor during his/her lifetime under his/her last will in case his/her executors or trustees are in need of cash, liquid assets, or income-producing assets with which to pay taxes, claims, or other estate or trust indebtedness, or in case such executors or trustees are in need of such property to properly exercise and discharge their discretion with respect to distributions to beneficiaries as provided for under such bills, declarations, or agreements. Such purchase may be in cash or may be in exchange for other property of this trust, and trustees shall not be liable in any way for any loss resulting to the trust estate by reason of the exercise of the authority.

o. To make loans or advancements to the executor or other personal representative of trustor's estate, the executor or other personal representative of trustor's husband's/wife's estate, and trustees of any agreement or declaration executed by trustor during his/her lifetime or under his/her last will in case such executors or trustees are in need of cash for any reason. Such loans or advancements may be secured or unsecured, and trustees shall not be liable in any way for any loss resulting to the trust estate by reason of the exercise of this authority.

p. To do all other acts and things not inconsistent with the provisions of this instrument which they may deem necessary or desirable for the proper management of the trusts herein created, in the same manner and to the same extent as an individual might or could do with respect to his or her own property.

SECTION ELEVEN
GOVERNING LAW

The validity, construction and effect of this agreement and of the trust created hereunder and its enforcement shall be determined by the laws of the State of _____.

In witness whereof, trustor and trustee have executed this agreement at _____ [designate p*lace of execution]* the day and year first above written.

_____

_____

[Signatures]

[Acknowledgments]

[Schedule A: Trust Estate]

Irrevocable "Minor's Trust"

23

Gifts in trust to minors are quite common, both as a means of building up a child's estate and as a way to minimize federal gift, income and estate taxes payable by the trustor or the trustor's estate. Under the present law, minor's trust is one of the most useful devices available to shield a person's assets from creditors by transferring them to the children, and simultaneously reduce current income tax and estate tax payable upon the death of the estate owner.

Impact of Tax Reform

The Tax Reform Act of 1986 did away with a number of popular income splitting techniques, such as Clifford and spousal remainder trust. It now is much more difficult to use trusts and custodianships to split family income. For instance, under the new law custodianships under the Uniform Gift to Minors Act have been negatively impacted in that it requires all unearned income in excess of $1,000 of a child under the age of 14 to be taxed at the rate of the child's parents.

Nevertheless, trusts created under Code § 2503(c) as "Minor's Trust" are a useful vehicle for shifting both wealth and income to younger members of the family. The use of a Minor's Trust is especially valuable after 1987 when the trustee must not only deal with the "under 14" rule, but must also consider how to make maximum use and effect of the trust's 15% income tax rate.

You can get around the problem of taxation of minor's income at the parents' supposedly higher tax rate by setting up a §2503(c) minor's trust, because the income that is accumulated in the trust is taxable to the trust in the year it is earned.

Taking Advantage of Gift Tax Exclusions

ERTA generously increased the unified credit. Under this credit a substantial amount of property can be transferred free of gift tax, but to the extent that the credit is "used up" by lifetime gifts, it is unavailable to reduce estate taxes.

Therefore, in order to obtain maximum tax savings, you should devise a gift program, spread over years, to take advantage of multiple annual $10,000 exclusions. If the grantor elects to split gifts with his spouse, the annual exclusion per donee is doubled to $20,000.

Compliance with §2503(c)

In order for the gift in trust to qualify for the annual gift tax exclusion, the agreement must conform to the requirements of Section 2503(c) of the Internal Revenue Code.

Generally, such gifts qualify for the exclusion if the property and the income therefrom may be expended by or for the benefit of the minor before he or she attains the age of 21 years, and will to the extent not so expended pass to the minor on his or her reaching 21; or, in the event the minor dies before attaining the age of 21, will be payable to the minor's estate or as the minor may appoint under a general power of appointment. The trustee may be given the power in the trustee's discretion to accumulate part or all of the income during the beneficiary's minority.

Additionally, the trust agreement must provide for invasion of corpus, and no substantial restriction can be imposed on the discretionary powers of the trustee to accumulate income or to invade the trust principal. In some circumstances, a gift of trust income alone, without any distribution of corpus, can be made to qualify for the exclusion, to the extent of such income interest. Thus, if the value of the income interest in the property transferred to trust will exceed the amount of the available exclusions, it is not necessary to give the trustee the same broad discretion over the principal. The trustee need only be given broad discretion as to income and accumulated income.

The Crummey demand trust is one under which a minor beneficiary or his or her guardian may make demand on the trustee for the distribution of an amount equal to the gifts to the trust in any given year by any single donor or of the amount of the annual gift tax exclusion then in effect per donor, whichever is less. Since the beneficiary has a present interest in the trust property subject to his or her demand right, the gifts to the trust qualify for the annual gift tax exclusion.

Advisability of a Minor's Trust

Despite its gift tax advantages, the minor's trust may not be advisable in all situations. The main problem with a minor's trust arrangement is that the beneficiary will obtain possession of trust property at age 21, whether or not he is mature enough to handle a large amount of inheritance at that age. Each situation should be evaluated carefully to determine if a trust of this nature would be suitable for the beneficiary.

It should be noted that the grantor will be taxed on the income of the minor's trust to the extent it is used to discharge his legal support obligations.

For example, caution must be exercised when such a trust is established to provide college education funds for the child. In some jurisdictions, college education is considered a parental obligation of support. If this is the case, payments made by a trust to furnish college expenses for the minor may be taxable to the parent who created the trust. You can, however, accumulate income within the trust and distribute it to the child the year before he enters college.

Again, if the grantor named himself as trustee or retained unrestricted power to remove the trustee and name himself as successor trustee, these broad powers would cause the principal of the trust to be included in his gross estate if he died before the trust is terminated.

Income Tax Aspects

After 1987, the top income tax bracket for estates and trusts fell to 28% as it did for individuals, and only the first $5,000 of taxable income receives the benefit of the 15% tax rate.

For the estate or trust which has taxable income exceeding $13,000, the 15% bracket begins to be phased out. The phase-out is accomplished by the imposition of 15% rate adjustment on taxable income between $13,000 and $26,000, forming this layer of income to be subject to a "phantom" marginal tax rate of 33%. The net result will cause an estate or trust having a taxable income of $26,000 or more to be subject to a flat tax of 28%.

In order to maximize income tax benefits under the new rules, the trustee should consider the beneficiary's age (i.e., whether the beneficiary is over or under the age of 14), the beneficiary's earned and unearned income, and the income of the trust after any income distribution to the beneficiary.

Prior to the enactment of the Tax Reform Act of 1986, a trustee had the right to select any month of the year in which to end the trust fiscal year. However, under the 1986 tax act, this favorable tax saving opportunity has been repealed by a provision mandating that the fiscal year of a trust be the calendar year.

The following sample irrevocable minor's trust agreement illustrates a trust for a minor terminating at age 21. It is designed to shift the income on the corpus away from the grantor, remove the corpus from his estate, take maximum advantage of the annual $10,000 gift tax exclusion, and avoid the "kiddie tax" imposed by the Tax Reform Act of 1986.

Setting up such a trust has many personal, financial and tax implications. Guidance of a competent professional is strongly recommended.

§2503(c) Minor's Trust Agreement

Trust agreement made _____ 19____, between _____ _____ of _____ [address], City of _____, County of _____, State of _____, herein referred to as trustor and _____ of _____ _____ [address], City of _____, County of _____, State of _____, herein referred to as trustee.

In consideration of the mutual covenants and promises set forth herein, trustor and trustee agree:

SECTION ONE
TRANSFER IN TRUST

Trustor hereby transfers and delivers to trustee all of the property described in Exhibit "A," attached and incorporated by reference. The receipt of such property is hereby acknowledged by trustee. Such property, together with any other property that may later become subject to this trust, shall constitute the trust estate, and shall be held, administered and distributed by trustee as provided in this agreement.

SECTION TWO
ADDITIONS TO TRUST

Trustee may, in its discretion, accept additions to the trust from any source, provided all such additions shall be irrevocable.

SECTION THREE
DISPOSITION OF PRINCIPAL AND INCOME

Trustee shall hold, manage, invest, and reinvest the trust estate, and shall collect and receive the interest, income, and profits therefrom for the benefit of _____

_____, hereinafter called beneficiary, upon the following terms:

a. Trustee may distribute to or expend for the benefit of the beneficiary, until said beneficiary attains the age of 21 years, so much of the principal and the current or accumulated income therefrom, for his health, maintenance, and education (including college education, both graduate and undergraduate), at such time or times and in such amounts and manners as shall be determined in trustee's sole discretion. Any amounts of income which trustee shall determine not to distribute to or expend for the benefit of beneficiary may be accumulated.

b. When beneficiary reaches the age of 21 years, he may withdraw any part or all of his share. Trustee shall notify the beneficiary in writing of his right of withdrawal. Beneficiary may exercise his right of withdrawal only by written request delivered to trustee no later than 30 days after the later to occur of trustee's mailing or delivering of the notice and beneficiary's attaining the age of 21 years.

c. After beneficiary has reached the age of 25 years, he may withdraw any part or all of his share at any time or times by written request delivered to trustee.

d. If beneficiary is not living on the termination of the trust, trustee shall pay the trust property to, or hold the same for the benefit of, such person or persons or the estate of beneficiary, in such amounts and proportions, and for such estates and interests, and outright, or upon such terms, trusts, conditions, and limitations as beneficiary shall appoint by will; and if, or to the extent that, beneficiary does not effectively exercise such power to appoint by will, trustee shall pay the trust property to the heirs at law of beneficiary.

e. Trustee may make payments for the benefit of and directly to beneficiary, or to the guardian of the person of said beneficiary, or to any other person deemed suitable by trustee, or by direct payment of expenses incurred for beneficiary's benefit.

f. Each share of the trust estate which is distributable to a person who has not reached the age of 21 years shall immediately vest in the person, but trustee shall establish with the share a custodianship for the person under a Uniform Gifts or Transfers to Minors Act.

SECTION FOUR
POWERS OF TRUSTEE

In addition to any powers granted under applicable law or otherwise, and not in limitation of such powers, but subject to any rights and powers which may be reserved expressly by trustor in this agreement, trustee of each trust established hereunder are authorized and empowered to exercise the following powers in their sole and absolute discretion:

a. To hold and retain any or all property, real, personal, or mixed, received from trustor's estate, or from any other source, regardless of any law or rule of court relating to diversification, or non-productivity, for such time as trustee shall deem best, and to dispose of such property by sale, exchange, or otherwise, as and when they shall deem advisable; notwithstanding this provision or any other contained herein, trustees shall stand without power to sell or otherwise dispose of any interest in a closely-held business unless they shall have consulted with all of the adult beneficiaries and the legal representatives of all the minor beneficiaries of this trust, and they shall have agreed to such sale or other disposition by an affirmative vote of a majority of such beneficiaries and representatives.

b. To sell, assign, exchange, transfer, partition and convey, or otherwise dispose of, any property, real, personal or mixed, which may be included in or may at any time become part of the trust estate, upon such terms and conditions as deemed advisable, at either public or private sale, including options and sales on credit and for the purpose of selling, assigning, exchanging, transferring, partitioning, or conveying the same, to make, execute, acknowledge, and deliver any and all instruments of conveyance, deeds of trust, and assignments in such form and with such warranties and covenants as they may deem expedient and proper; and in the event of any sale, conveyance or other disposition of any of the trust estate, the purchaser shall not be obligated in any way to see the application of the purchase money or other consideration passing in connection therewith.

c. To invest and reinvest or leave temporarily uninvested any or all of the funds of the trust estate as said trustees in their sole discretion may deem best, including investments in stocks, common and preferred, and common trust fund, without being restricted to those investments expressly approved by statute for investment by fiduciaries, and to change investments from realty to personality, and vice versa.

d. To lease any or all of the real estate, which may be included in or at any time become a part of the trust estate, upon such terms and conditions deemed advisable, irrespective of whether the term of the lease shall exceed the period permitted by law or the probable period of any trust created hereby, and to review and modify such leases; and for the purpose of leasing said real estate, to make, execute, acknowledge and deliver any and all instruments in such form and with such covenants and warranties as they may deem expedient and proper; and to make any repairs, replacements, and improvements, structural and otherwise, of any property, and to charge the expense thereof in an equitable manner to principal or income, as deemed proper.

e. To vote any stock, bonds, or other securities held by the trust at any meetings of stockholders, bondholders, or other security holders and to delegate the power so to vote to attorneys-in-fact or proxies under power of attorney, restricted or unrestricted, and to join in or become a party to any organization, readjustment, voting trust, consideration or exchange, and to deposit securities with any persons, and to pay any fees incurred in connection therewith, and to charge the same to principal or income, as deemed proper, and to exercise all of the rights with regard to such securities as could be done by the absolute owner.

f. To borrow money for any purpose in connection with the administration of any trust created hereby, and to execute promissory notes or other obligation for amounts so borrowed, and to secure the payment of any such amounts by mortgage or pledge or any real or personal property, and to renew or extend the time of payment of any obligation, secured or unsecured, payable to or by any trust created hereby, for such periods of time as deemed advisable.

g. To compromise, adjust, arbitrate, sue or defend, abandon, or otherwise deal with and settle claims, in favor of or against the trust estate as trustees shall deem best and their decision shall be conclusive. Trustees, however, shall not be required to take any action until indemnified to their satisfaction.

h. To make distributions in cash or in kind, or partly in each, at valuations to be determined by trustee, whose decision as to values shall be conclusive.

i. To determine in a fair and reasonable manner whether any part of the trust estate, or any addition or increment thereto be income or principal, or whether any cost, charge, expense, tax, or assessment shall be charged against income or principal, or partially against income and partially against principal.

j. To engage and compensate, out of principal or income or both, as equitably determined, agents, accountants, brokers, attorneys-in-fact, attorneys-at-law, tax specialists, realtors, clerks, custodians, investment counsel, and other assistants and advisors, to delegate to such persons any discretion deemed proper, and to do so without liability for any neglect, omission, misconduct, or default of any such agent or such agent or professional representative, provided he or she was selected and retained with reasonable care.

k. To apportion extraordinary stock and liquidating dividends between the income and principal in such manner as shall fairly take into account the relative interests of the beneficiaries and to determine what constitutes such dividends.

i. To hold and administer the trusts created hereby in one or more consolidated funds, in whole or in part, in which the separate trusts shall have undivided interests.

m. To rely upon any affidavit, certificate, letter, note, telegraph or other paper, or on any telephone conversation, believed by them to be sufficient and to be protected and held harmless in all payments or distributions required to be made hereunder, if made in good faith and without actual notice or knowledge of the changed condition or status of any person receiving payments or other distributions upon a condition.

n. To purchase securities, real estate, or other property from the executor or other personal representative of trustor's estate, the executor or other personal representative of trustor's husband's/wife's estate, and trustees of any agreement or declaration executed by trustor during his/her lifetime under his/her last will in case his/her executors or trustees are in need of cash, liquid assets, or income-producing assets with which to pay taxes, claims, or other estate or trust indebtedness, or in case such executors or trustees are in need of such property to properly exercise and discharge their discretion with respect to distributions to beneficiaries as provided for under such bills, declarations, or agreements. Such purchase may be in cash or may be in exchange for other property of this trust, and trustees shall not be liable in any way for any loss resulting to the trust estate by reason of the exercise of the authority.

o. To make loans or advancements to the executor or other personal representative of trustor's estate, the executor or other personal representative of trustor's husband's/wife's estate, and trustees of any agreement or declaration executed by trustor during his/her lifetime or under his/her last will in case such executors or trustees are in need of cash for any reason. Such loans or advancements may be secured or unsecured, and trustees shall not be liable in any way for any loss resulting to the trust estate by reason of the exercise of this authority.

p. To do all other acts and things not inconsistent with the provisions of this instrument which they may deem necessary or desirable for the proper management of the trusts herein created, in the same manner and to the same extent as an individual might or could do with respect to his or her own property.

SECTION FIVE
IRREVOCABILITY OF TRUST

This trust is irrevocable and shall not be subject to amendment, alteration, or change. Trustor hereby expressly acknowledges that trustor shall have no right or power, whether alone or in conjunction with others, in whatever capacity, to alter, amend, revoke, or terminate the trust, or any of the terms of this agreement, in whole or in part, or to designate the persons who shall possess or enjoy the trust property or the income therefrom. By this agreement trustor intends to and does hereby relinquish absolutely and forever all possession or enjoyment of, or right to the income from, the trust property, whether directly, indirectly, or constructively, and every interest of any nature, present or future, in the trust property.

SECTION SIX
SPENDTHRIFT PROVISION

No title or interest in the money or other property constituting the principal of the trust estate, or in any income accruing therefrom or thereon, shall vest in any beneficiary during the continuance of the trust created hereby. No such beneficiary shall have the power or authority to anticipate in any way any of the rents, issues, profits, income, monies, or payments hereby provided or authorized to be paid to such beneficiary, or any part thereof, nor to alienate, convey, transfer or dispose of the same or any interest therein or any part thereof in advance of payment. None of the same shall be involuntarily alienated by any beneficiary or be subject to attachment, execution, or be levied upon or taken upon any process for any debts that any beneficiary of the trust shall have contracted or shall contract, or in satisfaction of any demands or obligations that any beneficiary shall incur. All payments authorized and provided to be made by trustee shall be made and shall be valid and effectual only when paid to the beneficiary to whom the same shall belong, or otherwise, as herein provided.

SECTION SEVEN
ACCOUNTING BY TRUSTEE

Trustee shall render an account of his receipts and disbursements at least annually to each adult beneficiary then entitled to receive or have the benefit of the income from the trust.

SECTION EIGHT
SUCCESSOR TRUSTEE

On the resignation, removal, incompetency, or death of trustee, _____ _____ of _____ *[address]*, City of _____, County of _____, State of _____ shall become the successor trustee on such successor's written acceptance of the duties of trustee hereunder. On resigning, trustee shall transfer and deliver to such successor trustee the then entire trust estate and shall thereupon be discharged as trustee of this trust and shall have no further powers, discretions, rights, obligations, or duties with reference to the trust estate, and all such powers, discretions, rights, obligations, and duties of trustee shall inure to and be binding on such successor trustee.

SECTION NINE
TRUSTEE'S BOND

Trustee, or the successors, shall not be required to give bond or security for the faithful performance of duties as such, nor shall they be required to file an accounting with any court.

SECTION TEN
COMPENSATION OF TRUSTEE

The individual trustee shall be entitled to receive a fair and just compensation for trustee's services hereunder, and shall also be reimbursed for all reasonable expenses incurred in the management and protection of the trust estate.

SECTION ELEVEN
RESIGNATION OF TRUSTEE

Trustee, and any successor trustee, may resign at any time on giving written notice _____ days before such resignation shall take effect, to trustor or, after the death of trustor, to all adult beneficiaries and to the guardians, conservators, or other fiduciaries of the estates of any minor or incompetent beneficiaries, who may then be receiving or entitled to receive income or principal hereunder.

SECTION TWELVE
EXPENSES OF TRUST

Trustee shall pay from the trust estate all expenses incurred in the administration of this trust and the protection of this trust against legal attack, including counsel fees and compensation for trustee's own services as trustee, which expenses and compensation constitute a first lien on the trust estate.

SECTION THIRTEEN
ACCEPTANCE OF TRUST; GOVERNING LAW

This trust has been accepted by trustee and will be administered in the State of _____, and its validity, construction, and all rights thereunder shall be governed by the laws of that state. Neither the creation of this trust nor any distribution of principal or income hereof shall be deemed or considered to discharge or relieve trustor from trustor's obligation to support any dependent of trustor.

In witness whereof, trustor and trustee have executed this agreement at _____ _____ *[designate place of execution]* the day and year first above written.

_____

_____

[Signatures]

[Acknowledgments]

[Attach exhibit]

Life Insurance Trust as Asset Protection Device 24

Inter vivos trusts of life insurance policies have come into wide use as estate planning devices. Principal advantage of insurance trusts is that they permit a greater flexibility in investment and distribution of trust estate than may be possible under settlement options generally available in the policies themselves. Another advantage is that such trusts, like other gifts of insurance policies, may afford substantial estate tax savings.

Of course, a significant benefit of setting up an irrevocable insurance trust is to protect the policies from attachment by creditors of the policyowner.

Insurance Trust

An insurance trust may be either funded or unfunded, revocable or irrevocable, and may be created by either the insured or another. In an unfunded insurance trust, either the policy is paid up or the trustor, or another, contemplates making future periodic premium payments.

Revocable Insurance Trust

A revocable life insurance trust involves transferring insurance policies to a trust during the insurer's lifetime. Generally, the insured retains ownership of the policies rather than assigning them to the trust.

When an insured creates an unfunded revocable life insurance trust, just the life insurance policies are transferred to the trust. The insured remains obligated to pay the insurance premiums. A funded revocable life insurance trust is created when the insured also transfers income-producing property (e.g., cash or securities) with which the future premiums on the insurance policies can be paid.

Since the trust is revocable, the grantor can change its terms to suit his changing plans; he can change the trust provisions during his lifetime, cancel the policies, or cancel the trust. Thus, he retains all rights in the policies during his lifetime. At the grantor's death, the trust becomes irrevocable.

Limitations and Benefits

There are no estate tax savings in setting up a revocable trust because the grantor retains taxable powers over the policy during his lifetime. Therefore, the trust property is included in his estate upon his death. Nor are there any income tax savings, since if the trust is funded, income generated from the property transferred to the trust is taxable to the grantor.

A revocable life insurance trust nonetheless holds several other advantages:

1. The expenses and publicity of probate are avoided;

2. The need for a guardian is eliminated;

3. The trustees can collect the life insurance proceeds much faster after a settlor's death because they don't have to wait for the will to be probated and testamentary trust set up; and

4. A revocable living trust gives grantor the opportunity to see how the trust is operated while he's alive; if he doesn't like it, it can be changed or revoked.

A revocable life insurance trust offers no benefit against the claims of creditors. A creditor can compel the grantor to revoke the trust and take the assets back in order to satisfy a judgment.

Irrevocable Insurance Trust

An irrevocable life insurance trust can be created by irrevocably transferring ownership of the policies to the trust. The trust may be funded or unfunded. An unfunded irrevocable trust is created by an irrevocable transfer of only the life insurance policies. Since the trustee of the trust will have no funds with which to pay premiums, another party, e.g., the insured or trust beneficiary, must pay the premiums.

A funded irrevocable trust is created when transfer is made to the trust of the policies plus income-producing property, the income being used to pay the premiums.

The irrevocable insurance trust serves the useful function of insulating the donor's insurance policies from the claims of creditors.

Estate Tax Savings

In addition to shielding assets from creditors, an insurance trust, can provide significant estate and income tax savings, and possibly, may have gift tax consequences.

If the donor irrevocably transfers to the trust all "incidents of ownership" in the policies, and the proceeds are payable to the trustees, the proceeds generally are not included in the donor's gross estate. Note, however, that any gift to the trust made within 3 years of death will automatically be included in the decedent's estate.

Suppose an insured wants to leave life insurance policies to his wife and children in such a way so as to avoid including the proceeds in either his or his wife's estate. He can transfer the policies to an irrevocable trust. He can give his wife a life income in the proceeds, with the principal passing to his children on her death.

More flexibility can be added, however, without sacrificing the estate tax advantage. For instance, the insured can give trustee the discretionary power to use principal for the wife's benefit. He can also give his wife a limited power to appoint the principal among the children without having the proceeds included in her estate.

Incidents of Ownership

Under Section 2042 of Internal Revenue Code, the gross estate includes the proceeds of life insurance on the decedent's life if the decedent possessed any incident of ownership in the policy at his death or if the proceeds were payable to the decedent's executor or for the benefit of the decedent's estate.

The term "incidents of ownership" in a life insurance policy refers to the economic benefits of the policy, including the right to change the beneficiary of the policy, to surrender, cancel, or assign the policy, or to borrow on its cash value. If the decedent possesses any one of the incidents of ownership on the policy on his life (or if he had relinquished such interest in contemplation of death), the proceeds of the policy are included in his gross estate.

If the decedent did not possess any incidents of ownership at the time of his death, such proceeds are still includible in the decedent's gross estate under Section 2035 if the decedent made the transfer with respect to the policy within three years of death.

Income Tax Savings

It is possible to set up an irrevocable inter vivos life insurance trust that has income tax advantages as well as estate tax advantages, if the trust is funded with income-producing property. Unless the trust is funded with income-producing property, there is no income tax advantage. Therefore, the grantor must give up ownership and control of the property.

If the income is or may be used to pay premiums of insurance on the life of the grantor or his spouse, such income will be taxed to the grantor under Section 677 of Internal Revenue Code. However, it is possible to avoid taxation to the grantor if an adverse party must consent to the use of the trust funds for premium payment purposes. An adverse party includes a beneficiary who stands to lose if trust money is used to pay premiums. However, the beneficiary holding that power may then be taxed on the income used to pay the premiums.

Illustration: Grandfather sets up an irrevocable funded life insurance trust with insurance on his (the grandfather's) life for the benefit of his grandchildren and provides in the trust instrument that trust income will be used to pay the premium unless his son (the father of the grandchildren) demands that the income should be paid to him.

In this case, the income would be taxed to the son, which is fine if the son is in a relatively low bracket. If the son is in a high tax bracket, however, giving the son the right to require that the income either be paid to him or accumulated for his benefit as decided by the trustee may be a way around the tax. In such case, the income would probably be taxed to the trust because the son's power over the income is not held solely by himself.

Illustration: Father creates an irrevocable life insurance trust for his two daughters and transfers to the trust various income-producing properties. Assume father's income is in the 28% income tax bracket, and the daughters' incomes are taxed at the minimum rate of 15%. The trustee distributes to the two daughters income that each one uses to pay premiums on life insurance policies on their father's life.

Say the premiums on the policies cost $1,000. Due to his higher tax bracket, father would have had to have pre-tax income of $1,400 in order to have a $1,000 left after taxes to pay the premiums. However, by distributing the income to the daughters and using that income to pay the premiums, daughters would need to have income in the aggregate amount of $1,170 in order to have a $1,000 left after taxes to pay the premiums, thereby realizing a saving of $230.

Gift Tax Consequences

A gift of an insurance policy to an irrevocable trust or a gift of premiums to the trust is subject to the usual gift tax rules. If the beneficiaries of the trust have no present right to income or principal, the gift is one of future interest, and no annual gift tax exclusion is allowable.

On the other hand, if the trust contains a Crummey power permitting the beneficiaries to withdraw the value contributed to the trust in the particular year, or the amount of the available annual exclusions, whichever is smaller, then the grantor and the spouse of the grantor may claim the annual gift tax exclusions.

> **Drafting of an irrevocable life insurance trust requires professional expertise. In addition, there are significant financial and tax consequences that should be fully understood by a trustor. You should seek competent professional advice before proceeding.**

Irrevocable Funded Life Insurance Trust

Trust agreement made _____, 19____, between _____ _____, of _____ [address], City of _____, County of _____, State of _____, referred to as trustor and _____, of _____ [address], City of _____, County of _____, State of _____, referred to as trustee.

In consideration of the mutual covenants and promises set forth herein, trustor and trustee agree:

SECTION ONE
TRUST ESTATE

Trustor hereby transfers and delivers to trustee the securities and other property described in Exhibit "A", attached and made incorporated by reference, the receipt of which property is hereby acknowledged by trustee; and the insurance policies on the life of trustor described in Exhibit "B," attached and incorporated by reference, the receipt of which is hereby acknowledged by trustee. Trustor hereby releases to trustee all rights in the insurance policies described in Exhibit "B." Such insurance policies, securities and other property set forth in Exhibits "A" and "B," together with all insurance policies and other property hereafter subject to this trust, shall constitute the trust estate and shall be held, managed, administered and distributed by trustee as provided in this agreement.

Trustor reserves the right to add to this trust from time to time additional policies of insurance on his life and any other property, including cash, which, when delivered to trustee, shall be held by trustee in every respect subject to the terms of this agreement.

SECTION TWO
TRUSTEE'S RIGHTS IN POLICIES

Trustee is hereby vested with all right, title, and interest in and to such policies of insurance, and is authorized and empowered to exercise and enjoy, for the purposes of the trust herein created and as absolute owner of such policies of insurance, all the options, benefits, rights, and privileges under such policies, including the right to borrow upon such policies and to pledge them for a loan or loans. The insurance companies which have issued such policies are hereby authorized and directed to recognize trustee as absolute owner of such policies of insurance and as fully entitled to all options, rights, privileges, and interests under such policies, and any receipts, releases, and other instruments executed by trustee in connection with each policy shall be binding and conclusive upon the insurance companies and upon all persons interested in this trust. Trustor hereby relinquishes all rights and powers in each policy of insurance which are not assignable and will, at the request of trustee, execute all other instruments reasonably required to effectuate this relinquishment.

SECTION THREE
PAYMENT OF PREMIUMS

During the lifetime of trustor, trustee shall hold such insurance policies and shall hold, manage, invest and reinvest such securities or other property, collect the income derived therefrom, and after payment of all proper charges and expenses, apply such income in the following manner:

(a) The net income of the trust shall be applied to the payment of premiums and other charges on any and all insurance policies that are, or may become, part of the trust estate.

(b) Any net income in excess of the amount needed to pay such premiums and other charges during any year, if any, shall be accumulated and added to the principal of the trust estate at the end of that year.

(c) Trustee shall be under no obligation to pay the premiums which may become due and payable under the provisions of each policy of insurance, or to make certain that such premiums are paid by trustor or others, or to notify any persons of the nonpayment of such premiums, and trustee shall be under no responsibility or liability of any kind in case such premiums are not paid, except that trustee shall apply any dividends received on such policy to the payment of premiums thereon. Upon notice at any time during the continuance of this trust that the premiums due upon such policy are in default, or that premiums to become due will not be paid, either by trustor or by any other person, trustee within its sole discretion, may apply any cash values attributable to such policy to the purchase of paid-up insurance or of extended insurance, or may borrow upon such policy for the payment of premiums due thereon, or may accept the cash values of such policy upon its forfeiture. In the event that trustee receives the cash value of such policy upon its forfeiture for nonpayment of premiums, trustee shall add such amount to the principal of the trust to be disposed of in accordance with its terms. If trustor receives the cash value of such policy upon its forfeiture for nonpayment of premiums, this trust shall terminate with respect to such policy and the amount received shall be forthwith paid over, free and clear of the conditions of this trust, to _____ _____, the wife of trustor, if she is alive, or if she is then dead, to trustor's issue, in equal shares, per stirpes. If the insured under such policy of insurance, becomes totally and permanently disabled, within the meaning of such policies, and because thereof the payment of premiums, or any of them, shall, during the pendency of such disability, be waived, trustee upon receipt of such knowledge, shall promptly notify the insurance company which has issued such policy, and shall take any and all steps necessary to make such waiver of premium provisions effective.

SECTION FOUR
COLLECTION OF INSURANCE PROCEEDS

On the death of trustor, trustee shall take all necessary steps to collect the proceeds of any and all insurance policies in the trust estate, including double indemnity benefits if such are payable. In order to facilitate prompt collection of such sums, trustee shall furnish the necessary proof of death to the respective insurance companies and is authorized and empowered to do any and all things that in trustee's discretion are necessary to collect such proceeds, including, but not limited to, the power to execute and deliver releases, receipts and all other necessary papers; the power to compromise or adjust any disputed claim in such manner as seems just; and the power to bring suit on any policy, the payment of which is contested by the insurer, and to pay the expenses of any such suit, including attorneys' fees, from the principal of the trust estate or from any other insurance proceeds or from the net income, provided, that trustee shall be under no obligation to bring suit unless it is advisable in the opinion of trustee's counsel and unless trustee shall have either adequate funds with which to pay the expenses of such suit or indemnification to trustee's satisfaction against any laws, liability, or expenses that may be incurred in bringing such suit.

On the collection of the proceeds of any insurance policy in the trust estate, trustee shall add such proceeds to the trust estate and shall hold, manage, invest and reinvest such proceeds, collect the income therefrom, and pay and distribute the income therefrom and the principal thereof in the manner provided herein.

SECTION FIVE
DISPOSITIVE PROVISIONS

(a) If the trustor's wife, _____, and his children, _____ and _____, shall all predecease trustor, this trust shall terminate upon the death of the last of them to die, and all trust property shall forthwith be paid to such persons who would be entitled to the same if trustor had then died intestate, a resident of the State of _____, and the owner of the property constituting the principal of the trust.

(b) Upon the death of trustor, if the trust has not been theretofore terminated, trustee shall receive the proceeds of all policies of insurance forming a part of this trust, and shall hold, manage, invest and reinvest such proceeds, together with any other property acquired hereunder for the following purposes:

(i) To pay or apply the net income therefrom in annual or more frequent installments to or for the benefit of _____, wife of trustor, during her lifetime.

(ii) Upon the death of _____, this trust shall terminate, and its net assets shall be distributed in equal shares, per stirpes, to the then- living issue of trustor.

(c) Notwithstanding anything herein to the contrary, trustee shall distribute, from the date of the inception of this trust, the net income therefrom, in annual, semi-annual or quarterly installments (as trustee in its absolute discretion determine) to _____ and shall at any time or from time to time distribute to _____ so much or all of the principal of this trust as the trustee may, in its absolute discretion, deem advisable for her maintenance, support, comfort or welfare.

(d) In addition to the foregoing, trustee shall, during the life of _____, distribute so much or all of the principal of this trust to the trustor's issue, share and share alike, per stirpes, and in such manner as she may at any time or from time to time appoint by an instrument in writing.

SECTION SIX
IRREVOCABILITY OF TRUST

This agreement and the trust created hereby shall be irrevocable, and shall not be altered, amended, revoked or terminated by trustor or any other person. No part of the principal or income of the trust shall ever revert to, or be used for, the benefit of trustor, or be used to satisfy any legal obligations of trustor. Trustor hereby renounces for _____ [himself] and _____ [his] estate any interest, either vested or contingent, including any reversionary right or possibility of reverter, in the principal and income of the trust, and any power to determine or control, by alteration, amendment, revocation, termination, or otherwise, the beneficial enjoyment of the principal or income of the trust.

SECTION SEVEN
POWERS OF TRUSTEE

In addition to all other powers and discretions granted by law or by this agreement, trustee shall have the following powers and discretions, all of which shall be exercised in a fiduciary capacity:

(a) To arrange for the automatic application of dividends in reduction of premium payments, with regard to all policies of insurance held in the trust estate. Otherwise, such dividends shall be treated as income and shall be applied to the payment of such premiums.

SECTION EIGHT
SUCCESSOR TRUSTEES

Trustee shall have the power to appoint a successor trustee. If trustee shall die, resign, become incapacitated, or refuse to act further as trustee hereunder, without having appointed a successor, the successor trustee shall be _____ *[designate]*. Any successor trustee shall have all the duties and powers assumed and conferred in this agreement on trustee, including the power to appoint a successor. Any appointment of a successor trustee shall be made by an acknowledged instrument delivered to trustor, if living, and to _____ *[designate]*, should trustor then be deceased.

SECTION NINE
TRUSTEE'S BOND

No trustee or successor trustee shall be required to give any bond or other security.

SECTION TEN
ACCOUNTING

Trustee shall maintain accurate accounts and records, and shall render periodic statements to trustor while living and thereafter to the adult beneficiary or beneficiaries who may then be entitled to receive income hereunder. The statements shall show receipts and disbursements of principal and income of the trust estate. Written approval of such statement by the person or persons entitled to such accounting shall, as to all matters and transactions stated therein or shown thereby, be final and binding on all persons, whether in being or not, who are then or may thereafter become interested in or entitled to share in either the income or the principal of this trust. However, nothing contained in this section shall be deemed to give such person acting in conjunction with trustee the power to alter, amend, revoke or terminate this trust.

SECTION ELEVEN
GOVERNING LAW

This agreement shall be governed by the laws of the State of _____.

SECTION TWELVE
NAME OF TRUST

This trust shall be designated as the _____ FAMILY TRUST.

IN WITNESS WHEREOF, trustor and trustee have hereunto set their hands and seals the day and year first above written.

_____
Trustor

_____
Trustee

Witnesses:

_____

_____

[Acknowledgment]

Exhibit "A"

Cash $100.00

Exhibit "B"

Prudential Insurance Company of America:
Group Policy #E 0001-018113
Group Policy #E 0001-018112

Equitable Life Insurance Company, Inc:
Policy #GT00787143

Protection of Assets in a Revocable Living Trust

25

A revocable trust generally offers no protection to the grantor against attachment of trust assets by his creditors. The grantor, by reserving the power to amend or revoke the trust, retains the right to take the assets back from the trust. Therefore, the grantor's creditors, in an action against the grantor, can compel him to revoke the trust and apply the trust assets to satisfy the judgment claims.

There are a few minor variations in statutes and court rulings on this matter from state to state but, as a matter of practice, it would be inadvisable to rely upon a revocable living trust to shield your assets against the claims of creditors. Keep this point in mind while reading the following discussion of legal theories and differing interpretations by courts.

Limited Protection against Creditors

A revocable living trust offers, under certain circumstances, a limited exemption from attachment of trust assets. Depending upon the applicable state law, the trust assets may be protected against the claims of the settlor's creditors even though he has reserved the power to revoke the trust, the right to receive the trust income and other rights and powers.

In many jurisdictions, the settlor's creditors may not reach the trust assets in satisfaction of their claims unless the transfer in trust had been made with an intent to defraud the creditors, or the settlor had retained both a life estate and a general power of appointment as to the remainder, a combination of interests deemed equivalent to substantial ownership of trust assets, or unless the trust had been created for the sole benefit of the settlor.

Settlor: The Absolute Owner

In at least ten states, however, there are statutes which provide that a settlor who retains an unlimited power of revocation is to be deemed the absolute owner of the trust property insofar as creditors and purchasers are concerned. For example, in Ohio a revocable trust is valid as to all persons even though the creator of the trust reserves the requisite powers to amend or revoke, except that any beneficial interest retained by the creator is reachable by his creditors, and a creditor can compel the exercise of settlor's power of revocation in court proceedings.

In Michigan the statute provides that if the grantor dies without exercising his power of revocation, his personal representative on behalf of his creditors can reach the trust assets if (a) a claim is filed and allowed and, (b) probate assets are insufficient to pay the claim, except that no creditor has the right to obtain insurance or employee benefit proceeds.

(A list of ten states mentioned above covers Alabama, Indiana, Kansas, Michigan, Minnesota, Ohio, Oklahoma, South Dakota, Wisconsin and North Dakota.)

Creditors' Claims after the Grantor's Death

Are the assets contained in a funded revocable living trust at the time of the grantor's death subject to the claims of his general creditors for debts incurred during the grantor's life?

The answer to this question is far from clear. In the absence of statute, most courts have concluded that the grantor's creditors cannot reach the assets of a revocable trust established for others at a time when the grantor was solvent. See *Guthrie v. Canty*, 53 N.E.2d 1009 (Mass. 1944); *Van Stewart v. Townsend*, 28 P.2d 999 (Wash. 1934). Of course, the creditors can reach the assets if the grantor revokes the trust and takes possession of them.

Several states have statutes that allow the grantor's creditors to reach the assets of a revocable trust. They include Florida (Fla. Stat. Ann. 726.08 (West 1969), Indiana (Ind. Code Ann. 30-1-9-14 (Burns 1972)), Kansas (Kan. Stat. Ann 58-2414 (1976)), and Michigan (Mich. Stat. Ann. 26.155(118) (1974)).

If the transfer is made in fraud of the creditors, it stands to reason that the creditors may assert their claims against the trust. In *Estate of Heighs v. Heighs*, 186 CaAp2d 360, 9 Cal 196 (1960), it was held that if the transfer renders the grantor insolvent, the trust assets may be subjected to the decedent's creditors. This may, however, be difficult to establish since the grantor retained the power to revoke the trust and reclaim the trust assets.

On the other hand, the *Estate of Camm v. Brooks*, 76 CaAp2d 104, 172 P2d 547 (1946), holds that where the grantor reserves the lifetime benefits from a trust, such as income, the grantor's creditors may collect their debts after the grantor's death out of the assets which were payable to the grantor, even in the absence of the grantor's fraud or insolvency.

If, under state law, the trust assets are not subject to the decedent's creditors, the payment by the trust to such creditors is not deductible for federal estate tax purposes, unless the payment is made prior to the time for filing the federal estate tax return (including extensions). I.R.C. 2053(c).

General Power of Appointment

In some states creditors are allowed to reach property of a trust over which the grantor retained a general power of appointment. Others limit their reach to trusts in which the grantor also reserved a life interest. Where the grantor reserved an inter vivos power exercisable in his or her own favor, creditors should be able to reach the assets of the trust a la the Bankruptcy Code.

Other Creditors of a Deceased Grantor

The extent to which the grantor's creditors can reach the assets of a revocable trust following the grantor's death is uncertain in most jurisdictions. Unless the grantor retained a beneficial interest in the trust the creditors may be unable to reach the assets.

In *State Street Bank & Trust Co. v. Reiser,* 389 N.E.2d 768 (Mass. App. 1979), the court held that "where a person places property in trust and reserves the right to amend and revoke, or to direct disposition of principal and income, the settlor's creditors may, following the death of the settlor, reach in satisfaction of the settlor's debts to them, to the extent not satisfied by the settlor's estate, those assets owned by the trust over which the settlor had such control at the time of his death as would have enabled the settlor to use the trust assets for his own benefit."

Also, a relatively recent New York decision held that the assets of a revocable trust are subject to claims of the deceased grantor's creditors. In re *Matter of Granwell,* 228 N.E.2d 779 (N.Y. 1967). The decision was based on New York law, under which the grantor of a revocable trust is considered to have retained ownership of the trust assets until death insofar as creditors are concerned.

The possibility that the assets of a revocable trust cannot be reached by the grantor's creditors following the grantor's death is cited by some planners as an additional advantage of establishing a revocable trust. The advantage may be illusory, and costly if the trustee is required to engage in litigation after the grantor's death.

Protection of Death Benefits

In some states, upon death of the estate owner creditors may be able to reach assets in a revocable inter vivos trust that the decedent has established. Even in these states, payment of employee death benefits to a revocable inter vivos trust established by the decedent is not considered the equivalent of payment to the executor, and the employee death benefits are not reachable by creditors. The reasoning behind this is that since the employee death benefits were not reachable by the creditors during the settlor's lifetime, they are similarly not reachable after his death.

"Secret" to Protection of Assets in a Revocable Living Trust

In order to obtain complete protection of assets against judgment creditors, you would need to set up an irrevocable trust which, in essence, cedes the ownership of property irrevocably to the trust. Since you no longer own the property, it cannot be attached by your creditors. This would be true as long as the transfer was not made in fraud of the creditors.

But most people are not prepared to relinquish their assets irrevocably to a trust. They want to retain ownership and control of their assets during their lifetime while ensuring that those assets do not go through the tortuous process of probate. They can accomplish this objective - avoiding probate - by setting up a revocable living trust.

The question that arises is, how immune are these assets against the attacks of judgment creditors? What can be done to achieve even the minimal protection against seizure by creditors of the the settlor?

Let's take the case of a husband and wife where husband, due to his profession or business, faces tremendous exposure to lawsuits and possible loss to judgment creditors. In such a case, it would be advisable for him to set up two separate revocable living trusts, one for himself, the other for his wife. By so doing, the assets in the wife's trust would generally not be reachable by the husband's creditors. Except in situations where the wife acquired her property from her husband in fraud of his creditors, the separate assets of the wife ordinarily be not liable to satisfy her husband's debts, although, but for the transfer, they could have gone to pay his debts. 41 Am. Jur. 2d. *Husband & Wife* 324.

> The revocable living trust has its principal, and undeniably the most important, application in probate avoidance upon the death of the trustor. By avoiding probate, you'll minimize attorney's fees and court costs, avoid lengthy delays before the beneficiaries can claim their inheritance and eliminate the publicity attendant to the probate process. Just as the revocable living trust offers no protection of assets against the claims of creditors, there are no tax advantages or disadvantages to setting up the trust. All trust incomes, losses and deductions are reflected on the personal tax return of the grantor.
>
> For a complete discussion of the revocable living trust as a vehicle to avoid probate along with actual forms and step-by-step instructions to set up and implement the trust, write to: Homestead Publishing Company, 4455 Torrance Blvd., Suite 220, Torrance, CA 90503. (800) 423-7521(CA), (800) 247-2940(USA).

Business Trusts

26

Business trusts have been around for a long time and their origin can be traced to Massachusetts. Generally speaking, they have the advantage of providing limited liability protection to the certificate holders without the constraints and duties normally imposed on a corporation. Thus, it can be an excellent asset protection device - if properly used. State laws vary greatly in this regard and you should investigate the applicable state law to determine the feasibility and potential benefits of a business trust before proceeding.

Nature and Origin

The "business trust," "Massachusetts trust," or "common law trust" is one of several forms of business organization possessing mixed features of partnerships and corporations. As a result, it has been described "hybrid" in nature.

For many years, the trust had been used in Massachusetts as a form of business organization, as substitute for incorporation. In the years following the First World War, the device came to be widely used elsewhere, especially in Texas and other southern states. The term "common law trust" used to describe such an organization underlines the fact that the organization is one formed without the aid of statute.

The origin of the business trust in Massachusetts has been attributed to the fact that corporations were not at that time permitted to be organized under the general incorporation statutes for the purpose of developing and dealing in real estate. But the use of business trusts has not been limited in Massachusetts or elsewhere to real estate enterprises. The trust device has been used to secure some of the advantages of incorporating without actually forming a corporation.

For example, business trust was often used to secure limited liability for its members without the payment of taxes and fees required of corporations and without the filing of detailed periodic reports of operations and financial condition. It also allowed its organizers to secure capital by the sale of shares without compliance with the "blue sky" laws. A business trust allowed its trustees to do business in foreign states without compliance with the requirements imposed upon foreign corporations.

Decline of Business Trusts

The use of business trust as a device to circumvent the incorporation statutes produced a sort of backlash against its use in many states. Courts in many states held that the beneficiaries of such trusts do not escape personal liability for the debts of the enterprise. Such rulings have pretty much destroyed the use of business trusts in these states.

Business trusts also lost their popularity on another front. In the past, the use of a trust to conduct a business could provide many of the advantages of the corporate form but without the major disadvantage of double taxation at the corporate level and again at the shareholder level upon distribution of corporation profits. However, federal tax regulations have largely removed this federal income tax advantage where the trust actively conducts a business for profit.

Definition of a Business Trust

The most significant characteristic of a business trust, and the most important distinction between a business trust and ordinary trusts established by a will or inter vivos, lies in its life and its profit-making function. While an ordinary trust is for the holding and conservation of a particular property with incidental powers of sale and investment vested in its trustee, the business trust is a vehicle for the conduct of a business and sharing of its profits.

In a business trust a going business is held by the trustees who are its managers. The beneficiaries are also the equitable owners of the property and assets, and they share the profits.

A business trust, as defined by the Supreme Court, is essentially "an arrangement whereby property is conveyed to trustees, in accordance with the terms of an instrument of trust to be held and managed for the benefit of such persons who, from time to time, may be the holders of transferable certificates issued by the trustees, showing the shares into which the beneficial interest in the property is divided."

In simpler terms, a business trust is an association in which (1) trustees hold and own as principals the property, (2) of a business which they manage as trustees, (3) pursuant to an indenture or agreement of trust, (4) for the benefit of shareholders who share the profits. In the absence of any one of these features, the association is not a business trust.

Business Trust - Is It a Corporation or Partnership?

While a business trust is neither a corporation nor a partnership in legal principle, it does have certain attributes of both forms of business organizations. A business trust is similar to a corporation in that the corpus of the trust corresponds to the capital of the corporation. The trustees are analogous to the board of directors of a corporation; the beneficiaries of the business trust and the trust certificates they hold correspond to the stockholders of a corporation and their shares of stock, and the trust declaration performs a function similar to that of the corporate charter or articles of incorporation. Furthermore, each form of business organization has limited liability, continuous existence, and freely transferable ownership.

There are substantial differences between the business trust and partnership. In the business trust, liability is limited, the organization is not changed by a transfer of the beneficial ownership, and legal title to the trust rests in the trustees; in the partnership, the liability of partners is not limited, a new partnership exists with the addition of new partners and title to the partnership assets is held by the partners. There are some similarities, however, between these two types of business organizations. For example, each is created by agreement, and some courts have even held that business trusts are partnerships and the certificate holders of a business trust are to be treated as partners, at least for certain purposes.

So in essence a business trust combines the favorable features of both partnership and corporation, while avoiding their shortcomings. A business trust, which in effect is a contract between trustees and beneficiaries, can be made as general and flexible as a contract. It enjoys greater freedom from statutory regulation and more favorable state tax treatment than corporations. A business trust has a more-centrally organized management than a partnership, and does not dissolve on the transfer of a beneficial share, nor upon the death, insanity or bankruptcy of a shareholder. Beneficiaries of a business trust enjoy greater protection against liability to third persons than partners of a partnership, and in some states even more than stockholders of a corporation.

Note: For a sample form to set up a business trust, see Appendix, P. 349.

Validity of Business Trusts

The practice of business trusts points out that it essentially is an effort to secure some of the advantages of incorporation without incorporating, for the primary objective of achieving limited liability status for its shareholders.

As a result, they have been regarded in many states as schemes to circumvent constitutional and statutory provisions for the protection of creditors and shareholders. In some states, the primary benefits of business trusts may not be available. In no state, however, is the business trust illegal, meaning null and void, and wholly unenforceable, as against public policy.

Perhaps the most disfavored status accorded to the business trust is in the state of Washington. There, it has been held that a business trust has no legal status and is without legal standing in the courts of that state. Even in Washington, however, business trust instruments and agreements are enforceable as between the parties thereto, it being held that the state is the only one that can complain of their invalidity.

In several other states business trusts have likewise been held to be without legal standing. In a majority of states, however, the business trust is recognized as a wholly valid and legal form of business organization. Such a trust has the right to do business, hold and convey real and personal property, make contracts and enforce its rights in court. Arkansas, California, Idaho, Illinois, Maryland, Massachusetts, Michigan, Minnesota, Mississippi, Missouri, Montana, New Jersey, New York, Oklahoma, Pennsylvania, West Virginia and Wisconsin are some of the states that fall under this category.

In some states the validity of the business trust as a form of business association is recognized by statute. California, Massachusetts, Wisconsin and Oklahoma are some of the states that have such statutes on their books.

Some jurisdictions do not accord to the business trust the right to offer shareholders immunity from personal liability, or freedom from corporate regulations. In Arizona, Kansas, and Louisiana, a trust is regarded as a corporation, and failure to comply with incorporation laws results in the imposition of individual liability upon the shareholders. In Kentucky and Indiana, a business trust is held to be a partnership for purposes of imposing personal liability. In Texas, a business trust is treated as a joint-stock company, and shareholders bear personal liability. However, even in these states the courts will sustain the trust agreement to some extent.

In an action at law, the property of a business trust is not available to third persons unless this remedy is expressly provided for in the trust instrument or by statute. Therefore, the trust estate will not be held liable to third parties upon the theory of implied authority held by the trustees, even where the trust receives the benefit of a contract between the trustees and third persons. Nor can a creditor of an individual shareholder or trustee enforce his claim against the trust estate, unless the trustee is also the sole shareholder of the trust.

Liability of Shareholders

The principal attraction of a business trust form of organization is possible exemption for its shareholders from personal liability to creditors of the trust. If exemption from personal liability cannot be achieved by the use of the trust, it has few advantages over the joint stock association.

Control over Operation

The determining factor allowing exemption from personal liability is the control exercised by shareholders over the operation of the business. If the shareholders have reserved no powers of control over the business or in which the powers reserved are not extensive, the shareholders would generally not be individually liable for the debts of the trust in the majority of jurisdictions.

If the beneficiaries are able to dictate on questions of the management of the trust they are liable for the debts. This liability is usually based upon the theory that the organization is not a trust but a partnership or joint stock association in which the trustees are mere agents.

In a small number of states, shareholders of business trusts are personally liable for debts of the trust regardless of the extent of control exercised. Texas is one such state, where business trusts are deemed to be joint stock companies and the liability of shareholders or members of joint stock companies is statutory.

"Pure Trust"

In Massachusetts a distinction has been developed between a "pure trust," where the beneficiaries reserved little or no powers of control over the trustees, and a trust which constituted partnership because of the reservation of too much control. The beneficiaries of the "pure trust" escaped personal liability for the debts of the enterprise under the general theory that the trustee and not the beneficiary is liable for debts incurred in the administration of the trust.

Courts have found nothing contrary to public policy or legislative intent in permitting entrepreneurs to achieve freedom from personal liability without complying with either the corporation or the limited partnership statutes. The states of Arkansas, California, Illinois, Missouri, New York and Rhode Island have adopted the Massachusetts rule.

Even in jurisdictions which follow the Texas rule imposing personal liability on shareholders, or even if the powers reserved to them are sufficient to subject them to liability under the Massachusetts rule, creditors frequently find themselves precluded from suing the shareholders. This would be the case where the creditor has the knowledge of the fact that the enterprise with which he is dealing was organized under an indenture purporting to exempt the beneficiaries from liability.

A provision in the trust agreement negating the liability of the shareholders is effective as between the members themselves, so that a person who takes shares in the trust as part payment for products or services sold to the trust may not hold the other shareholders personally liable under contract.

Formation of Business Trusts

The essential act in the creation of a business trust is the execution of a trust instrument or agreement. No particular form or particular words are required, such as the use of the word "trust" or "trustee." The effect must be, however, to vest property in the ownership of trustees who'll use it in the operation of a business. A valid business trust must have all the essential features that were discussed earlier in this chapter.

A typical business trust agreement is a declaration of several persons, constituting themselves trustees and agreeing to hold specified property in trust, for the benefit of certificate holders. Provisions are made for the issuance and transfer of certificates, meetings of shareholders, election of trustees, removal and powers of trustees, duration of the trust, liability of trustees, and amendment of the trust instrument.

The recording of business trust instruments is governed by statute. Most jurisdictions do not make special provisions for the recording of business trust agreements.

Any person who has the legal capacity to take and hold property may be the trustee of a business trust. Trustees are principals vested with the control and management of the business, subject to the terms of the trust instrument. Trustees of a business trust are potentially liable to two classes of persons: to third persons who deal with the trust, and to shareholders of the trust.

SECTION IX

Prenuptial Agreements 27

No discussion regarding lawsuits and asset protection would be complete without a discourse on prenuptial agreements. Divorce rates are at their highest level across the nation and a person with even a moderate estate contemplating a marriage would be well-advised to consider a prenuptial agreement as an essential tool to avert any future legal problems or dissipation of assets.

An agreement that defines the property rights of each party would go a long way toward keeping the lawyers and courts out of the lives of divorcing spouses, if that eventuality did ever occur.

Validity of Antenuptial Property Agreement

Generally speaking, prospective spouses may enter into a marital property agreement with one another and determine thereunder the status of the property of the parties, provided the agreement does not contravene public policy or the law of the jurisdiction where it is to be enforced. Such agreements are subject to the limitations and restrictions that apply to contracts generally, and they should be in writing and subscribed by the parties.

As with all other contracts, competency of the parties, consideration, appropriate subject matter, and a meeting of the minds are elements necessary to the validity of an antenuptial property agreement.

Purpose

Prenuptial agreements are generally intended to define the duties, property rights and expectations of the parties. The rights of the parties in the event that the marriage ends through death or dissolution are established by the agreement, and are not subject to judicial determination or statutory distribution schemes.

The negotiation, drafting and signing of prenuptial agreements has been termed "private ordering" because contracting parties are exempting their marital estate plan from the operation of law.

There are many possible purposes for a prenuptial agreement, including:

(1) Protecting and preserving the identity of separate property (i.e., that which is already owned prior to marriage, or which is received by gift or inheritance, or is derived from the proceeds of the sale or exchange of separate property during the marriage);

(2) Defining which assets or properties accumulated or earned during the marriage will be separate and which will be joint;

(3) Insulating certain properties for family members or others (e.g., children from a previous marriage) who might not otherwise have an unassailable claim to such property as beneficiaries of the grantor's estate.

(4) Simplifying accounting and management so as to avoid the tracing problems inherent in the event of inadvertent commingling of funds;

(5) Preventing undue expectations, ambiguities or misunderstandings between the partners about the economic aspects of the marriage relationship; and

(6) Avoiding the estate plan which would otherwise be devised for the couple by the courts or the general operation of law.

In short, the purpose of the agreement is to alter the property rights which are otherwise governed by statute. In many cases, judicial intervention in the private ordering of property rights is avoided altogether.

Prohibited Provisions

The area of antenuptial agreements is relatively new and legislatures and courts are constantly defining what constitutes a valid agreement. There are certain provisions that may be held against public policy or inherently unfair to a party. Consult someone familiar with this subject in your state since there is no uniformity of law in this area.

Below is a list of provisions generally considered prohibited in California.

(1) Do not include waiver by either spouse of other's duty to support him or her during marriage. Every person has a statutory duty to support his or her spouse [Civ. Code § 242]. The obligee spouse may enforce this duty or, if that spouse becomes indigent and must turn to public funds for support, the county furnishing that support may invoke the duty of the obligor spouse in seeking reimbursement from that spouse [see Civ. Code § 248].

(2) Do not include provision for lump sum payment in lieu of court-ordered support in event of marital dissolution [see *Pereira v. Pereira* (1909) 156 Cal. 1, 4-5, 103 P. 488].

(3) Do not include provision under which one prospective spouse agrees, in exchange for payment of money or transfer of property by other spouse, to provide following services during marriage [see *Brooks v. Brooks* (1941) 48 Cal. App. 2d 347, 119 P. 2d 970]:

    a. Domestic; and/or
    b. Nursing.

Note: An exchange of money or property for housekeeping and nursing violates public policy since spouses are considered to owe one another these duties by virtue of the marriage relationship [see *Estate of Sonnicksen* (1937) 23 Cal. App. 2d 475, 479, 73 P.2d 643 (referring to duty of wife)]. However, it is possible that a court would uphold the validity of a premarital agreement containing two independent convenants: one under which a spouse agrees to transfer money or property to the other spouse and another under which the other spouse promises to perform nursing and household services.

(4) Do not include limitation on spousal support in event of marital dissolution [see *Barham v. Barham* (1949) 33 Cal. 2d 416, 428, 202 P. 2d 289].

(5) Do not include limitation on attorney's fees in event of legal separation and/or marital dissolution [see *Pereira v. Pereira* (1909) 156 Cal. 1, 4-5, 103 P. 488].

The form on the following pages is a complete premarital agreement covering the property rights of the prospective spouses. It is designed to be used by prospective spouses who do not wish to mingle or share their interests in property earned, accumulated, or in any other way received by either of them during their marriage or brought to that marriage by either of them.

This form provides for a complete separation of the property interests of the prospective spouses, since it specifies that their respective incomes and accumulations during marriage will be deemed the separate property of the spouse receiving those earnings or accumulations. It also contains a complete mutual release of all marital rights to the property of each spouse.

You must consult a competent local professional who's conversant with the laws of your state for aid in drafting a premarital agreement.

Premarital Agreement Requiring Complete Separation of Prospective Spouses' Interests in Property Brought to or Acquired after Marriage

1. Parties. _____, of _____
_____, and _____,
of _____, in contemplation of their future
marriage, do hereby enter into this Premarital Agreement.

2. Purpose. The parties enter into this Agreement for the purpose of defining their respective property rights following their contemplated marriage. They intend that all property owned by either of them at the time of the marriage, and all additional property of any nature which either of them acquires after marriage, shall be the separate property of the party who receives and owns that property. The parties further intend to avoid any interests which, except for the operation of this Agreement, each of them might acquire in the property of the other as incidents of their marital relationship.

3. Disclosure of Property. Each party has made a full and complete disclosure to the other party of all property which he or she owns. A list of all property owned by the first prospective spouse, _____, along with encumbrances, is set forth in Exhibit A, which is attached to and made a part of this Agreement. A list of all property owned by the second prospective spouse, _____, along with encumbrances, is set forth in Exhibit B, which is attached to and made a part of this Agreement.

The parties understand that the figures and amounts set forth in Exhibits A and B are approximately correct and not necessarily exact, and that they reflect the values of the listed property on or about the date of this Agreement.

Each party acknowledges that he or she has read Exhibits A and B, that he or she is entering into this Agreement freely and voluntarily, and that he or she understands the contents of this Agreement.

4. Children of Prospective Spouses. First prospective spouse, _____
_____, is the mother of the following children:

_____   _____ years of age.

_____   _____ years of age.

Second prospective spouse, _____, is
the father of the following children:

_____   _____ years of age.

_____   _____ years of age.

5. Property of Each Spouse to Be Separate. First prospective spouse, _____
_____, agrees that all property of any nature or in any place,
including but not limited to the earnings and income resulting from the personal services, skill,
effort, and work belonging to the second prospective spouse, _____
_____, at the commencement of the marriage, or acquired by or coming to this spouse
by purchase, gift, inheritance, or other means during the marriage, shall be the separate
property of the second prospective spouse, and shall be subject to that person's disposition
as separate property, in the same manner as if no marriage had been entered into.

Second prospective spouse, _____, agrees that all
property of any nature or in any place, including but not limited to the earnings and income
resulting from the personal services, skill, effort, and work belonging to the first prospective
spouse, _____, at the commencement of the marriage, or
acquired by or coming to this spouse by purchase, gift, inheritance, or other means during the
marriage, shall be the separate property of the first prospective spouse, and shall be subject
to that person's disposition as separate property, in the same manner as if no marriage had been
entered into.

6. Waiver of Maintenance Obligations. The parties agree that if their marriage is
terminated at any time by divorce, annulment, or dissolution, neither party shall be liable for
the maintenance of the other. If there are issue of the marriage, this Agreement between the
parties will not in any way affect the rights of the children to support from both of their parents.

7. Release of Marital Rights to Separate Property. The parties mutually agree to
waive and release any and all equitable or legal claims and rights, actual, inchoate, or
contingent which he or she may acquire in the separate property of the other by reason of their
marriage, including but not limited to:

    (a) The right to a family allowance.

    (b) The right to a probate homestead.

    (c) The right to claims of dower, curtesy, or any statutory substitutes provided
        by the laws of the state in which the parties or either of them die domiciled
        or in which they own real property.

(d) The right of election to take against the will of the other.

(e) The right to a distributive share in the estate of the other should he or she die intestate.

(f) The right to act as administrator of the other.

Nothing in this Agreement shall be deemed to constitute a waiver by either party of any bequest or devise that the other party may choose to make to him or her by will or codicil. However, the parties acknowledge that neither of them have made promises of any kind to the other regarding any bequest or devises.

8. Execution of Other Instruments. Each party agrees, upon the request of the other, to execute, deliver, and properly acknowledge whatever additional instruments may be required to carry out the intention of this Agreement and to execute, deliver, and properly acknowledge any deeds or other documents in order that good and marketable title to any separate property can be conveyed by one party free from any claim of the other party acquired by him or her by reason of their marriage.

9. Representation by Separate Counsel. Each party acknowledges that he or she has been represented by independent counsel in the negotiation of this Agreement; that counsel representing each party is one of his or her own choosing; and that each party has read this Agreement and that the meaning and legal consequences of this Agreement have been explained to them by their respective counsel.

10. Binding Effect. This Agreement shall bind and inure to the benefit of the parties and their respective heirs, personal representatives, successors, and assigns.

11. Integration Clause. This Agreement constitutes the entire understanding between the parties concerning the subject matter that it covers. Any oral representations or modifications made prior to or after execution of this Agreement concerning the subject matter of this Agreement shall have no force or effect; provided, however, that this Agreement may be subsequently modified by a writing specifically referring to this Agreement and signed by both parties.

12. Effect of Partial Invalidity. If any term, provision, promise, or condition of this Agreement is determined by a court of competent jurisdiction to be invalid, void, or unenforceable, in whole or in part, the remainder of this Agreement shall remain in full force and effect and shall in no way be affected, impaired, or invalidated.

13. Governing Law. This Agreement shall be governed by the laws of the State of
_____.

IN WITNESS WHEREOF, the parties have executed this Agreement at _____
_____ on _____, 19_____.

_____
First Prospective Spouse

_____
Second Prospective Spouse

Attachments:

Exhibit A - List of Property Owned by First Prospective Spouse
Exhibit B - List of Property Owned by Second Prospective Spouse

Acknowledgment

State of _____

County of _____

    On this _____ day of _____ in the year of 19 _____,
before me, _____ a notary public,
personally appeared _____ and _____
                  Name of first prospective spouse
_____ personally known to me or proved to
    Name of second prospective spouse
me on the basis of satisfactory evidence to be the persons whose names are subscribed to this
instrument, and acknowledged that they executed the same.

[*Notarial Seal*]

_____
Notary Public

Certification of Attorney for First Prospective Spouse

The undersigned hereby certifies that _____ [he *or* she] is an attorney licensed to practice and admitted to practice in the State of _____; that _____ [he *or* she] has been retained by _____ [*name of first prospective spouse*], a party to this Agreement, and that _____ [he *or* she] has advised that party with respect to this Agreement and has explained to _____ [him *or* her] its meaning and legal effect; and that _____ [*name of first prospective spouse*] has acknowledged _____ [his *or* her] full and complete understanding of the Agreement and its legal consequences, and has freely and voluntarily executed the Agreement in my presence.

_____ [*name of attorney*]

By _____ [*signature*]

[*typed name and title*]

Certification of Attorney for Second Prospective Spouse

The undersigned hereby certifies that _____ [he *or* she] is an attorney licensed to practice and admitted to practice in the State of _____; that _____ [he *or* she] has been retained by _____ [*name of second prospective spouse*], a party to this Agreement, and that _____ [he *or* she] has advised that party with respect to this Agreement and has explained to _____ [him *or* her] its meaning and legal effect; and that _____ [*name of second prospective spouse*] has acknowledged _____ [his *or* her] full and complete understanding of the Agreement and its legal consequences, and has freely and voluntarily executed the Agreement in my presence.

_____ [*name of attorney*]

By _____ [*signature*]

[*typed name and title*]

Postnuptial Agreements

28

Postnuptial Agreement

Generally speaking, husband and wife may enter into any transaction with each other that may determine the ownership or distribution of property between them. Thus, they may contract or agree between them to change the status of the property owned by either or both of them. Such contracts may relate to currently-owned property, to an expectancy, or to after-acquired property. Either spouse may file an inventory of his or her separate personal property in the office of the county recorder of the county in which the parties reside, which act will constitute prima facie evidence that title is in the party so filing.

Postnuptial property agreement is executed by spouses during their marriage. It is designed so that the parties may determine and settle their respective rights to property and avoid misunderstandings regarding the use, management, control, and devolution of that property. The form shown here is not designed to be used by parties contemplating or in the process of a marital dissolution.

Unlike antenuptial agreements, postnuptial agreements between husband and wife respecting property need not be in writing. It is recommended, nevertheless, that any contemplated postnuptial agreement be in writing, since a properly drafted instrument facilitates proof of the details of the transaction, indicates the actual intent of the parties, and demonstrates that the transaction resulted from good faith, arms length negotiation.

Caution: Postnuptial agreements affect property rights of husband and wife. All such agreements should be undertaken only after a frank and thorough discussion between the two marriage partners and then in consultation with independent counsel retained by each party.

Postnuptial Property Agreement - General Form

THIS AGREEMENT is made on _____, 19_____ between _____
_____, Husband, and _____
_____, Wife, who have been married since _____, 19_____, and who
reside at _____, City of _____,
County of _____, State of _____.

This agreement is made with the intent and desire to define and specify the respective and collective rights of the above-named parties in the separate, joint and community property of the parties, and without the intent of either party to obtain a divorce or legal separation.

1. Stipulation of Parties. The parties stipulate as follows:

a.   Husband's Separate Personal Property. _____
_____, Husband, owns as his separate property the following personal property:

Description	Location	Value
_____	_____	$_____
_____	_____	$_____

b.   Husband's Separate Real Property. _____
_____, Husband, owns as his separate property the following real property:

Description	Location	Value
_____	_____	$_____
_____	_____	$_____

c.   Wife's Separate Personal Property. _____
_____, Wife, owns as her separate property the following personal property:

Description	Location	Value
_____	_____	$_____
_____	_____	$_____

    d. Wife's Separate Real Property. _____

_____, Wife, owns as her separate property the following real property:

Description	Location	Value
_____	_____	$_____
_____	_____	$_____

    e. Community Personal Property. _____, Husband, and _____,Wife, own, as husband and wife, the following community personal property:

Description	Location	Value
_____	_____	$_____
_____	_____	$_____

    f. Community Real Property. _____, Husband, and _____, Wife, own, as husband and wife, the following community real property:

Description	Location	Value
_____	_____	$_____
_____	_____	$_____

    g. Personal Property Held in Joint Tenancy. _____, Husband, and _____, Wife, own the following personal property in joint tenancy:

Description	Location	Value
_____	_____	$_____
_____	_____	$_____

h. Real Property Held in Joint Tenancy. _____
_____, Husband, and _____,
Wife, own the following real property in joint tenancy:

Description	Location	Value
_____	_____	$_____
_____	_____	$_____

i. Affirmation of Full Disclosure. Each party individually affirms that a complete disclosure has been made to the other of all real and personal property owned, in whole or in part, by each respective party.

2. Property Rights of Parties. The parties agree:

a. Husband's Separate Personal Property. All of the following-described personal property, heretofore the separate property of the Wife or the community property of the parties or held by the parties in joint tenancy, shall become the separate personal property of _____, Husband:

Description	Location	Value
_____	_____	$_____
_____	_____	$_____

b. Husband's Separate Real Property. All of the following-described real property, heretofore the separate property of the Wife or the community property of the parties or held by the parties in joint tenancy, shall become the separate real property of _____ _____, Husband:

Description	Location	Value
_____	_____	$_____
_____	_____	$_____

c. Wife's Separate Personal Property. All of the following-described personal property, heretofore the separate property of the Husband or the community property of the parties or held by the parties in joint tenancy, shall become the separate personal property of

_____, Wife:

Description	Location	Value
_____	_____	$_____
_____	_____	$_____

d. Wife's Separate Real Property. All of the following-described real property, heretofore the separate property of the Husband or the community property of the parties or held by the parties in joint tenancy, shall become the separate real property of

_____, Wife:

Description	Location	Value
_____	_____	$_____
_____	_____	$_____

e. Community Personal Property. All of the following-described property, heretofore the separate property of the Wife or Husband or held by the parties in joint tenancy or as community property, shall become the community personal property of the parties:

Description	Location	Value
_____	_____	$_____
_____	_____	$_____

f. Community Real Property. All of the following-described real property, heretofore the separate property of the Wife or Husband or held by the parties in joint tenancy or as community property, shall become the community real property of the parties:

Description	Location	Value
_____	_____	$_____
_____	_____	$_____

g. Tenancy in Common. All of the following-described property shall be owned by _____, Husband, and _____, Wife, as tenants in common with all of the rights and incidents pertaining to such tenancy in common:

Description	Location	Value
_____	_____	$_____
_____	_____	$_____

h. Joint Tenancy. All of the following-described property shall be owned by _____, Husband, and _____, Wife, as joint tenants with all of the rights and incidents pertaining to such joint tenancy:

Description	Location	Value
_____	_____	$_____
_____	_____	$_____

i. Cooperation in Execution of Instruments. Each of the parties to this agreement shall cooperate fully in executing and delivering all instruments necessary to carry into effect the provisions of this agreement.

3. Stipulation of Representation by Counsel.

We, _____, Husband, and _____ _____, Wife, acknowledge that we have been represented by counsel during negotiations for this agreement, that our rights in the real and personal property described in this agreement have been fully explained, that the legal consequences of this agreement have been fully explained, and that we understand our legal rights in the property and the legal consequences of this agreement.

Dated: _____, 19_____.   _____

                                                                                    Husband

                                                                   _____

                                                                                    Wife

[Acknowledgment]

Property Agreements between Husband and Wife

29

Agreements between husband and wife that convert separate property into community property or vice versa are very common and generally accepted in law. Such agreements have the advantage of delineating property rights between the spouses.

Generally, statutory procedures are available for the transmutation, transfer, or partition of community property. Agreements between husband and wife may be made in contemplation of separation, or they may be made for other purposes, such as tax advantage, estate planning, defining property rights of each spouse, etc.

Agreements between married persons that transmute, transfer, or partition community property must, of course, contain the essential elements of a valid contract generally. Such agreements should, where appropriate, make provision for property that has not yet been acquired or come into existence.

Where the spouses wish to convert separate property into community property, a schedule of the spouse's separate property to be transferred should be included in or appended to the agreement.

Reminder: Contracts effecting a transfer or conveyance of community real property must be subscribed, acknowledged, and recorded in order to be valid.

Caution: Property agreements between husband and wife are, by their very nature, private and must be tailored to meet the specific, individual requirements of the parties. The standards for legal sufficiency also vary from jurisdiction to jurisdiction. It is essential that you consult the local law and seek out competent professional advice.

Postnuptial Agreement
to Convert Separate
Property into Community Property

Agreement made _____, 19_____, between _____
_____ *[husband]* and _____ *[wife]*,
husband and wife, both of _____ *[address]*, City
of _____, County of _____, State of _____.

RECITALS

A. *Status and Property of Parties.* The parties intermarried on _____, 19____,
at _____ *[marriage domicile]*, and since the above date have been and
now are living together as husband and wife. The parties during their marriage have acquired
certain property which, by virtue of the laws of the State of _____ *[if appropriate, add:* and by virtue of a written agreement between the parties dated _____,
19_____]*, is the community property of the parties, and which property is listed and described
in Schedule "A" which is annexed to this agreement and incorporated by reference.

B. *Intent of Parties.* The parties desire that their respective rights and interest in and
to all their community property be expressly set forth and established in accordance with the
terms and provisions of this agreement.

AGREEMENT

In consideration of the mutual convenants contained hereinafter, the parties agree as
follows:

SECTION ONE
SEPARATE PROPERTY TRANSMUTED TO COMMUNITY
PROPERTY

All property now owned as separate property by _____
_____ *[husband]* and by _____
[wife], respectively, which separate property is listed and described in Schedule "B" is
declared by the parties to be, and it hereby is, their community property.

SECTION TWO
MANAGEMENT BY HUSBAND/WIFE

All of the interests of the parties in their community property during continuance of the marriage are, and shall be subject to, the sole management, control, and disposition of _____ *[husband/wife]* as set forth in _____ _____ *[statute]* of the laws of the State of _____.

SECTION THREE
AFTER-ACQUIRED PROPERTY

All property hereafter acquired by the parties, or either of them, whether earned by capital or by personal efforts or otherwise acquired, and regardless of whether it is real, personal, or mixed, shall be deemed to be, and is hereby declared to be, the community property of the parties.

SECTION FOUR
FULL DISCLOSURE BY PARTIES

Each of the parties has made a full disclosure to the other party of all property owned or otherwise held by each respective party, as is shown in Schedule "B" attached.

SECTION FIVE
EXECUTION OF NECESSARY INSTRUMENTS

Each party shall cooperate fully with the other party in preparing, executing, and delivering all instruments necessary to carry into effect the provisions of this agreement.

SECTION SIX
PARTIES REPRESENTED BY COUNSEL

The parties acknowledge that they, and each of them, have been represented by counsel of their choice in the preparation of this agreement; that their rights in the property described in this agreement and in Schedule "A" and "B" have been fully explained to them; that the legal effect of this agreement has been fully explained to them; and that they understand the terms, provisions, and legal effect of this agreement.

In witness whereof, we have executed this agreement at _____
_____ *[place of execution]* the day and year first above written.

_____

_____

                                                                    [Signatures]

[Acknowledgment]

Schedule "A": List community property
Schedule "B": List separate property of each spouse

Postnuptial Agreement
to Convert Community
Property into Tenancy in Common

Agreement made _____, 19_____, between _____ _____ [husband] and _____ [wife], husband and wife, both of _____ [address], City of _____, County of _____, State of _____.

SECTION ONE
DESCRIPTION OF COMMUNITY PROPERTY

The parties have accumulated and acquired certain real and personal property subsequent to their marriage, which was solemnized on _____, 19_____, at _____ _____ [address], City of _____, County of _____, State of _____. All of such property has been and is community property _____ [under the laws of the State of _____ or pursuant to a written agreement of the parties], as set forth and described below:

Real Property	Value	Personal Property	Value
_____	$_____	_____	$_____
_____	$_____	_____	$_____
_____	$_____	_____	$_____

SECTION TWO
INTENT OF PARTIES

The parties have, from _____, 19_____, to the present, held title to all of the above-described property as community property, and now intend and desire to divide and separate the property and hold the property as tenants in common with equal undivided interests therein.

SECTION THREE
CONVEYANCE

The parties agree to convey, by deed, all of the above property, heretofore held as community property, and to convey to each of them an undivided one-half interest to be held as tenants in common, within _____ days from the date of this agreement.

SECTION FOUR
DOCUMENTS OF TITLE

Each party convenants to execute and deliver to the other such bills of sale, deeds, and other documents and instruments necessary to convey the title to the above property to each of them as tenants in common.

SECTION FIVE
SEPARATE PROPERTY

The parties expressly declare that the purpose and intent of this agreement is that each party is to acquire and own one-half of all the property above referred to, in his or her individual right and as his or her sole and separate property, including the rents, issues, and profits therefrom, so that each may convey, transfer, assign, or otherwise transfer to his or her heirs at law, devisees, assignees, or legatees, without the interference or necessity of or by the other party consenting or signing any instruments in connection therewith.

SECTION SIX
WAIVER OF RIGHTS

Each of the parties agrees to waive all and every right whatsoever he or she might have or acquire by law in the community property of the marriage, whether now owned or hereafter to be acquired, and each party shall have sole control and management of, and the right to sell, convey, or transfer any and all of their properties transferred pursuant to this agreement, without signature or joining in by the other, to the extent permitted by the laws of the State of _____ respecting tenancy in common.

In witness whereof, we have executed this agreement at _____ _____ *[place of execution]* the day and year first above written.

_____

_____

[Signatures]

[Acknowledgments]

Postnuptial Agreement
Earnings to Be Separate Property

Agreement made _____, 19_____, between _____ _____ [husband] and _____ [wife], husband and wife, both of _____ [address], City of _____, County of _____, State of _____.

RECITALS

A. The parties married each other on _____, 19_____, at _____ [city and state], and since this date have been and are now living together as husband and wife.

B. The parties desire that earnings from personal activities shall hereafter be the separate property of the party earning such income.

AGREEMENT

In consideration of the above recitals and the mutual covenants of the parties, the parties agree as follows:

All earnings of either party earned on or after the date of execution of this agreement and arising from any and all sources, contingent or otherwise, and all income and profits from the investment or use of such earnings from such personal activities, ability, or capacity of either party, and regardless of which party controls and invests such earnings, shall be the separate property of the party earning or investing such income and shall not be community property.

In witness whereof, the parties have executed this agreement at _____ _____ [place of execution] the day and year first above written.

_____

_____

[Signatures]

{Acknowledgement]

SECTION X

Appendix: Sample Form for Business Trust

Protecting a Professional Client's Assets from the Potential Claims of Creditors

30

Doctors, lawyers and other professionals are increasingly concerned about safeguarding their assets from malpractice or tort claim judgment creditors. The authors examine available methods that do not involve fraudulent transfers.

by **RICHARD P. KESSLER, JR.,** *and* **ZOE M. HICKS,** *Attorneys, Atlanta, Georgia*

Clients who practice in professions where there is a high risk of malpractice claims require special attention so that their assets may be protected from potential judgment creditors. For such clients, a judgment that is not fully covered by liability insurance can mean the loss of most substantial personal assets. In order to safeguard the wealth of the highly exposed professional, the estate planner must be aware of the applicable state law of fraudulent conveyances and the Federal Bankruptcy Code. Ignorance of these laws could cause the planner to advise the client to engage in transfers of assets which would be fraudulent as to creditors. There are, however, techniques available to protect those clients who bear a high risk of exposure to lawsuits.

Fraudulent transfers

The Federal Bankruptcy Code and state fraudulent transfer statutes give creditors or trustees in bankruptcy specific rights to property that has been transferred with the intent to hinder, defraud, or delay creditors, or with respect to which the transfer necessarily had that effect. Fraudulent transfers may be actual or constructive.

Actual fraudulent transfers are those in which the client intended to hinder, delay or defraud his or her creditors. The creditors or the trustees in bankruptcy are given the difficult task of establishing fraudulent intent. Since intent is seldom susceptible of direct proof, courts have relied on "badges of fraud," *i.d.,* objective, observable facts which are evidence of fraudulent intent, in finding that the transferor meant to defraud his or her creditors.

Constructive fraudulent transfers are those that are deemed in law to be fraudulent without regard to the actual intent of the transferor. They include transfers without adequate consideration by an insolvent, or a near-insolvent transferor. Constructive fraudulent transfers fall into three categories:

1. A transfer for less than fair consideration when the transferor is or will be thereby rendered insolvent.

2. A transfer for less than fair consideration when the transferor fails to retain sufficient assets or capital to meet likely future business needs.

3. A transfer for less than fair consideration when the transferor fails to retain enough property to meet his or her likely future debts as they become due.

Most fraudulent-transfer litigation involves a constructive fraudulent transfer. The judgment creditor or the trustee simply shows the objective fact that a transfer was made by an insolvent or near-insolvent transferor for less than adequate consideration. The judgment creditor or the trustee is not required to establish any intent to hinder, delay or defraud creditors; as a matter of equity, the creditors own the property.

Limitation period. State statutes of limitation for fraudulent conveyances vary. In some states, the right of a creditor to set aside a fraudulent transfer has been limited to three years after the transfer. In other states creditors have had as long as ten years to bring an action. Under Section 548 of the Bankruptcy Code, fraudulent transfers made within one year preceding the filing of the bankruptcy petition can be set aside.

Transfers to family members

Transfers made to relatives have not been regarded as badges of fraud sufficient to set aside the transfer when unaccompanied by any other evidence of fraud. However, courts have uniformaly recognized that such transfers warrant close scrutiny, including the nature and extent of the consideration exchanged.

Gift. Gifts to family members are probably the easiest conveyances to set aside. All a judgment creditor or a trustee in bankruptcy has to do is to ascertain the circumstances of the donor. If they are such that the transaction could be described as fraudulent, the donee must yield to the donor's creditor. Transfers to a spouse for "love and affection" are gifts, since they are not based on consideration. Thus, if such a transfer is made with the intent to defraud creditors or if the transferor is insolvent or is rendered insolvent by the transfer, the creditors can set aside the transfer.

Sale. Transfers to family members for fair consideration and in which the family member takes the property in good faith and without knowledge of a fraud on creditors are valid and will not be set aside. Normally, courts will scrutinize the transfer on the basis of the adequacy of consideration. For example, a transfer by an insolvent to his children in return for a promise of support for life and a transfer by an insolvent to family members in return for a promise to pay were not supported by fair consideration.

Where the family member is aware that the transfer is fraudulent, courts will set it aside, even though the family member gave adequate consideration for the transfer.

Joint ownership. Depending on state law and how assets may be titled thereunder, joint ownership of assets may offer the exposed professional some protection from creditors' claims.

For professionals residing in community property states, statutes may make the community property liable for the community debts of the spouses incurred after the marriage. However, while it may still be true in some states that the community property is liable for the husband's debts (a corollary to his right to manage and control the community), it does not necessarily follow that the community property is liable for the wife's separate debts.

Tenants in common have independent and distinct titles and estates. Thus, since the interest of each tenant in common is subject to the claims of his or her creditors, this type of joint ownership is helpful only with respect to the interest of a nondebtor spouse.

Property held in joint tenancy with right of survivorship (equal rights to share in the property during the joint tenants' lives, with the entire estate going to the surviving joint tenant) or in tenancy by the entirety (a type of survivorship joint tenancy available only to spouses) may, under state law, be exempt from the separate debts of either spouse. In such jurisdictions, property owned individually by one spouse may be effectively protected by creating a tenancy by the entirety. In other states, however, property owned as a joint tenancy with right of survivorship may be reached by the creditors of one of the joint tenants, causing a severance of the joint tenancy.

Safe harbor assets

State laws that give creditors and trustees in bankruptcy the means to set aside fraudulent transfers also permit certain assets to be exempt from the claims of creditors. For example, in Texas up to 200 acres in a rural area is exempt, and in Florida up to 160 acres (plus livestock) is exempt. In both states the exemption is permitted regardless of the value of the land. In other states, the exemption is limited to a dollar amount, which is sometimes minimal; for instance, in Georgia only $5,000 in value is exempt.

Most states have enacted statutes which exempt insurance proceeds from the claims of creditors. The plain purpose of such statutes is to encourage insurance protection for the benefit of families. Most statutes that exempt life insurance do so even though the owner has the right to change the beneficiary. Some states include the cash surrender value of the policy within the insurance exemption, while other states do not. Under some statutes, the exemption is unlimited, but other states impose limitations. Some statutes have been interpreted to exempt life insurance proceeds from the claims of the beneficiary's creditors as well as the owner's creditors.

The proceeds of annuity contracts are exempt under some statutes, and some states even exempt the proceeds of disability, health and accident insurance.

In addition, there are a variety of miscellaneous exemptions in each state, which may include tools and implements used in the professional's trade or business, animals, household goods and furniture, wearing apparel, jewelry, crops and claims for personal injury or death. Dollar amounts vary from state to state.

The exemptions under Federal law are contained in Section 522 of the Bankruptcy Code. These exemptions permit a debtor to exit a bankruptcy case with sufficient assets to allow him or her to obtain a "fresh start."

Many states follow the rule that the conversion of non-exempt property into exempt property does not constitute a fraudulent conveyance. The rule has also been applied to one already owning a homestead of less than the maximum legal value who purchases the adjoining lot or lots to bring the homestead up to the maximum value. While the general rule appears to give the client maximum flexibility, some states have narrowed its application.

Qualified retirement trusts

After re-titling property where practicable and counseling the professional to place as much net worth as possible in exempt assets, the estate planner may seek further shelter through trusts.

Often, the professional's major asset is an interest in a qualified retirement plan. Because plan assets are subject to ERISA, whether the assets are protected from future judgment creditors must be considered in and out of the context of a bankruptcy proceeding. ERISA, which preempts state law, prohibits the assignment or alienation of benefits provided by a qualified plan.

Therefore, in a nonbankruptcy setting, ERISA should protect plan benefits against claims of future judgment creditors. The planner should note, however, that in egregious factual situations, for example, where criminal activities are involved, a court may still find exceptions to the ERISA nonalienation provisions.

Individual retirement accounts (IRAs) are not subject to the anti-alienation provisions of ERISA. Therefore, they are not protected from judgment creditors.

In a bankruptcy setting, it is generally held that the Bankruptcy Code prevails over ERISA to the extent the two statutes are inconsistent. The planner, of course, not knowing whether the professional client will be involved in a bankruptcy proceeding, must assume that the Bankruptcy Code provisions (which are far more difficult than ERISA) will apply.

On its face, the Bankruptcy Code appears to provide many opportunities for the professional to protect qualified retirement plan assets from a judgment creditor. For example, Bankruptcy Code Section 541 excludes from the debtor's estate any trust which is subject to a restriction on transfer enforceable under applicable nonbankruptcy laws (i.e., a spendthrift trust). Further, under Bankruptcy Code Section 522(b)(2), a debtor may elect to exempt property exempted under applicable state law or under other Federal law. Alternatively, the debtor may exempt certain classes of property as provided in Bankruptcy Code Section 522 (d)(10)(E), including payments from a pension or profit-sharing plan to the extent "reasonably necessary" for the support of the debtor and any dependents. In lieu of the classes of property listed in the Bankruptcy Code, however, the states may determine what is exempted.

Unfortunately for the professional client, the judicial interpretations of these Bankruptcy Code provisions indicate that they are not as broadly protective as they might seem. For example, the provision excluding spendthrift trust assets from the debtor's estate has been held to apply only to traditional spendthrift trusts (discussed below). Therefore, unless the qualified plan is a traditional spendthrift trust under state law, it might be included in the client's bankruptcy estate. This is a major problem for the professional who normally creates the trust and is the primary beneficiary, thus preventing the trust from qualifying as a traditional spendthrift trust under state law.

If a professional's pension plan trust cannot qualify as a spendthrift trust under state law, can the plan assets be exempt under law other than the Bankruptcy Code? Although ERISA is another Federal law which protects assets from alienation, the courts have generally held that ERISA was not the kind of "other Federal law" exemption anticipated in the Bankruptcy Code, making it difficult for the planner to rely on this statutory exemption. This leaves the bankrupt professional with the exemptions available for certain listed classes of property, including payments from qualified retirement plans to the extent reasonably necessary for support. Even if the professional client meets the "reasonably necessary" test, the standard used is property sufficient to sustain basic needs, but not necessarily to sustain the debtor's accustomed standard of living. For most professionals, this would likely result in a drastic change in lifestyle.

Other safe harbor trusts

A spendthrift trust provides that the beneficiary's interest terminates upon an attempt to transfer or reach the interest, or upon bankruptcy. The provision, if effective, merely prevents creditors from reaching the interest while still in trust. However, one cannot create a spendthrift trust for one's own benefit; creditors can reach the assets, but the trust is otherwise valid.

A discretionary trust gives the trustee absolute latitude to pay or apply income or principal to or for a beneficiary. As with the spendthrift trust, the grantor cannot create a discretionary trust solely for the grantor's benefit and protect the trust from creditors. There is some authority, however, that where there are other current beneficiaries of the discretionary trust, the rule does not apply.

In some jurisdictions, the grantor-beneficiary of a discretionary trust exposes to his or her creditors whatever the trustee *could*, under the terms of the trust, pay to or apply for the benefit of such person. Thus, if the trustee has discretion to invade principal for the benefit of the grantor, the creditors can also reach the principal even where there is a remainder over to other beneficiaries. However, where the remainder interest in principal is indefeasibly vested in others, with no discretion in the trustee to pay principal to the grantor, the creditors cannot reach the principal.

Where a trust imposes a duty on the trustee to distribute income and principal for the grantor-beneficiary's maintenance and support under a fixed and ascertainable standard, creditors may be able to compel the trustee to pay to them the maximum amount which could be paid to or applied for the benefit of the grantor.

Gift tax issues

A conveyance in trust is not subject to gift tax where the transferor retains dominion and control over the property transferred. Thus, if a transfer in trust is made to protect assets from creditors, and the transferor wants to avoid payment of gift tax, sufficient dominion and control over all or part of the assets transferred should be retained to avoid having the transfer deemed a completed gift.

Under Reg. 25.2511-2(b), a gift to a discretionary trust, where the trustee can distribute income and principal to the grantor with no reversion in the grantor, is normally a completed gift for gift tax purposes. However, in *Rev. Rul.* 76-103, where the grantor's creditors could reach the trust property under state law, no completed gift was made because the grantor effectively could terminate the trust by relegating creditors to the trust for settlement of their claims.

What if the property *is* protected from creditors under state law? Has a taxable gift occurred despite the rules that might otherwise apply? Assume a grantor transfers property to an irrevocable trust, retaining an income interest for life with remainder to those persons among his spouse and descendants as he may appoint by will. While his creditors can generally reach his income interest, the remainder interest, in which the grantor retains no interest, cannot be reached. Under Reg. 25.2511-2(b), however, a donor's retained testamentary power to appoint the remainder among his descendants would prevent the transfer from being a completed gift. This Regulation appears to allow avoidance of a completed gift while protecting the remainder interest from creditors.

Other trust provisions, although successful in some states to protect all or part of the trust's assets from creditors, have been held to result in taxable gifts. For example, a provision allowing distributions to the grantor only with the consent of a party with a substantial adverse interest, and a provision vesting the remainder interests in named persons (with no reserved powers to change by the grantor's will) have been held completed transfers for gift tax purposes.

Planning suggestions

How might a professional, concerned about a future judgment creditor, establish a trust that will protect the underlying property but will still allow the professional to enjoy some current benefits?

Discrepancies in state laws make uniform guidelines impossible, but two recent cases may be helpful. In *DiMaria v. Bank of California,* 237 Cal. App. 2d 254, 46 Cal. Rptr. 924 (1965), a widow with two adult children executed an irrevocable trust agreement transferring her assets to a bank as trustee. The trust provided that all of the income would be paid to the widow during her lifetime with the remainder on her death to her two children equally. It also gave the trustee the power to apply for the widow's benefit so much of the principal as the trustee deemed advisable, if, in the trustee's discretion, the trust income together with the widow's income from other sources was insufficient to provide for her reasonable support, medical care and comfort.

When a judgment creditor attempted to reach the trust principal without showing the inadequacy of the widow's income from the trust and other sources for her support, the court refused the creditor and held that to allow the creditor access to the principal would give the creditor greater rights in the trust than the beneficiary herself had.

The court distinguished the trust from a spendthrift trust or a fully discretionary trust, noting that such trusts were "mere subterfuge[s] to insure the unbridled financial demands of the Settlor and, at the same time, insulate his estate against the just claims of creditors." While here the trust income had to be paid to the grantor and thus was subject to alienation and to the claims of her creditors, the trustee's discretion over principal was limited.

The court concluded that the purpose of the trust was not to avoid the widow's just obligations but rather to free herself from the constant demands of her own children. Further, because the trust property passed to the widow's children at her death, the children had vested remainder interests which could not be defeated by creditors except in strict compliance with the trust instrument.

In *Estate of German*, 55 AFTR 2d 85-1577 (Ct. Cls., 1985), the court interpreted Maryland law with respect to whether the decedent's creditors could reach the principal and income of trusts created by her for the benefit of her sons. The sons were co-trustees. Each trust provided that the trustees should accumulate the net income and add the accumulated net income to principal at the end of each year. After the decedent's death, the trust property was held for the sons and their families. However, during the decedent's life, the trustees had the power at any time, in their absolute and uncontrolled discretion, to pay to or apply for the grantor's benefit all or part of the net income and principal, with the written consent of the respective beneficiary of the particular trust from which the distribution was made.

The decedent's estate maintained that Maryland law did not give creditors access to the trusts, that gifts were completed at the time she transferred assets to the trusts, and that the assets were no longer subject to estate tax. The court agreed.

Although the trustees had discretion to distribute income and principal to the decedent, if not distributed income and principal would pass to specified remainder beneficiaries. Before the decedent could receive any distribution, the consent of a beneficiary having an adverse interest had to be obtained. Finally, the trust made dispositions of property upon the death of the decedent, giving her sons' families vested remainder interests, and was not intended solely to shield her assets from her creditors.

In drafting a trust for a professional who needs to be fully or partially protected from a future judgment creditor, the practitioner should consider implementing the following provisions under applicable state law:

1. Seek reasons other than protection of assets from future judgment creditors for establishing the trust (*e.g.*, to protect assets from demanding children; for estate planning purposes).

2. Unless the professional resides in a state where creditors cannot reach property in a totally discretionary trust, do not give the trustee absolute discretion to distribute income and principal to the professional alone. This could expose assets to creditors. Therefore, the trustee's powers on behalf of the professional should be tightly restricted.

3. Consider adding additional beneficiaries to a trust to protect the professional's interest. Some statutes providing that a transfer in trust for the use of the grantor is void as against creditors apply only where the grantor is sole beneficiary of the trust.

4. Consider vested remainders in persons or a class of persons. (In *DiMaria* and *German*, the fact that the grantor's children had vested remainders subject to defeasance if the principal had to be invaded for the grantor was important to the courts.)

5. If gift tax considerations are paramount and if no part of the transfer is to be a taxable gift, retain an income interest for the professional's life, and have the professional retain the right to name the remainder beneficiaries from a designated class.

6. If the professional is creating a trust for his or her benefit, consider omitting any type of spendthrift clause. The clause is invalid with respect to the professional and lessens the court's opportunity to find other reasons for the professional's establishment of the trust.

Estate planners should familiarize themselves with the laws concerning fraudulent conveyances before counseling their exposed clients. Valid techniques are available, but caution must be exercised to avoid fraudulent transfers.

RICHARD P. KESSLER, JR., is a partner in the Atlanta, Georgia, law firm of Macey, Wilensky, Cohen & Wittner. He is a member of the ABA General Practice Section's Bankruptcy Committee and the Bankruptcy Sections of the State Bar of Georgia and the Atlanta Bar Association. Mr. Kessler has previously written on bankruptcy issues for Prentice-Hall, Inc. ZOE M. HICKS is an attorney in Atlanta and a member of the ABA Tax Section's Estate and Gift Tax Committee, and has previously written for THE JOURNAL OF TAXATION *and other professional publications.*

Reprinted with permission from:
ESTATE PLANNING
Nov./Dec. 1986, P. 340-344

WARREN, GORHAM, & LAMONT, INC.
210 South Street
Boston, MA 02111

How Family Partnerships Can Be Used to Shift Income and Capital Appreciation

31

A family partnership, if structured properly, can be a useful tool in shifting income and appreciation of capital assets to other family members. This article explains what an estate planner must watch out for when setting up a family partnership

by DAVID GERSON, CPA, *New York City*

TECHNIQUES THAT result in future appreciation and income flowing to younger family members are of special importance to estate planners. This is especially true as a result of the unification of gift and estate tax rates and the ERTA phase-in of increases in the unified credit. However, most clients will be unwilling to give up complete control over family assets. A well-structured family partnership can accomplish the shifting of future appreciation and income to the younger generation while retaining significant controls in the older generation.

The family partnership also provides flexibility to meet changing circumstances. Except in the case of an investment company, under Section 721 no gain or loss is recognized by a partnership or its partners upon the contribution of property to the partnership. Further, except for current year's income and cash received in excess of basis, under Section 731 gain or loss is generally not recognized upon the liquidation of a partnership. It is therefore possible to liquidate a partnership arrangement without severe income tax consequences if it no longer serves the purposes for which it was formed. Alternatively, the partnership agreement can be amended to meet changed circumstances. The family partnership also obviates the unreasonable accumulation, personal holding company and preferred stock bailout problems inherent in family corporations.

Income tax considerations

While the tests for determining whether a family partnership will be effective for estate tax purposes are different from those for income tax purposes, the estate planner must be aware of the income tax consequences of the creation of a family partnership. In certain instances, a family partnership designed to achieve estate tax results will be ineffective for income tax purposes. This may bring about additional estate tax savings, resulting from the payment of income tax by the older family member on income attributable to the younger generation. However, a client willing to divert future income to heirs usually is not willing to be taxed on such income on a continuing basis.

The income tax rules governing family partnerships are incorporated in Section 704(e) and its Regulations. As described in Reg. 1.704-1(e) (1) (i) the purpose of the section is to insure in the family partnership area that "income be taxed to the person who earns it through his own labor and skill and the utilization of his own capital" and to insure that the regular assignment-of-income rules are not violated. Under Section 704(e)(1), a person will be recognized as a partner for income tax purposes if capital is a material income-producing factor and the person owns a capital interest in the partnership, whether the interest is derived by purchase or gift.

Capital is a material income-producing factor under Reg. 1.704-1(e)(1)(iv), "if a substantial portion of the gross income of the business is attributable to the employment of capital in the business conducted by the partnership." Capital is not a factor where the income of the business is derived from personal services. Where capital is not a material income-producing factor a partnership will be recognized under the tests set forth in case law, in particular the Supreme Court's decision in *Culbertson*. There, the Court held that in such circumstances the basic consideration is whether "the parties in good faith and acting with a business purpose intend to join together in the present conduct of the enterprise." Generally speaking, one will be recognized as a partner in a personal-service partnership only if significant services as a partner are rendered in the conduct of the partnership's business.

Regulation 1.704-1(e)(2)(i) states that "[w]hether an alleged partner who is a donee of a capital interest in a partnership is the real owner of such interest, and whether the donee has dominion and control over such interest, must be ascertained from all of the facts and circumstances of the particular case." Control retained by the donor may cause the donee not to be treated as a partner. Under Reg. 1.704-1(e)(2)(ii), this can include:

1. Control over the distribution of income.

2. Control over the right of the donee to liquidate or sell the interest in the partnership.

3. Control over assets essential to the business.

4. Retention of management powers inconsistent with normal relationship among partners.

However, the following types of retained control will not defeat the income tax effect of an assignment of a partnership interest:

1. The right as a managing partner to retain income necessary for the reasonable needs of the business.

2. A buy-sell agreement providing for the purchase at fair market value.

3. Retention by the donor of voting control which is common in ordinary business relations, provided the donee is free to liquidate the partnership interest without financial detriment.

Trustees. A trustee will be recognized as a partner for income tax purposes if unrelated to and independent of the grantor, and receives income distributable from the partnership to the trust. Where a grantor acts as a trustee or the trustee is not independent of the grantor, the trust will be recognized as a partner according to Reg. 1.704-1(e)(2), if the trustee "actively represents and protects the interests of the beneficiaries in accordance with the obligations of a fiduciary and does not subordinate such interests to the interests of the grantor. That Regulation also states that particular consideration will be given to whether the trust is recognized as a partner in business dealings and income is distributed annually for the benefit of the beneficiaries of the trust. The identity of the trustee is, of course, also relevant in connection with the "grantor trust" rules of Sections 671 and 679.

Minors. Where a partnership interest is given directly to a minor, not in trust, the minor will be a partner for income tax purposes if competent to manage property and participate in partnership activities, or if the control of the minor's property is exercised by a fiduciary (subject to judicial supervision) for the sole benefit of the minor. This requirement will not present a problem in a jurisdiction which permits partnership interests to be held by a custodian under a Uniform Gifts to Minors Act.

Limited partners. An interest of a donee as a limited partner will be recognized even though the donee does not participate in the management of the partnership, provided that the general partner retains no control which substantially limits any of the rights which would ordinarily be exercisable by unrelated limited partners and if the limited partner's right to transfer or liquidate the interest is not subject to substantial restrictions. In a traditional limited partnership arrangement, the general partner exercises exclusive control over the partnership activities. Accordingly, the formation of a limited partnership having the older generation member as a general partner with control over the partnership affairs will appear to accomplish the purposes of the family partnership, provided Section 2036 problems (discussed below) are avoided.

Allocations. Under Section 704(e)(2), a donee partner's distributable share of partnership income must be determined after allowing the donor partner reasonable compensation for services rendered to the partnership, and cannot be proportionately greater than the share allocable to the donor's capital interest. This rule is intended to thwart an attempt to shift a greater portion of the partnership's income to the donee partners than would be the result if such income were allocated in accordance with the capital account balances. However, this rule only comes into effect in the case of partnership interests created by gift of partnership interests from family members, *i.e.,* spouses, ancestors and lineal descendants. A capital contribution from a source derived from an indirect gift from a family member will be considered acquired by gift and not by purchase. Accordingly, a transfer of property by an older-generation family member to a third party who in turn transfers such property to a younger-generation member for contribution to the partnership, or contributions to a partnership by a younger-generation family member from a source traceable to an older-generation family member will be considered partnership interests acquired by gift.

If a contribution is made by purchase and not by gift, under Section 704(b) the partnership agreement will determine the allocation of income provided such allocation has "substantial economic effect." The allocation will have substantial economic effect under Reg. 1.704-1(b)(2) if it will "actually affect the dollar amount of the partners' shares of the total partnership income or loss independently of tax consequences." So long as allocations of income and deduction reflect the amounts actually distributable to a partner, such allocations generally will be allowed.

In addition, specific items of income and expenses may be allocable among the partners in accordance with the partnership agreement. Items of tax-free income and depreciation can be allocated to specific partners provided such allocation has a "substantial economic effect." In the case of a depreciable asset held by the partnership, the depreciation deduction may be allocated to the older-generation family member, with such member's capital account being restored at the time of the sale of such asset by his or her recognition of gain. The special basis adjustment election of Section 754 should also be considered.

Estate tax considerations

Section 2036 provides that a decedent's gross estate will include the value of all property transferred (except for a bona fide sale) to the extent that the decedent during life retained either the enjoyment of or the rights to the income from the property, or the power to designate the persons to receive such rights.

These considerations are important even where a younger-generation partner acquires the partnership interest by way of a purported contribution by such partner because of the danger that, in view of valuation problems discussed below, the transaction might be considered a partial gift. In that situation, Section 2036 would come into play.

In *Ltr. Rul.* 7824005, the Service took the position that if the creator of a family partnership retains control over the partnership property and all of the income from the partnership, any transferred interest in such partnership will be includable in the creator's estate under Section 2036. The facts there were particularly unfavorable to the taxpayer because the income generated from the partnership was insufficient to pay the income reserved by the creator of the partnership, and there was no possibility that the transferees would receive any income from the partnership during the creator's lifetime. However, the Service's position would not appear tenable in the usual family partnership where the purpose is to transfer significant income to younger-generation family members. In addition, the Service's position in *Ltr. Rul.* 7824005 is not supported by analogous situations in the corporate context.

In the landmark *Byrum* case, the Supreme Court held that the retention of the power to vote stock in a closely-held corporation did not require the stock to be included in a decedent's gross estate. In response to this decision, an anti-*Byrum* provision was enacted as Section 2036(b). That section provides that "the retention of the right to vote (directly or indirectly) shares of stock of a controlled corporation shall be considered to be a retention of the enjoyment of transferred property." However, it is the retained right to vote the *transferred* stock which causes the inclusion, not the right to vote the *retained* stock.

Because of the lack of authority dealing with retained rights in the partnership area and because of *Ltr. Rul.* 7824005, it may be helpful to make the partnership situation more analogous to the corporate situation. This can be done by making a corporation the managing general partner of the family partnership. If the older-generation partner retains control over the partnership by holding the stock in the general partner, it would appear that the arrangement would satisfy the *Byrum* rules. The transferred partnership interests would not be included under Section 2036(b) because voting control would be in retained stock.

Gift tax considerations

The formation of a family partnership presents a two-tiered valuation problem to the older-generation family member. In the first instance, the value of the property contributed to the partnership must be ascertained since, to the extent that such value exceeds the amount credited to the older-generation partner's capital account, a gift is made to the younger-generation partners. The valuation concepts contained in Section 2512, the Regulations, and *Rev. Rul.* 59-60 are, of course, relevant. Inasmuch as valuation is not an exact science, there is a significant danger that a gift will result upon the creation of the partnership. It is therefore strongly recommended, particularly where amounts involved are significant, that the services of a valuation expert be retained in connection with such formation. The expert should be called upon to appear at conferences with IRS representatives in case of an audit and to be available to testify in case of court proceedings.

The second valuation issue concerns the extent of the partnership income retained by the older-generation partner and the amount of such income, in substance, transferred to the younger-generation partners. To the extent that the income rights retained are less than current yields and are less than the older-generation partner's proportionate share of capital, the present value of the contributed capital is diluted, resulting in a transfer to the younger-generation partners. As a result of prevailing interest rates, a significant gift may result in the case of the retention of relatively low income rights unless other features are given to enhance the older-generation partner's interest. The older-generation partner should be given the power to compel the partnership to liquidate the interest at the value of the initial capital contribution. It is difficult to see how the Service could successfully argue that a gift has occurred no matter what portion of the income is retained, if the older-generation partner can recover the contribution to the partnership at the same instant that such contribution is made. Another feature which may be given to the older-generation partner is the ability to convert a preferred income right to a larger participation in the general income of the partnership. The retention of control through the corporate managing partner described above will also bolster the value of the older-generation's partnership interest.

Formation of the partnership

A typical family partnership may be created under the following plan:

1. An older-generation family member would transfer to the partnership assets having significant potential for appreciation or generating significant amounts of income, in exchange for a limited partnership interest in the partnership.

2. A corporation wholly-owned by the older-generation family member would act as managing general partner of the partnership and would have a nominal interest in the partnership.

3. Younger-generation family members would transfer to the partnership cash or other assets (derived from sources other than the older-generation partner) in exchange for general partnership interests in the partnership.

4. The limited partnership interest would be entitled to a noncumulative preferential distribution of cash flow. The income distributed to the limited partner will presumably be significantly less than the total income generated by the partnership, allowing excess income to be available for distribution to the general partners. However, to bolster the value of the limited partnership interest, such interest should participate to some small extent in the cash flow remaining after the preferential distribution.

5. The limited partner would be given a right to compel the partnership to liquidate the limited interest and distribute to the limited partner assets having a value equal to the partner's original capital contribution.

6. The limited partnership interest would be convertible into a general partnership interest based on the values of the limited partnership interest and the general partnership interests at the time of conversion.

7. Depreciation deductions would be allocated to the limited partnership interest. The capital account of the limited partnership interest would be restored upon the sale of the underlying depreciable property, to the extent of such depreciation, by the recognition of gain on such sale. Any tax-exempt income would be allocated to the limited partnership interest.

8. The general partners would share to the greatest extent in cash flow in excess of the preferential distribution to the limited partner.

Conclusion

A properly structured family partnership can be an effective technique for transferring assets to younger-generation family members free of estate, gift and income taxes. However, care must be exercised in drafting the partnership agreement to avoid the many potential problems which may be encountered in accomplishing this end. The practitioner must not let the volume of detail obscure the need to fit the arrangement to the client's situation and sensibilities, since it is the client who must live and work within the framework.

DAVID GERSON, CPA, is with the New York City office of Ernst & Whinney. He is also a member of the New York, New Jersey, and Florida Bars.

Reprinted with permission from:
ESTATE PLANNING
March 1983, Pg. 86-89

WARREN, GORHAM & LAMONT, INC.
210 South Street
Boston, MA 02111

All Rights Reserved

32

Offshore Havens

What are the general characteristics and advantages of an offshore haven?

First and foremost characteristic of an offshore haven, of course, is the assurance of secrecy with respect to offshore financial transactions, amounts, and holders of accounts, and beneficial ownership of companies or securities. As a rule, the governments in these offshore havens do not enter into international agreements that would force them to reveal the identity of their foreign clients or the nature of their business transactions. Anyone looking for an offshore haven for his money or investment would want to investigate if any international treaty exists that may defeat the objective of anonymity.

Havens do not tax or have vary low taxation on foreign funds locally administered. Currency exchange controls are non-existent. Some havens do not even tax locally-earned funds. Havens also are typically free from many regulations that govern banking practices.

Corporate clients may even enjoy benefits beyond secrecy. They do not have to bother with shareholder disclosure requirements, annual reporting, or public auditing of corporate books, and filing requirements with respect to stock ownership, sale or transfer, and reporting of dividends.

There's one other important consideration to keep in mind when choosing a haven, which is convenience. If you live in New York, Pacific Islands are not convenient; you would want to use a Caribbean nation instead. The Bahamas are more convenient in terms of travel time to Miami than Panama, but Panama is more reliable with respect to electronic communication. Hong Kong may be more desirable to those looking for large financial markets, but its uncertainty may be an offsetting factor and, the convenience of English language even as a second language used in business should not be overlooked.

List of Offshore Financial Havens

There's no official list that defines a particular country as an offshore haven. Each country offers its own advantages and disadvantages, but the following countries are generally recognized as offshore financial havens: Bahamas, Bermuda, British Virgin Islands, British Antilles including Montserrat, Anguilla, Caymans, Nevis, St. Kitts, Antigua, Dominica, St. Lucia, St. Vincent, Costa Rica, Netherlands Antilles, Panama, Bahrein, Hong Kong, Liberia, Liechtenstein, Luxembourg, and Switzerland.

Using an Offshore Haven

Blum in his book *Offshore Haven Banks, Trusts and Companies* recounts many interesting strategies for use of offshore havens for tax evasion purposes. They range from the simplest to the most complex.

Everyone has thought of this one. Simply carry the money in a suitcase to the Caymans. Establish a bank account in the name of the company that your Cayman lawyer created the day before.

You can go one step further. Create your company in the Caribbean. Then find an existing U.S. company to launder your funds. Any cash-generating retail business will do. You may have to pay a small commission for the special services. The funds are transferred through wire transfer instructions. The advantage of wire transfers is that, unlike cash transfers, wire transfers are not reported to the IRS. To quell any probing inquiries, you may want to establish a business reason for such wire transfers.

Here's another strategy. Say you're in the business of importing goods from abroad. Ask your supplier to overbill you for the purchases, and arrange to have the excess payments you are making to be transferred to your numbered account in Switzerland or Panama. Your money now has left the country beyond the reach of creditors or the IRS. If this sounds too difficult, create a business partnership in an offshore haven. Pay them for some phony services billed. This money is deposited in an offshore account and whenever you need it you can "borrow" it back at a going interest rate, making your interest payments tax-deductible.

Of course, you can do what financial wizards have always done: make your paper trail impossible to trace. Create several different companies with interlocking, seemingly-legal business relationships. Make one company buy from the other, second company overcharges for the goods, while the third company holds title to real estate or rights to merchandise and receives royalties. The parent company receives dividends from various companies. Portions of stock in various companies are owned by you, your relatives, or the companies you control. It will take a determined sleuth to sort the entire thing out.

Bringing Money Home

Sending money abroad is only the first leg of the journey. There is no particular advantage in keeping the money outside of the country indefinitely. You can spend only so much money on travel, entertainment, and retirement villas. Your very objective in transporting money abroad was to launder it and bring it back in legal form so that it can be freely declared, spent and enjoyed. Here's a brief overview of some of the methods of bringing money home:

• One common strategy is to find an international bank with branches in an offshore haven and headquarters in, say, Canada, Europe, and preferably branches in the U.S. Ask to borrow money secured by your income-generating assets in the haven. Even your foreign bank accounts maybe collaterized for this purpose. The U.S. branch of the bank will originate the loan to you on which you will make interest payments with reportable income, the payments, of course, being tax-deductible. The loan generated by the U.S. branch will arouse less scrutiny by the IRS whereas a loan from a bank in an offshore haven may raise a red flag. We're assuming that you have investigated and satisfied to yourself the confidentiality protocol of the bank.

• Arrange a loan from the offshore entity. This probably is the most effective way of bringing money home, although any loan originated in an offshore haven is likely to raise questions from the tax authorities. The questions can be easily answered if you have been able to set up even a semblance of business or investment facade in the offshore country. Once a loan has been made, it need not be paid back although interest payments must be made, which themselves are tax-deductible.

• You can use your offshore money to finance purchase of vacation retreats, boats, aircraft, and other amenities, ownership of which can easily rest in the offshore business you have created.

• Lend your personal services as a consultant or employee to the offshore business or its U.S. subsidiary. This money can now be reported to the IRS as lawful income.

• You can also arrange to have your illicit money converted to legal gambling "wins." You may have to pay a commission to the casino operator for his cooperation. The wins will have to be declared and they will be taxed but their origin will remain unprobed.

• Your offshore business can also make investments in the U.S. in real properties or other businesses. Then you can acquire these assets at favorable prices and terms yielding high legitimate profits.

Traps in Offshore Havens

So far we have discussed only the advantages and means of setting up business and investment entities in offshore havens for the purpose of concealment of illicit profits or shielding of assets from the IRS or creditors. What we've discussed above may appear attractive and plausible on paper, but in reality the practice may have many traps for the unwary. The results could range anywhere from unpleasant surprises to outright loss of capital.

What should you be aware of? In your pursuit of protecting your assets what should you protect yourself against?

The first rule, recommended by every authority on this subject, dictates that you should stay away from any organization that operates only in one (or other) offshore haven. In other words, if a bank or trust company operates only in Antigua the protection enjoyed by your assets or deposits is limited to whatever that particular organization is able to muster up. You must also realize that no matter how much background information you may have gathered on a bank in an offshore haven, in the end much of it may turn out to be totally false. Few offshore havens have anything even remotely resembling FDIC or Department of Corporations or insurance commissioner to protect or advise you against unscrupulous operators. There are no SEC filings or disclosure statements that would guide you in your investment plans.

Confidentiality or secrecy assured in banking and business dealings, which may have attracted you to the offshore haven in the first place, ironically may work against you once you are there. The same secrecy will prevent you from gathering information about banks and other organizations that you need to make intelligent decisions about your investments.

The biggest trap may lie in lack of administrative and judicial protections that we take for granted in the U.S. As a rule, there is no rule of law in most offshore havens. You may be entirely at the mercy of your local liasion, attorney or a trust officer who face no ethical or disciplinary constraints.

You may think that you are avoiding U.S. taxes, but in reality you may pay another kind of tax. Your local attorney or trust officer of the local bank may "tax" you, knowing full well that you are there for the sole purpose of concealing illicit money from the U.S. authorities or courts. It is not entirely uncommon for the tax to be 50 percent or in extreme cases even confiscatory. In other words, you may lose your entire investment. Your remedy against such predatory practices may be none, for there's no regulatory or judicial mechanism for you to turn to.

Corruption and bribes in banking and government circles are quite normal and, given sufficient inducement, your confidentiality may be breached. Even governments that boast of having no international treaties allowing for exchange of information may be quite willing to transmit information upon receipt of probable wrongdoing under certain circumstances. You'll have no protection of laws concerning illegal search and seizure routinely enjoyed in the U.S.

If you are still determined to find an offshore haven for your capital, you should limit your search to large, reputable international banks and trust companies with branches or headquarters in the U.S. You should never lose sight of the fact that every benefit carries with it a measure of risk.

Other references:

Blum, Richard H. (1984). *Offshore Haven Banks, Trusts, and Companies.* New York: Pracger Publishers.

Institute for Lawsuit and Asset Protection: David Tedder, attorney. 3601 S.E. Ocean Bl., #103, Stuart, FL 34996. (800) 922-1771, (407) 220-4800.

APPENDIX

Sample Form for Business Trust

Declaration of Trust

Agreement and declaration of trust made _____ *[date]*, between _____ of _____ *[address]*, City of _____, County of _____, State of _____, and _____, of _____ *[address]*, City of _____, County of _____, State of _____, _____, *[repeat for other trustees]* herein referred to as trustees, for the purpose of enabling the trustees to hold and manage the trust estate and to carry on business as provided below in this declaration.

Trustees declare that all property now held or acquired after the effective date of this declaration by them or either of them or their successors, as trustees, and all income and profits from such property, shall be by them managed, administered, received, collected, disposed of, and distributed for the benefit of such persons as may from time to time be owners of certificates of shares evidencing beneficial interests in this trust estate, in the manner and subject to the terms and conditions set forth in this instrument and any amendments to this instrument.

The property now held by trustees subject to the terms of this trust consists of the following:

_____

_____

_____

1. Character of the Organization It is hereby expressly declared that there is created a trust, of the type commonly termed a business trust, and not a partnership, a corporation, or a joint-stock association.

2. Name and Location A. Trustees may be collectively designated as _____ _____ *[adopted business name of trust]*, in which name they make and execute contracts and all kinds of instruments, conduct business, acquire, and convey real or personal property, and sue and be sued.

B. The principal office of the trust shall be at _____ *[address]*, in the City of _____, State of _____, unless and until it is changed by trustees.

3. Capital Stock and Shares A. The beneficial interest in the trust shall be divided into _____ (____) shares _____ [of the par value of _____ Dollars ($ _____) each *or* without par value.]

B. Trustees may sell or exchange such shares to such persons, for such sums or other consideration, and on such terms, as they may deem expedient.

C. Trustees shall issue or cause to be issued to subscribers for or purchasers of such shares, certificates in such form as trustees deem proper, evidencing the beneficial interests of such share owners.

D. The certificates shall be personal property and shall entitle owners of such certificates to participate in all dividends and other distributions of income or principal in the proportion which the number of shares of each owner bears to the total number of shares issued and outstanding.

E. Any trustee of the trust may acquire, hold, and dispose of shares in the trust to the same extent and in the same manner as if he or she were not a trustee and without affecting in any way his or her status or power as such.

4. Transfer of Shares   A. The shares of the trust shall be transferable by an appropriate instrument in writing and by the surrender to trustees or to the person designated therefor by them, but no transfer shall be of any effect as against trustees until it has been recorded upon the books of trustees kept for that purpose. On the transfer and surrender, and recording in the trust books, a new certificate shall be issued to the transferee. In case of a transfer of only a part of the shares evidenced by a certificate, a new certificate for the residue shall be issued to the transferor.

B. The person in whose name shares stand on the books of the trust shall be deemed to be and treated as the absolute owner of such shares for all purposes of this instrument, and until the existing certificate is surrendered and transfer is recorded as required above, trustees shall not be affected by any notice, actual or constructive, of any transfer.

C. Any person becoming entitled to become a shareholder in the trust as a result of the death or bankruptcy of any shareholder, or in any way other than by transfer in accordance with the above provisions of this section, may receive a new certificate for the share and be recorded on the books of the trust as the owner of such share, upon the production of proper evidence of his or her entitlement to such share and the delivery of the existing certificate to trustees or any person designated by them. Until such evidence is produced and the existing certificate is surrendered, trustees shall not be affected by any notice of the change in title.

5. Loss or Destruction of Certificate   In case of the loss or destruction of a certificate of shares, a new one may be issued in its place, on such conditions as trustees may deem necessary and proper.

6. Effect of Death of Shareholder or Transfer of Shares   A. The death, insolvency, or incapacity of one or more of the shareholders, or the transfer of shares, shall not operate to terminate or dissolve the trust or affect its continuity in any way, nor shall such event entitle any legal representative or other person to dissolve the trust or to partition the trust property or to demand an accounting.

B. In the event of the death of a shareholder, or a transfer of shares, the transferees, heirs, legatees, or legal representatives of the decedent or transferor shall succeed to his or her rights.

7. Inspection of Stock Books The stock books of the trust, showing the ownership of all shares of the trust and recording all transfers of such shares, shall be subject to inspection by any shareholder or his or her attorney or agent at all reasonable times, under such reasonable conditions as the trustees may prescribe.

8. Dividends Trustees may, from time to time, declare and pay out of the net earnings received by them such dividends as they, in their discretion, deem proper and advisable.

9. Rights of Shareholders   **A.** The rights of shareholders and of transferees and other persons becoming entitled to shares of the trust shall be subject to all the terms and conditions of this declaration of trust.

B. The shares of the trust shall be personal property, and the ownership of such shares shall not give any person any legal or equitable title in or to the trust property or any part of such property, but shall only entitle the owners of shares to their proportionate shares of dividends and distributions as provided above.

C. No shareholder shall have any rights to manage or control the property, affairs, or business of the trust, or any power to control trustees in these respects.

D. No shareholder shall have any right to a partition of the trust property or to an accounting during the continuance of the trust.

10. Liabilities of Shareholders **A.** Shareholders shall not be liable for any assessment, and trustees shall have no power to bind the shareholders personally.

B. All persons dealing with or having any claim against trustees or any officer or agent of the trust shall look only to the funds and property of the trust for the payment of any debt, claim, damage, judgment, or decree, or of any money or thing that may become due or payable in any way, whether founded on contract or tort, and the shareholders shall not be personally or individually liable for any such debt, claim, damage, judgment, or decree.

C. No amendment shall ever be made to this declaration of trust increasing or enlarging the liability of shareholders, without the written consent of all the shareholders.

D. In every written order, contract, instrument, or obligation given or executed by trustees or under their authority, it shall be the duty of trustees to insert or cause to be inserted a stipulation to the effect that the shareholders shall not be liable for any debt, demand, or liability incurred by or under the authority of trustees, and reference shall be made to this declaration of trust. The letterheads and other stationery used in transactions or correspondence with outsiders shall contain a brief notice to the same effect. However, no failure of trustees or of the officers or agents of the trust in this regard shall have the effect of rendering any shareholder personally

352

liable.

11. Shareholders' Meetings; Elections **A.** The shareholders shall meet at the principal office of the trust on _____ *[date]*, and shall hold meetings at such office on the _____ *[third]* _____ *[Monday]* of _____*[month]* each year thereafter, for the purpose of electing trustees and of exercising and discharging any other powers or duties vested in them by this instrument.

B. Trustees may call special meetings of shareholders at any time.

C. Trustees shall notify all shareholders of the time and place of all meetings of shareholders, whether regular or special, and, in the case of special meetings, shall also give notice to all shareholders of the general purpose of the meeting and the nature of the business to be considered at such meeting, and such special meetings shall be limited to the business thus specified in the call, unless the owners of at least _____ percent (_____%) of all outstanding shares consent in writing to the consideration of other matters.

D. Notice mailed to a shareholder directed to him or her at the address shown on the books of the trust shall be deemed sufficient for the provisions of this section and for all other purposes unless written notice of change of address is given to trustees.

E. At all meetings of shareholders, the president named by trustees, or such other person as may be designated by trustees, shall preside. Each share shall be entitled to one vote, and shareholders may vote by proxy. The owners of _____ *[one-half]* of the issued and outstanding shares, or their proxies, shall constitute a quorum for the purposes of any meeting. In the election of trustees, and on other matters except where it is otherwise provided in this instrument, a majority of the shares represented and voting at the meeting shall control.

12. Number, Election, and Tenure of Trustees **A.** There shall be _____ *[number]* trustees. The above-named persons are hereby designated as trustees of this trust, and they and their successors shall hold for a term of _____ (_____) years and until their successors are elected and qualify.

B. The death, incapacity, resignation, or removal of any or all of the trustees shall not terminate the trust or in any way affect its continuity.

C. Any vacancy among the trustees occurring during a term of office shall be filled by the remaining trustees for the unexpired portion of such term.

D. Every _____ (_____) years following the date of this instrument, trustees shall be elected by the shareholders at meetings held and conducted as provided above.

13. Resignation of Trustees **A.** Any trustee may be removed during his or her term at any regular meeting of trustees or at any meeting specifically called by any trustee for that purpose, by a majority of all trustees for any cause by them deemed sufficient.

B. Written notification of any special meeting called for the purpose of considering the removal of any trustee shall be given or mailed to each trustee at least _____ (___) days prior to such meeting, but no such notification shall be necessary in the case of a regular meeting of trustees.

14. Meetings of Trustees; Manner of Functioning A. Regular meetings of trustees shall be held at the principal office of the trustee at least once a month, at such times as they may from time to time fix, and they may hold meetings at any time for the transaction of any business upon the call of any trustee. The president or, in his or her absence, any other person as trustees may designate, shall preside at such meetings.

B. No informality or defect in the manner of calling or holding meetings, and no failure to call or hold such meeting, shall affect the validity of any action taken by a majority of all trustees.

C. A majority of trustees shall constitute a quorum; and the concurrence of all trustees shall not be necessary to the validity of any action taken by them, but the decision or action of a majority of trustees present and voting any meeting shall be conclusive and binding as the act and decision of the trustees as a body.

D. Trustees may delegate to any one or more of their number the exercise of any power or the performance of any duty that trustees as a body might exercise or perform.

15. Reports by Trustees Trustees shall annually make a written report of their operations during the preceding fiscal year, showing their receipts, disbursements, and earnings, and the assets and condition of the trust estate. Such report shall be kept on file at the principal office of the trust at all times, and shall be subject to inspection by any shareholder or his or her attorney or agent at any reasonable time; and a copy or summary of such report shall be furnished to any shareholder upon written request.

16. Officers and Agents A. Trustees shall appoint from among their number a president and a treasurer, and shall appoint from among their number or otherwise a secretary, and such officers shall have such authority and shall perform such duties as trustees shall prescribe and such as are usually incident to those offices in the case of corporations, so far as applicable and in the absence of the adoption of contrary provisions by trustees.

B. The terms of all officers shall be fixed by trustees, and trustees may at any time, with or without cause, remove or discharge any such officer or any agent or employee; provided, that the removal of an officer as such shall not affect his or status as trustee.

17. Compensation of Trustees Trustees shall receive such compensation, regular or special, as they shall deem reasonable and proper. They shall fix the compensation, if any, of all officers and agents appointed by them.

18. General Powers and Function of Trustees **A.** Trustees shall hold the legal title to all property at any time belonging to the trust, and shall have absolute and exclusive control, management, and disposition of such property, and absolute and exclusive power and control over the management and conduct of the businesses and affairs of the trust, free from any power of control on the part of the shareholders.

B. Trustees may hold, manage, deal with, and dispose of the property and business of the trust in the same manner as if they were the absolute owners of such property, subject only to the specific limitations placed on their powers by this instrument.

C. The enumeration of powers contained in this section shall not be construed as limiting in any way the general powers hereby conferred on trustees. They shall have all powers necessary, convenient, or appropriate to the purposes and ends of this trust, and are authorized to take any action that they may deem proper to carry out such purposes.

D. Trustees shall have the powers, among others, to purchase or otherwise acquire property, and to sell, exchange, lease, mortgage, pledge, or in any manner dispose, encumber, improve, or deal with the property of the trust, or any part of such property or any interest in such property, on such terms and for such consideration and purposes as they deem proper.

E. Trustees may engage in business, manufacture, and deal in goods, wares, and merchandise, incur indebtedness, borrow or loan money with or without security, enter into contracts of all kinds, execute, accept, discount, negotiate, and deal in commercial paper and evidences of indebtedness, execute conveyances, mortgages, deeds of trust, leases, and any other instrument in writing; they may invest and reinvest the trust funds; they may compromise or settle any suits, claims, or demands, or waive or release any rights, relating to the trust estate or business; they may appoint and employ officers, agents, and attorneys.

F. Trustees may sue and be sued and prosecute and defend any and all actions affecting the trust or its business or property, either in the name of the trust or in their own names.

G. Trustees may adopt and enforce such bylaws or rules and regulations, not inconsistent with the provisions of this instrument, as they may from time to time deem expedient; they may adopt and use a common seal; they may vote in person or by proxy any stock belonging to the trust estate, and receive the dividends on such stock.

19. Application of Trust Funds **A.** Any act or thing done by trustees, or by the officers or agents of the trust under authority from trustees, shall, as to strangers dealing with such trustees, officers, or agents, be conclusively deemed to be within the purposes of this trust and within the powers of trustees.

B. No person dealing with trustees or any of them, or with any officer or agent of the trust, shall be bound to see to the application by the trustees of any funds or property passing into their hands or control.

20. Liability of Trustees   A. No trustee shall be liable for any act or omission whatsoever of any other trustee or of any officer, agent, or employee of the trust.

B. No trustee shall be liable for any negligence or error in judgment, or for any act or omission, except for his or her own willful breach of trust.

C. No trustee shall be required to give any bond or surety to secure the performance of the trust.

D. Every act or thing done or omitted, and every power exercised or obligation incurred by trustees or any of them in the administration of the trust or in connection with any business, property, or concern of the trust, whether ostensibly in their own names or in their trust capacity, shall be done, omitted, exercised, or incurred by them as trustees and not as individuals.

E. Every person contracting or dealing with trustees or having any debt, claim, or judgment against them or any of them shall look only to the funds and property of the trust for payment or satisfaction. No trustee, officer, or agent of the trust shall ever be personally liable for or on account of any contract, debt, tort, claim, damage, judgment, or decree arising out of, or preservation of, the trust estate or the conduct of any business of the trust. A stipulation or notice to this effect may be inserted in any contract, order or other instrument made by trustees or their officers or agents, and on stationery used by them, but the omission of such stipulation or notice shall not be construed as a waiver of the above-stated provision, and shall not render trustees, officers, or agents personally liable.

21. Reimbursement and Indemnification of Trustees Each trustee shall be indemnified by and reimbursed from the trust estate for any personal liability, loss, or damage incurred or suffered by him or her, including liability, loss or damage resulting from torts, in the administration of the trust estate or in conducting any business or performing any act authorized or permitted by this declaration of trust or any amendment to this declaration, except such as may arise from his or her own willful breach of trust; but such indemnity or reimbursement shall be limited to the trust estate, and no shareholder shall be personally or individually liable for such indemnity or reimbursement to any extent.

22. Amendment This declaration of trust may be amended in any particular, except as regards the liability of shareholders, by trustees, but only with the consent of the owners of at least _____ *[two-thirds]* of the shares, or their proxies, voting at a meeting called for that purpose pursuant to notice given as provided in this instrument and specifying the purpose of the meeting and the nature of the proposed amendment.

23. Duration and Termination A. This trust shall continue for a period of _____ (___) years from the date of this instrument, unless sooner terminated.

B. Trustees may terminate and dissolve this trust at any time, but only with the assent of the owners of at least _____ *[two-thirds]* of the shares, or their proxies, voting at a meeting called for that purpose pursuant to notice given as provided in this instrument and specifying the purpose of the meeting.

C. On the termination of this trust by any cause, trustees shall liquidate the trust estate, wind up its affairs, and dispose of its property and assets at public or private sales, and, after discharging all legal obligations of the trust, shall distribute the proceeds among the shareholders in proportion to their interests, and for these purposes trustees shall continue to act until such duties have been fully performed.

24. Governing Law This instrument and the trust shall be governed by, construed, and enforced in accordance with the laws of the State of _____.

In witness whereof, the parties have executed this declaration of trust at _____ *[designate place of execution]* the day and year first above written.

_____

[Signatures]

[Acknowledgments]

SOURCE: Am Jur Legal Forms

Also see *Rabkin & Johnson, Current Legal Forms with Tax Analysis,* Vol. 1A, Form Nos. 2A.22-2A.27.